KU-074-799

Contents

Preface   ix

Introduction   xiii

PART I   COMPONENTS OF THE SOCIAL SELF

Chapter 1	**Self-esteem: A Social Approach**	**3**
	Theory	4
	Measurement	9
	Validation	11
	Research	16
	Overview	23
Chapter 2	**Social Interest**	**27**
	Theory	27
	Measurement	33
	Research	34
	Related Concepts	38
	Summary	44
Chapter 3	**The Marginal Man**	**46**
	Communication of Marginality	48
	Validation	49
	Overview	54

PART II   PATTERNS OF SELF–OTHER ORIENTATION

Chapter 4   **The Alienation Syndrome: A Triadic Pattern of**
                 Self–Other Orientation   **61**
             Self–Other Orientation and Alienation   62
             Self–Other Orientation Tasks   66
             Behavior Problem Children   67
             Neuropsychiatric Patients and the Aging   68
             The American Negro   72
             Summary   75

Chapter 5   **A Political Personality Syndrome**   **76**
             Self-esteem and Responsiveness   77
             Complexity of the Self Concept and Responsiveness   78
             The Self-esteem–Complexity Matrix (Integration–
                 Differentiation)   81
             Conclusion   89

PART III   DEVELOPMENT OF SELF–OTHER CONCEPTS

Chapter 6   **Consistency and Change of the Social Self**   **93**
             Sullivan's Interpersonal Approach   94
             Sarbin's Cognitive Approach   95
             Brim's Resocialization Orientation   96
             Kuhn's "Who Am I?" Technique   96
             Development of Self–Other Orientation   97
             Summary   100

Chapter 7   **The Ecology of the Social Self**   **102**
             Familial Correlates of the Self System   102
             Locus of Reinforcement   105
             Self–Other Orientations of Asian Indian Children   106
             Self–Other Orientations of Kibbutz Children   112
             Changing Group Membership   116
             Geographic Mobility   118
             Overview   125

The Social Self

ROBERT C. ZILLER, Ph.D.

University of Florida

LIBRARY
I.M. MARSH COLLEGE OF PHYSICAL EDUCATION
BARKHILL ROAD, LIVERPOOL, 17.

PERGAMON PRESS INC.

OXFORD · NEW YORK · TORONTO
SYDNEY · PARIS · BRAUNSCHWEIG

U.K.	Pergamon Press Ltd., Headington Hill Hall, Oxford OX3 0BW, England
U.S.A.	Pergamon Press Inc., Maxwell House, Fairview Park, Elmsford, New York 10523, U.S.A.
CANADA	Pergamon of Canada, Ltd., 207 Queen's Quay West, Toronto 1, Canada
AUSTRALIA	Pergamon Press (Aust.) Pty. Ltd., 19a Boundary Street, Rushcutters Bay, N.S.W. 2011, Australia
FRANCE	Pergamon Press SARL, 24 rue des Ecoles, 75240 Paris, Cedex 05, France
WEST GERMANY	Pergamon Press GMbH, D-3300 Braunschweig, Postfach 2923, Burgplatz 1, West Germany

Copyright © 1973 Pergamon Press Inc.

All Rights Reserved. No part of this publication may be reproduced, stored in a retrieval system or transmitted in any form or by any means: electronic, electrostatic, magnetic tape, mechanical, photocopying, recording or otherwise, without permission in writing from the publishers

First edition 1973

Reprinted 1976

Library of Congress Catalog Card No. 72-77402

Printed in Great Britain by A. Wheaton & Co., Exeter

0 08 017030 7 (H)
0 08 017250 4 (F)

PART IV   THEORIES OF PERSONAL CHANGE AND STABILITY

Chapter 8	**Toward a Theory of Self–Other Orientation**	**129**
	The Social Self	129
	Self–Other Conflict	131
	Overview	140
	Self–Other Orientation	142
Chapter 9	**A Helical Theory of Personal Change**	**147**
	A Helical Theory	147
	Assumptions of the Personal Change System	151
	Cognitive, Conative, and Affective Components	156
	A Synthesis of Four Micro-theories of Personal Change	156
	Overview	177
	New Directions	179
Appendix A	**Examples of Items from the Self–Other Orientation Tasks**	**181**
References		187
Author Index		199
Subject Index		203

Preface

To see others as others see themselves is the quest of those who study the self concept. The study of the self concept has enjoyed a rebirth in the last decade (Wylie, 1961; Diggory, 1966; Coopersmith, 1967; Manis & Meltzer, 1967; Gordon & Gergen, 1968). In part, the renewed interest may stem from the recent emphasis on humanism in the social sciences. Humanism stresses the significance of the individual as an individual rather than as a member of a collective. Humanism also emphasizes a personal frame of reference rather than group norms as guides to behavior. The question asked repeatedly is "Who am I?"

A second impetus to the study of the self concept may be a reconsideration of the cognitive as opposed to the behavioral approach to the study of human experience. The behavioral view emphasizes the direct association of stimulus and response. For the behaviorist the self concept is an unnecessary complication, a will-o'-the-wisp. In the cognitive view, on the other hand, the self concept obtrudes between the stimulus and response. The stimulus is translated in terms of the self concept, and the individual's behavior is associated with the person's view of himself. In the cognitive approach, human behavior is viewed as determined, in part, by the prism effect of the individual on the stimulus.

Unfortunately, the reviews of the literature already cited are subject to severe limitations and criticism because of the limitations of earlier measurements of the self concept. The measures used throughout are based on verbal self reports. The person is asked directly how he evaluates himself. Can the individual, in fact, tell us who he is, using the usual methods of communication?

It is proposed here that the inherent shortcoming of self reports is that they are subject to distortion by the individual. In order to avoid this, the present approach is based upon non-verbal measures of the self concept. The individual is asked to locate himself in relation to a field of significant others, represented in a variety of geometric arrangements using symbols of the self and others (*see* Appendix A).

Also, in contrast to most earlier work, a multifaceted analysis of the self concept is presented. Earlier analyses were concerned largely with self-esteem. Here self-esteem is considered along with self-centrality, self-complexity, social interest, identification, power, marginality, openness, and majority identification.

As already indicated, the social nature of the self is assumed. Humanists are concerned with the question, "Who am I?" Social psychologists concerned with interpersonal perception ask, "Who are they?" In the present approach, these two questions are combined and we ask, "Who am I in relation to them?"

Finally, from these new directions, a new theoretical framework evolves which addresses the yang and yin of the social sciences, stability, and change. On the one hand, stability in interpersonal relationships makes for predictability and satisfaction of mutual expectations. On the other hand, change is inherent in social relations. The control of this inherent conflict is a demand of any self–other system. A large body of literature, in the areas of personality and social psychology dealing with the confluence of the individual and the group under conditions of change is organized by the Theory of Self–Other Orientation and the Helical Theory of Personal Change.

The work is intended for all students of social psychology, personality, sociology, and education regardless of academic level who are interested in a new look at the self concept, its measurement, and theoretical considerations. The content evolves from a description of some of the basic components of the self system including self-esteem, social interest, and marginality. The text moves toward more complex analyses including the alienation syndrome and the political personality which involves two or more of the components of the social self. A third section describes the development of the self concept and examines such variables as socio-economic background and the history of geographic mobility of the child.

As already indicated, in the final section a reintegration is proposed of earlier self theories which deal with the classic dilemma of personal stability and change. The book ends with the presentation of a "Helical Theory of Personal Change." This framework combines theories of attitude and value change, behavior modification, role theory, and the self concept into an open ended theoretical statement of the change-stability cycle.

This book may be used as a text or a supplement to a text. It is used most effectively, however, if it is combined with experience in using the accompanying devices in the study of interpersonal perception, following up ideas presented in the text, or examining numerous ideas which will occur to the students.

This book is the result of happy and productive associations with my students and friends: Drs. Barbara H. Long, Edmund H. Henderson, Lynn Hunt Monahan, Beal M. Mossman, Mary Dell Smith, Joan Hagey, Bobbi Jo Stark, and Dalia C. Leslie. Dr. Barbara H. Long, in particular, was instrumental in developing several of the core studies.

The work was begun under a contract with the Veterans Administration Hospital of Elsmere, Delaware, with the gracious help of Dr. Searles A. Grossman. Later, a research program was supported by the National Science Foundation. The book was initially encouraged by Dr. Theodore M. Newcomb. The organization of the material was greatly improved through his gracious criticisms and adroit suggestions.

University of Florida   ROBERT C. ZILLER, Ph.D.

Introduction

Definitions of the field of social psychology differ, but almost all of them are concerned with the consequences of group membership for the individual. Examples of topics central to this relationship include conformity and deviation, interpersonal attraction, social learning, social status, social roles, personality and culture, aggression, and interpersonal conflict. The emphasis is on the individual, albeit within a social field.

It is proposed here that the confluence of the individual and the group is the most fundamental area of inquiry in social psychology. How is the classic conflict resolved between satisfaction of the needs of the individual and the needs of the group? Under what circumstances does an individual attempt to persuade the group? Under what circumstances is the individual willing to place his fate in the hands of others? What are the characteristics of individuals who withdraw from social groups under conditions of conflict? What individuals are most responsive to other people? How do social experiences affect interpersonal orientations?

One approach to this area of inquiry is to examine the individual's perception of himself in relation to significant other persons and significant groups. In this approach the crucial existential question "Who am I?" is extended to become "Who am I and Thou?" It is assumed that these self–other orientations are coded social experiences which act as guides for future social behavior. The answer to the question "Who am I?" derives in part from social experiences, and the answer then serves as a partial framework for responses to new social experiences. Indeed, once the question, "Who am I?", is presented, subsequent behavior is mediated by the concept of the self, but particularly the concept of the social self. Thus, self–other orientations become a basic unit for the understanding of social behavior, just as it is proposed by some (Rogers, 1951) that the self concept is a basic unit for the study of individual behavior.

The origins of the concept of the self have been traced at least as far back as Homeric times (Reeves, 1958). Translations of these writings express the distinction between the physical human body and some non-physical counterpart described as "soul," "spirit," or "psyche." One of the best definitions of the self is also one of the simplest: "The self is the individual as known to the individual" (Murphy, 1947). The self theorists assume that the self is one of the most central and focal objects within the life space of the individual because of its primacy, ubiquity, and continuity. Its origins are early. Once developed, the self concept tends to mediate stimulus and response much as a lens might mediate the perception of objects. Finally, the self concept appears to be resistant to change, but not totally.

The utility of self theory has fallen far short of its promise, however. After an exhaustive review of the literature pertaining to the self concept, Diggory (1966) concluded that "All the extant theories of the self are sterile from the point of view of scientific knowledge" (p. 63).

Although a variety of reasons are offered to explain the lack of utility of the self theories (Wylie, 1961), it is enough to point to the inadequacies of the validity and reliability of the measurement devices, together with the failure to view the self within a social context. The self can only be a hypothetical construct within a larger social framework. To study the self as separate from others is like an ecologist trying to study the habits of birds whose wings have been removed for purposes of experimentation.

The relationship between self and other was recognized long ago by the sociologists Baldwin (1897), Cooley (1899), and Mead (1925). Baldwin described the bipolar self which involves the self and other. The individual has more control over the sense of self as opposed to the other. The other frequently behaves in a way which the individual does not anticipate, but these variations in the behavior of the other lead to the development of a new self concept. Baldwin suggests a spiraling interaction between self and other leading to a complex self concept.

No discussion of the self concept is complete without including the contribution of Cooley (1899). Cooley, too, emphasizes the interaction of self and other in the development of the self concept.

To Cooley, the "self and society are twin-born..." (1918, p. 5). The self and other mutually define each other. Each concept serves as a point of reference for the other. Thus, the definition of the self necessarily involves the other and its reverse. In so doing, Cooley accords the other or the social factor an equal weighting with the self. This approach contrasts with earlier conceptions in which the self was dominant in a field in which the other formed the background.

Finally, Mead (1934) advanced the thesis of the social nature of the self concept when he introduced language as a connecting link. He noted that whereas a facial expression can be observed only by the other, vocal behavior may be attended by both the speaker and the other person. The individual may be both a speaker and a listener with regard to his vocalizations. In this way the vocalizations are a stimulus to which both the self and the other may respond, and it is a rather simple step for the speaker to put himself in the place of the other and take "the attitude of others toward himself" (Mead, 1934, p. 90). Moreover, when the speaker repeats his role taking behavior across situations, a concept of the "generalized other" emerges. The attitudes of others toward himself become organized and the individual becomes an object unto himself. It now becomes possible for him to conduct exchanges between the "I" and the "me."

Although early theorists referred to a variety of components of the self concept, such as complexity of the self concept, self-esteem, and self-centrality, most investigators have focused on the concept of self-esteem. This concept has presented a sufficient number of difficulties to the investigators, however, that extensions into new regions may have been discouraged. Nevertheless, a multifaceted approach is proposed here. The self–other concepts which will be considered include: self-esteem, social interest, marginality, self-centrality, complexity, identification, majority identification, power, and openness. In the brief definitions of these concepts which follow, the individual's point of view is emphasized. The approach is phenomenological.

Self-esteem is usually defined as the individual's perception of his worth. The evaluation of the self, however, is presumed to evolve within a social context of significant other people. Through a process of social comparison regarding the attitudes and abilities of the self and the other, the meaning of the self emerges. Self-esteem is relative—not absolute. Finally, it is proposed that self-esteem is associated with consistency of behavior across situations. Persons with high self-esteem as opposed to those with low self-esteem tend to control the environment, whereas persons with low self-esteem tend to be controlled by the environment. Evidence for this point of view is presented in Chapter 1.

Social interest is the individual's perception of himself as included within a field of significant others as opposed to being apart from others. Inclusion indicates a willingness to be subject to the field of forces generated among others and the self. This latter component suggests an association with social trust, a willingness to place one's fate in the hands of others. Theory, measurement, and research associated with this construct is presented in Chapter 2. The research suggests that social interest is associated with expectations of social support.

Marginality refers to the individual's perception of himself as being between two separate groups as opposed to being included with one of the two groups. The concept has its origin within the Lewinean framework when he discusses the marginal man whose life space is ambiguous and divided. Examples include racial minorities, adolescents, and foremen. In Chapter 3, salesmen as persons who hold linking positions between the organizations and buyers were found to represent themselves as marginal.

Self-centrality is defined as the perception of the social environment from the point of view of the perceiver rather than from the point of view of the other. In Mead's terms, self-centrality is associated with "I," whereas self-decentrality is associated with "me," that is, the self as an object as perceived by the other. Self-centrality is a key concept in the theory of alienation described in Chapter 4.

Complexity of the self concept is defined as the number of facets of the self perceived by the individual. The simplex individual in contrast to the complex is assumed to require fewer concepts to describe himself. High complexity was identified as a characteristic of the political personality (Chapter 5).

Identification is associated with the perception of similarity between the self and significant others such as parents, teachers, or friends. In a sense, identification may be associated with modeling behavior where significant others serve as models for the self. Identification with parents is shown to be a critical requirement in child development (Chapter 7).

Majority identification is the perception of similarity between the self and the majority of others, or the inclusion of the self with the more dominant or pervasive others. Majority identification, then, is a gross indicator of belongingness.

The construct of power derives from Adler's (1927) concept of "feelings of inferiority." The power component of self–other orientation is the perception of the self as consistently superior or inferior to specific others.

Openness refers to bridging the span between self and others, or in Horney's (1937) terms, "moving toward people." Again, the focus is on the self within a social field. The extent of associations is significant. Many as opposed to few perceived associations between self and other may indicate a willingness to risk social encounters (*see* Jourard, 1964).

The aforementioned definitions are broad gauged. The wide category widths of the definitions are consistent with the use by the subjects of symbols rather than words to describe the relationship between the self and the other. The advantages of the geometric arrangements of symbols to describe cognitive maps of self and other has been indicated. At once, however, symbols and cognitive maps are not as denotative as words and sentences. Symbols evoke a wide variety of associations, and the cognitive maps of self and other surely may be expected to possess broad meanings. Correspondingly, the definitions of the concepts are broad and connotative.

It was apparent from the definitions of the concepts that the point of view of the subject was emphasized. Here we are following the dictum of the phenomenologists who maintain that the first task of the psychologist is to establish the subject's point of view of himself in relation to his environment without regard to the conventional categories of the psychologist (MacLeod, 1947). The phenomenologist is convinced that a significant psychological process goes on "inside" in "private worlds" which is difficult to communicate by conventional methods. It is hoped, here, that some of the inherent shortcomings of the phenomenological approach may be avoided by an improved method of communication between the subject and scientist.

By going "inside," however, the investigator is compelled to have recourse to intervening variables and internal organizing constructs. The history of psychology records a large number of such constructs, such as the "mind" and "consciousness," but systems of thought which used such constructs have failed to become cumulative and have tended to generate endless ontological arguments. The wordy complexity of these systems was attacked by Watson (1913) who proposed that "mind" be banished from the lexicon of psychology, and with it any interpretation that an organism might make of stimuli. Explanations of an organism's responses were to be made entirely in terms of antecedent stimuli, untouched by human minds, if you will.

Nevertheless, psychologists repeatedly return to the cognitive approach in theory construction because the simple stimulus-response model is inadequate, restricting, and insufficiently veridical with regard to the complexities of human behavior (*see* Hebb, 1960; Mancuso, 1970). Hebb (1960), for example, proposes that the failure of experimental psychology to deal with the intervening variables of "I" or "ego" is a cause of its continual inadequacy with regard to clinical matters. He goes on to quote Bridgman concerning normative behavior in scientific inquiry: "The scientific method, as far as it is a method, is nothing more than doing one's damnedest with one's mind, no hold's barred."

Nevertheless, the criticism of the cognitive approach is well founded. Cognitive constructs invite speculation and endless circular arguments. It is proposed here, however, that the theory, measures, and research concerning self–other orientation provide a more systematic and less illusive approach than some earlier attempts.

Perhaps, much of the criticism of the cognitive approach has been misdirected. Measurement rather than the model itself may be the greatest shortcoming of cognitive approaches to social psychology, particularly where self–other concepts have been involved. Previous research has largely involved verbal self-report measures of self-esteem. The individual is asked directly to evaluate himself. Contamination of these reports by defense mechanisms and self-deception may well yield a distorted view of the self. For this reason, a more objective phenomenological approach will be emphasized here. Geometric configurations of the self and significant others serve as the media for communicating self–other orientations. Symbolic representations rather than words are assumed to facilitate the resolution of conflict between self and others.

But measurement must be integrated within a system of inquiry which includes theory and research. The interplay of theory, measurement, and research will be illustrated in the chapters dealing with self-esteem, social interest, and marginality. In these three sections, measurement is emphasized primarily because in the problem area of the social self, measurement has been the missing link. The area was in a state of disarray and doubt, although theory and research abounded. Without adequate measures and related research, theory tends to become spirals of gossamer discourse. On the other hand, without at least an incunabular framework, measurement and research may be characterized as buzzing confusion.

The presentation of this approach will begin with descriptions of some of the major components of self–other orientation. Most important, however, these sections illustrate the interplay of theory, measurement, and research in the development of the components and the evolving self-social system. This is followed by descriptions of two patterns of self–other orientation (the alienation syndrome and the political personality), the child's development of self–other concepts, environmental influences on self–other concepts, such as geographical mobility, cultures, and socioeconomic background, and finally, a two part theory section concerning concepts as they relate to personal stability and change. Again, the crucial problem of social psychology is assumed to be the synthesis of the self and significant others and the consequences of this synthesis for social behavior. A direction of this synthesis is proposed here.

Part I   Components of the Social Self

In this section, the theory, measures, and experiments concerning three of the components of the social self are described. The three components include self-esteem, social interest, and marginality. These examples were selected because the meaning of the self is described in relation to significant other people (self-esteem), in relation to significant categories of other people (social interest), and in relation to significant other groups (marginality). Measurement is emphasized and the topographical approach to communicating self–other orientations is described, but the tripartite nature of scientific inquiry including theory, measurement, and research is central to each of the chapters.

CHAPTER 1

Self-esteem: A Social Approach

Self-esteem is perhaps the most used and misused concept in the area of personality and social psychology. Individual behavior in a social setting is often explained in terms of the individual's "confidence in himself," "personal pride," or even his "inferiority complex."

Research abounds but so does misinformation because measures of self-esteem are of questionable validity. They may measure what the individual is willing to make public about himself. Theory derived from research based on these misleading measures have contributed little to our understanding of the concept. Indeed, the area of research was almost reduced to a wasteland because of the vast accumulation of poor research stemming from poor measures. Yet, the concept has survived.

The concept has survived because it is considered basic, measurement problems notwithstanding. Individuals evaluate themselves and behave on the basis of these evaluations even though some social scientists do not recognize the legitimacy of the concept of self-esteem. Now let us go on from this point. First, theories dealing with the concept of self-esteem will be discussed. This discussion is followed by a section describing the development of measures consistent with the framework of self–other orientation. Finally, a research section examines some of the fundamental principles of the framework.

*This chapter is a revision of an earlier paper by Ziller, Hagey, Smith, and Long (1969).

THEORY

The individual in a social setting is required to make a series of decisions to guide his behavior under conditions of rapid presentation of social events. In order to facilitate decision making, persons find it expedient to develop schemata which will aid in the processing of social information. For example, an individual in a discussion group may use the schema of his self ranking among the group members to help him decide whether or not to speak or how often he should speak. Schema refers to a cognitive mapping of elements, for example, an arrangement of persons in a hierarchy.

In the social psychological theory of personality proposed here, social adaptation is presumed to be mediated by self–other concepts. It is proposed that social stimuli are screened and translated into personal meaning through crude mappings of the self in relation to significant others. As opposed to Watson (1913), the organism is presumed to translate the stimulus and intervenes between the stimulus and the response. The organism is a controlling agent rather than being controlled by the stimulus (Social Stimuli → → Self–Other Schemata → → Social Response).

The fundamental framework of the theory of self–other orientation derives from Brunswik's (1956) theory of perception. Brunswik stressed the interaction of the organism and the environment. Cues of the environment are presumed to be processed by the individual in relation to his needs or sets. Certain cognitive processes intervene between the stimulus and the response. Stimuli must be selected and organized according to the needs of the organizer, and in terms of some system which reduces the information to be stored and facilitates information retrieval and general utility (*see* Neisser, 1967).

In terms of interpersonal perception, social stimuli are presumed to be mediated by schemata which map the relationship of self and other. Examples of social schemata include self above other, self with other, self more than other, self separated from other, self included with other, self similar or dissimilar to other, self more central than other, self close to others, or self connected with others. With the aid of these mappings of self and other, decision making for interpersonal behavior is facilitated in new situations. As will be shown later, for example, an individual who perceives the self above others tends to speak more frequently than others in a group discussion. Self–other concepts make for stability under kaleidoscopic social conditions. In this sense, self-social constructs act, to some degree, as defense mechanisms or control mechanisms as they might be labeled by ego psychologists. Through these concepts, the individual imposes himself on the situation or controls the situation to some extent and is thereby capable of regulating or stabilizing the environment somewhat.

Similarly, Klein (1951) has proposed that all theories of adaptation are concerned with the resolution of tension and an effort to establish equilibrium between the inner and outer systems. In his efforts to establish equilibrium, the individual puts to use his perceptual, cognitive, and motor processes. These processes mediate adaptation.

Among the equilibrating processes, Klein includes "leveling" and "sharpening." Leveling involves overlooking differences between objects in an array, whereas sharpening involves a heightened sensitivity to details (differentiation). It has been found that people develop definitive modes and patterns of perception which are adaptive for them. It is now proposed that self–other concepts are similar perceptual patterns or ego controls for interpersonal adaptation. Self-esteem is one such concept.

Heretofore, self-esteem and the self concept have been used almost interchangeably (Wylie, 1961), perhaps because other facets of the self concept have received little attention. James (1890) discussed self-esteem in a uniquely personal manner. For him, self-esteem was directly linked with success or failure. It remained for the individual to select the arena for contest. The arena for James was competence in the area of psychology. He was little concerned about his pole vaulting competence. In this personal arena, the individual is prepared to match himself with others and accept the outcome. It must be noted that a comparison of self with others was assumed.

Freud's use of the concept of self-esteem was overshadowed by his concern with the ego, id, and superego. Nevertheless, Diggory (1966) deduced Freud's concern with the self concept from his interest in "narcissism." Self-approval is reinforced by parents through the successful exercise of purposive motor acts such as sexual, eating, locomotion, and occupational activities. "Everything we possess or achieve, every remnant of the primitive feeling of omnipotence that experience has corroborated, helped to exalt the self regard" (Freud, 1914, p. 55).

It was Adler (1927), however, who first made self-esteem a major construct in personality theory. Ansbacher and Ansbacher (1956) repeatedly record Adler's emphasis upon the neurotic's concern with loss of self-esteem (inferiority complex) and his striving for superiority. In Adler's approach, however, self-esteem was considered along with the concepts of social interest and egocentrism, thereby introducing a component approach to the study of the self concept. For example, he attributes the fear of loss of the goal of superiority to an exaggerated longing to be pampered and to a lack of ability to cooperate (Ansbacher & Ansbacher, 1956, p. 109).

Self-esteem is usually defined as the individual's perception of his worth. A phenomenological orientation is taken; it is the subject's point of view rather than that of the scientist which is the central concern. Here the generality of Osgood's evaluative component with regard to meaning is assumed (Osgood, Suci, & Tannenbaum, 1957). In developing measures of meaning, Osgood found that three dimensions emerged. One of those was an "evaluative" dimension. The evaluative dimension evolves from ratings of a word (such as "self") on a scale defined by bipolar adjectives such as rough-smooth, warm-cold, and good-bad. In Osgood's terms, then, the evaluative component of the self concept is self-esteem.

In evaluating the self, few physical cues exist which provide a reliable basis for measurement. Certainly, one can obtain pieces of information about the self, such as running speed, height, and so forth, but an overall evaluation is more meaningfully obtained through comparisons with appropriate other persons as points of reference. For example, "I can run faster than John but not as fast as Jim." Thus self-evaluations are rendered in terms of a social frame of reference provided by significant others and an implicit location of the self within this frame of reference. Self-evaluation or self-esteem is not an absolute, but evolves from a series of self–other comparisons, or, exists only in a social context. Thus, interpretations of research findings concerning self-esteem must include considerations of the significant others used as points of reference by the subject.

Previous research has largely avoided the social context of self-esteem and attempted to develop a concept and accompanying measures which were not qualified by a social frame of reference. In so doing, however, the effectiveness of the theories and instruments in predicting social behavior may have been severely limited. It is now proposed that the self concept is a mediating agent between the organism and the environment, and that self-esteem is that component of the self system which is associated with the consistency of the organism's response to the environment.

More specifically, it is proposed that self-esteem is a component of the self system which is involved in the regulation of the extent to which the self system is maintained under conditions of strain, such as during the processing of new information relative to the self. Self-esteem in this context becomes a control mechanism. Thus, for example, evaluations by others of either a positive or negative nature do not evoke immediate, corresponding action by the individual with high self-esteem. New information relative to the self is examined in terms of its relevance and meaning for the self system. Some information may be discarded as irrelevant, or invalid. Even if the information is accepted, a person with high self-esteem will tend to assimilate the information rather than restructure the self system. In this way, persons with high self-esteem are somewhat insulated from the environment or are not completely subject to environmental contingencies. The individual is not a victim of events or does not feel compelled to accommodate the self to the situation. Events are assimilated within the self system.

Persons with low self-esteem, on the other hand, do not possess a well-developed conceptual buffer for evaluative stimuli. In Witkins' terms (*see* Witkins, Dyk, Foterson, Goodenough, & Karp, 1962), the person with low self-esteem is field dependent, that is, he tends to passively conform to the influence of the pervasive field or context. Since such a person's behavior is directly linked to immediate environmental circumstances and is not mediated or differentiated and integrated by the self concept, he is thereby inclined toward inconsistency. Low self-esteem is associated with short term adaptation and inconsistency, whereas high self-esteem is associated with long range adaptation and consistency. In yet another context, the adaptation system of persons with low self-esteem may be characterized by S-R models of learning (response is directly linked to stimulus), whereas persons with high self-esteem may be characterized by S-O-R models of learning (the stimulus is interpreted or mediated by the organism).

Again, it is seen that a cognitive orientation is assumed here. Various social concepts are assumed to mediate social stimuli and social behavior. Self-esteem is one such social concept. Through this representational concept, it is possible for the person to categorize and evaluate social stimuli and social acts. The social stimuli and acts are translated in terms of personal meaning by means of the personal abstraction, self-esteem. In this way, multiple situational cues are taken into account, but an integration is sought among the specific behaviors and stimuli in terms of self-esteem. For example, self-esteem facilitates the hierarchical ordering of self and others along some status dimension, and frequency of verbal participation in a social situation is congruent with the perceived status hierarchy. Persons with high self-esteem participate more frequently. As Aronfreed (1968) points out, "The mediational power of cognitive representation therefore allows the child's conduct to be governed with a certain amount of consistency that could not be produced if its actions were closely bound to immediate situational behavioral cues" (p. 69). Again, Fromm (1955) describes the emergence of the self as a response to the need for a stable and consistent way of apprehending the social environment. Thus, it is anticipated that the behavior of persons with high self-esteem is more integrated and that their cognitive processes are characterized by a selective consideration of relevant social elements.

The relationship between consistency and self-esteem may also be a function of self-reinforcement. In this approach self-evaluation is seen as providing a mediating link between previous socialization and a person's tendency to administer self-reinforcement (Bandura & Whalen, 1966; Kanfer & Marston, 1963). Here, it must be assumed that the child who is successfully inducted into the social system is frequently supported by the parents; high self-esteem results (*see* Coopersmith, 1967). In the process of socialization and self-acceptance, the child adopts the point of view of the parents and gradually substitutes self-reinforcement for parental reinforcement. At first, he identifies with the parents and reinforces himself on occasions similar to those when he has been supported by parents. In time and with the increased independence the self concept rather than the parent concept serves as a more meaningful and reliable model for the reinforcement process.

The self is more meaningful and reliable because it arises directly from the child's social experiences rather than through the indirect experiences transmitted by the parents. In addition, the self concept is more responsive to change than the parents' concept of the individual and therefore may be more situationally valid. The ubiquity of the self concept also serves as a more ready guide for self-reinforcement, thereby contributing to the consistency of behavior. Finally, consistency in behavior is more probable by persons with higher self-esteem because the person is less dependent upon external sources of reinforcement. The person with low self-esteem is compelled to be responsive to a wide variety of others leading to inconsistency. The person with high self-esteem is more inclined to be responsive to internal guidance mechanisms, to one abstract person, if you will, leading to a greater consistency in behavior.

Yet another way of viewing self-esteem is that the person with low self-esteem is required to monitor the behavior of many others before making a decision to act, whereas a person with high self-esteem only monitors the behavior of a few others before making a decision to act.

Self-esteem is a cognitive orientation of the self in relation to significant others along an evaluative dimension chosen by the evaluator himself. This orientation then serves to organize and assimilate social stimuli and serves as the basis of social behavior. The concept is broad gauged. It incorporates many facets of the concepts of earlier investigators, but the emerging concept is still very different.

In contrast to Freud and Adler, the concept of self-esteem as proposed here has a more positive orientation. Superiority-inferiority feelings are only tangentially related. The concern here is the individual's perception of his control over the environment and the consistency of his behavior in social situations.

Similarly, although the concept of self-esteem as used here is related to Lewin's (1935) concept of differentiation-integration, Witkins' concept of field independence, and Piaget's (1947) concept of assimilation-accommodation in that they all are concerned with cognitive structure, self-esteem is more concerned with social behavior and must be considered along with other self–other concepts such as social interest (*see* Chapter 4) and complexity of the self (*see* Chapter 5). Self-esteem is but a single component of the self system, and the self system in turn is but a part of a more inclusive personal system involving attitudes, values, behaviors, and roles (*see* Chapter 9). Again, self-esteem as viewed here is but a single component in the personal-social system.

The recurring propositions concerning self-esteem are: (1) persons with high as opposed to low self-esteem are more consistent in their social behavior, and (2) persons with high as opposed to low self-esteem have had a history of social reinforcement. These propositions will be examined in the research section of this chapter. First, however, the derivation of the measure of self-esteem is described.

MEASUREMENT

Previous research concerning self-esteem has not emphasized sufficiently the social nature of the self system. The failure to incorporate and weigh social factors within the self-evaluation framework may have contributed, in part at least, to the disappointing state of the investigation of self-esteem.

A second shortcoming of earlier studies in this area is their descriptive nature which, coupled with the serious shortcomings of the measurement techniques, have left the area at a low level of theoretical development.

Finally, and more serious, previous research has largely involved a verbal self-report measure of self-esteem. Kelly (1955) qualifies his assertions continuously by pointing to the most tenuous of his assumptions, that the subject's word labels for his constructs mean what the examiner thinks they mean. Finally, Kelly suggests (p. 268) that if a test "can be arranged to produce a kind of protocol which can be subjected to a meaningful analysis, independent of words, we shall have made progress toward a better understanding of the client's personal constructs."

The inadequacy of our language and concepts in dealing with interpersonal relations is often acknowledged with almost implied resignation. Thus, Polanyi (1966, p. 4) states that in certain realms ". . . we know more than we can tell." Polanyi may simply be lamenting the limitations of verbal communication. A system of communication may be functional optimally only within a given knowledge area. Thus, the message must be matched with an appropriate medium in order to maximize communication. The English language was not invented in order to help persons to communicate their self-evaluations to social scientists.

The method of communication between the subject and investigator used here involves the medium of a structured projective technique with limited verbal demands. The subject is asked to arrange symbols of the self and significant others. The arrangement is presumed to be an expression of his perceived relationships with others. The outcome may be referred to as a cognitive sociometric of self and other.

In developing theory and measures of self–other orientation, it was assumed that the human organism finds it expedient to order, map, or structure the multitude of social stimuli. The processes used by persons are expected to be somewhat idiosyncratic, but owing to commonality among human experiences, sensory processes, classification systems, and normative processes, the evolving abstraction systems possess sufficient similarity that a basis of a communication system exists.

The most relevant ordering process with regard to self-esteem is what DeSoto, London, and Handel refer to as "spatial paralogic" and "linear ordering." It is observed that people are prone to place elements in a linear ordering to the exclusion of other structures, and that they handle linear ordering more easily than most other structures (Coombs, Raiffa, & Thrall, 1954; DeSoto, London, & Handel, 1965). Indeed, DeSoto, London, and Handel note that serial ordering proceeds more readily in a rightward direction than in a leftward direction. The tendency to attribute greater importance to the object placed at the extreme left position in a horizontal display has been noted by Morgan (1944).

The measure of self-esteem developed here utilized the serial ordering predilection of the subjects within a social context. (*See* Item 1 in Appendix A.) The measure involves presenting a horizontal array of circles and a list of significant others such as "yourself," "a teacher," and "someone you know is unhappy." The task requires the subject to assign each person to a circle. The score is the weighted position of the self. In accordance with the cultural norm, positions to the left are assumed to be associated with higher self-esteem.

Item 1 is one of six items in the student form of the instrument. The other five self-esteem items involve the following sets of significant others: (a) doctor, father, friend, mother, yourself, teacher; (b) someone you know who is a good athlete, someone you know who is a good dancer, someone you know who is funny, someone you know who gets good grades, yourself, someone you know who is unhappy; (c) an actor, your brother or someone who is most like a brother, your best friend, a dean of students, yourself, a salesman; (d) someone you know who is cruel, your grandmother, a housewife, a policeman, yourself, your sister or someone who is most like a sister; (e) doctor, father, friend, nurse, yourself, someone you know who is unsuccessful. The list of significant others derive from Kelly (1955).

In a study involving 75 randomly selected students from grades 7 through 12, the split-half reliability (odd-even) was 0.80 corrected for length (Long, Ziller, & Henderson, 1968). Split-half reliability (odd-even) for the adult form* was 0.85, uncorrected for length, in a study (Mossman & Ziller, 1968) involving 60 neuropsychiatric patients. Test-retest reliability for 86 sixth and seventh graders was 0.54 for the student form. Thus, the measure was found to possess sufficient stability for purposes of research.

VALIDATION

The measure of self-esteem proposed here is assumed to involve social reasoning and a norm of hierarchical ordering of social objects in a horizontal line from left to right. This assumption was examined in a series of separate studies.

---

*The six sets of social objects included in the adult form of the instrument are: (a) doctor, father, a friend, a nurse, yourself, someone you know who is unsuccessful; (b) doctor, father, friend, politician, yourself, an employer; (c) someone you know who is a good athlete, someone you know who is popular, someone you know who is funny, someone who knows a great deal, yourself, someone you know who is unhappy; (d) an actor, your brother or someone who is most like a brother, your best friend, yourself, a salesman, a politically active person; (e) someone you know who is cruel, a judge, a housewife, a policeman, yourself, your sister or someone who is most like a sister; (f) a defeated legislative candidate, the happiest person you know, someone you know who is kind, yourself, someone you know who is successful, the strongest person you know.

In the first of these (Ziller, Megas, & DeCencio, 1964), 45 patients in an acute neuropsychiatric treatment ward were presented with seven circular pieces of white felt cloth two inches in diameter. The circles were marked by symbols indicating the person they represented. These persons included nurse (N), nurse's aide (NA), other patients in the ward (O), psychiatrist (Pi), psychologist (Po), social worker (SW), and yourself (Y). A list of the symbols and their referents were placed on a table in alphabetical order for the subject's information. These were also read to the subjects. The subjects were instructed to arrange the circles on a black felt board, $2 \times 2\frac{1}{2}$ yards, in any way that they wished. (*See* Kuethe, 1962.)

In support of the serial ordering tendencies proposed by DeSoto, London, and Handel (1965), the majority of subjects arranged the symbolic circles in a straight line from left to right. By assigning weights to the left-right positions and calculating the mean weighting of the seven symbols, the resulting order of the symbolized positions was: psychiatrist, psychologist, social worker, nurse, nurse's aide, other patients, and yourself. It is apparent that a left to right status hierarchy of the social objects emerges.

A similar analysis was made of the left to right location of a low status other person by college students using the student form (*see* Table 1.1). It was noted that the "unhappy" person was placed in the last position to the right 48% of the time; "someone you know who is unsuccessful," 56%; "someone you know who is cruel," 64%; and "someone you know who is flunking," 59%.

Further support for the assumption of a left to right paralogic was found in the association of the self-esteem score as previously derived and a second technique of scoring. This involved the identification of the most

Table 1.1 Distribution of the Location of the "Negative Significant Others" in Four Items of the Self-esteem Measures, Horizontal Arrangement Positions.

	6	5	4	3	2	1
Unhappy $N = 150$	16%	7%	7%	7%	15%	48%
Unsuccessful $N = 147$	21%	3%	5%	9%	5%	56%
Cruel $N = 154$	27%	2%	4%	1%	3%	64%
Flunking $N = 172$	31%	1%	2%	3%	4%	59%

negative, significant other for each set of significant others and calculating the distance, in number of circles, between the low status other and the self. (Only four items which involved a clearly differentiated low status other were included in this analysis. These items were a, b, d, and e.) This method of scoring was suggested when it was noted in Table 1.1 that the low status other was sometimes located in the left position, indicating that arrangement of the self and others may be based on other than a left to right hierarchical ordering in some cases.

The correlation between the scores derived by these methods was 0.33, $p < 0.05$ ($N = 163$ male and female college students). Only the results with regard to males were statistically significant, however ($r = 0.46$, $N = 61$, $p < 0.001$; females, $r = 0.14$, $N = 102$, $p < 0.10$).

A similar analysis of the two scoring methods was made using the adult form with male neuropsychiatric patients (Mossman & Ziller, 1968). The results corroborate the findings with regard to the male college sample ($r = 0.56$, $N = 60$, $p < 0.001$).

In yet another study of the left-right serial ordering phenomenon, a children's form of the self-esteem measure was used (Henderson, Long, & Ziller, 1965). The analysis involved the responses of 48 boys and girls ranging in age from 7 to 14 and who had applied for corrective training at a reading study center, plus 48 controls matched for age, sex, and general intelligence. The subjects were given a paper with a long horizontal line. They were next presented in random order six circles with pictures representing self, friend, and a "smart," "dumb," "funny," and "bad" classmate. The children were told to paste these symbolic circles in a row on the line. It was found that children placed the "smart" classmate to the left and a "bad" classmate to the right to a significant degree.

Evidence that the left-right serial ordering is not a phenomenon limited to persons within the United States is found in the analysis of the location of "someone you know who is unsuccessful" in the student form of item e. With regard to 92 boys and girls from Form I of the M.V.D.M. High School in Vesakapatnam, Andhra, South India, the frequency with which the "unsuccessful" person was located in the positions from *right to left* was 74, 9, 4, 0, 1, and 4. With regard to an American sample of 94 boys and girls, the corresponding frequencies were 53, 17, 15, 3, 3, and 3.

Another test of the left to right hierarchical ordering assumption was the association between the weighted position of "yourself" among five others, including "someone you know who is flunking," "the happiest person you know," "someone you know who is kind," "someone you know who is successful," and "the strongest person you know" under conditions where the social objects were to be arranged horizontally as in Table 1.2 and vertically. In the vertical display, the higher position of the self is assumed to represent higher self-esteem. The correlation between these two measures was 0.50 ($N = 82, p < 0.05$).

Table 1.2 Distribution of the Location of "Someone Who is Flunking" in Two Identical Self-esteem Items (Vertical vs. Horizontal Arrangements).

Location* Arrangement	6	5	4	3	2	1
Vertical	9%	0.6%	0.6%	3%	3%	84%
Horizontal	31%	1%	2%	3%	4%	59%

*In the vertical arrangement location "6" was the first or top position in the hierarchy. In the horizontal arrangement location "6" is the first position in the left-right hierarchy.

An analysis of the location of the lowest status other, "someone you know who is flunking," indicates (*see* Table 1.2) that the number of reversals in the placement of the low status other is reduced in the vertical arrangement (9% vs. 31%). The vertical arrangement may introduce greater item visibility, however.

A third approach to the validation of the social self-esteem (SSE) measure was a correlational analysis of SSE with existing measures of the construct. The measures selected for comparison were those most frequently referenced in the literature (Wylie, 1961), and a more recent device developed for research purposes by Culick and used by Diggory and her collaborators (Diggory-Farnham, 1964). With the exception of the SSE, all the measures were based on self reports. Thus, the Bills–Vance–McLean (1951) Index of Adjustment and Values required the subject to rate himself with reference to each of 49 adjectives as to how often he was "this sort of person." Six-week test-retest reliability was 0.90 ($N = 100$). Diggory's Self-evaluation Questionnaire asks the subject the percentage of time that he expected to succeed in eight given situations. The reliability is not reported.

Coopersmith's (1959) Self-esteem Inventory contains 54 items concerned with the subject's perceptions in four areas: peers, parents, school, and self. The form was modified slightly to make it more appropriate for a college population. The self-esteem score is twice the sum of the high self-esteem items (as agreed upon by five psychologists) marked "like me" and low self-esteem items marked "unlike me." Reported test-retest reliability after five weeks was 0.88.

In an earlier test of the relationship between the SSE and a single item overall self-evaluation (Ridgeway, 1965), a negative but not statistically significant relationship had been found ($r = -0.15$, $N = 100$, $p < 0.05$). Given the different theoretical frameworks and method of communication upon which the measures are based, a significant relationship was not anticipated in the present study. The purpose of this study in the program was to establish the independence of the SSE more systematically.

The correlation matrix for these three scales and the SSE for each set is shown in Table 1.3. None of the correlations with SSE were statistically

Table 1.3   Intercorrelation Matrix of Four Measures of Self-esteem.

		(2)		(3)		(4)	
		Males	Females	Males	Females	Males	Females
Bills–Vance– McLean Index	(1)	0.46xx	0.17	0.60xxx	0.29x	−0.10	−0.14
Coopersmith's Self-esteem	(2)			0.37x	0.23	0.02	0.04
Diggory's Self- evaluation	(3)					−0.09	0.21
Social Self- esteem							

xxx = $p < 0.001$
xx = $p < 0.01$
x = $p < 0.05$
N(males) = 33
N(females) = 53

significant. Once again, sex differences are quite apparent in the intercorrelations among the measures. For male subjects ($N = 33$), the highest correlation ($r = 0.60$), was between Diggory's and Bills' measures. Significant correlations with regard to male subjects were also found between Diggory's and Coopersmith's measures ($r = 0.37$), and Bills' and Coopersmith's ($r = 0.46$). The only significant correlation found for female subjects ($N = 53$) was between Diggory's and Bills' measures ($r = 29$). These results are worrisome, even though they were anticipated. Yet, the results may be interpreted to indicate that the SSE and the other measures of self-esteem are in different psychological domains. The SSE in contrast to the other devices is a non-verbal, "low visibility" instrument, and also incorporates a social frame of reference.

One of the universal criticisms of the most frequently used measures of self-acceptance is that they are about equally correlated with socially desirable responses as they are with each other (Crowne, Stephens, & Kelly, 1961). For example, the greater the tendency to deny negative characteristics about the self, the less the reported discrepancy between self and ideal self.

Using the Crowne–Marlowe (1964) measure of socially desirable response tendencies, and relating it to the SSE as well as Diggory's measure of self-evaluation, correlations of -0.36 and 0.65 ($N = 24, p < 0.05$ for both) were found for sophomore female volunteers for an experiment. Higher self-esteem as measured by the Diggory device was associated with a tendency to give socially desirable responses. The opposite relationship was found using the SSE. These results suggest that, whereas the usual measures of self-esteem invite the subject to disclose himself to others, the SSE asks the subject to disclose himself to himself.

These results need give us pause. The correlation between Diggory's measure of self-esteem and the measure of social desirability is higher than the correlation between Diggory's measure and any other measure of self-esteem or among any of the frequently used measures of self-esteem analyzed here. These data support the critical position taken here concerning verbal self reports. It must be acknowledged that some very sophisticated techniques have been devised to circumvent the inherent shortcomings of the verbal self report. Still, the obstacles for the verbal self report appear to be considerable. At the very least it is proposed here that studies which employ verbal self reports of self-esteem should also report results which employ less visible measures of self-esteem.

RESEARCH

The two major propositions associated with the self-esteem framework described here may now be tested. The most crucial proposition states that high as opposed to low self-esteem is associated with consistency of social behavior.

Self-esteem and Consistency of Social Participation

In an experiment by Mossman and Ziller (1968), it was hypothesized that self-esteem is: (1) positively related to frequency of participation in group discussion, and (2) is associated with the organism's consistency of response. Relative to the first hypothesis, it has already been demonstrated that high self-esteem is associated with social acceptance. This finding suggests that in a group discussion the individual with high self-esteem will receive and expects to receive verbal and non-verbal cues from the other members which invite or support his bid for participation. In addition, the high self-esteem–high socially accepted member may be expected to receive more social reinforcement for his participation. Thus, the high self-esteem–high socially accepted member is assumed to receive more self-reinforcement and social reinforcement for participation in group discussion, which results in a higher level of participation.

Here, high self-esteem is assumed to be associated with a higher potential for self-reinforcement and a higher probability of social reinforcement. To some extent, self-reinforcement and social reinforcement may be complementary. When social reinforcement is withheld, the individual with high self-esteem has recourse to self-reinforcement. The individual with low self-esteem is more dependent upon social reinforcement, leading, as we stated at the outset, to less stable participation.

Borgatta (1962, p. 256) demonstrated a significant correlation between Cattrell's Guilt Proneness versus Confident Adequacy subtests and total activity in a group discussion ($r = -0.34$, the more guilt, the less activity) and between Edward's Abasement subtest and total activity ($r = -0.30$, the less abasement, the more activity). The subjects in the study were 76 neuropsychiatric patients who were members of four "autonomous problem-solving groups" similar in purpose to those discussed by Fairweather (1964, p. 171). Each of the four groups were observed during one session a week over a three-week period. The observer recorded the total amount of interaction units per individual. The adult forms of the SSE were administered at the end of the third session.

The self-esteem scores were ordered as anticipated with regard to levels of verbal participation: high interactors (those who contributed more than 5% of the interaction units across the three sessions), 21.6 (the sum of six ratings); low interactors (those who contributed between 2% and 5% of the interaction units, 19.8; and the non-interactors (those who contributed 1% or less of the interaction units across the three sessions), 17.4. Furthermore, the results were statistically significant ($F = 3.37$, d.f. $= 1$ and 57, $p < 0.05$).

In order to test the second hypothesis, the variance of the relative frequency of interaction units across the three sessions was used as the measure of consistency of social behavior for each individual. A highly consistent interactor was defined as a group member whose relative frequency of interaction variance was 0.03 or less. The 0.03 point of division created two equal-size categories of subjects with regard to consistency of verbal participation. However, only the consistency of high interactors was analyzed since consistency among low interactors and non-interactors would be a statistical artifact stemming from a ceiling effect. As hypothesized, there was a significant difference ($p < 0.05$) in self-esteem scores between the high interactors–low consistency (SSE = 15.90, $N = 10$) and high interactors–high consistency (SSE = 26.73, $N = 11$) categories of subjects.

The second major proposition concerns the relationship between social support and self-esteem. In the following review of studies, high self-esteem was found to be associated with social acceptance, winning an election, socioeconomic status, and parental reinforcement; whereas low self-esteem was associated with institutionalization for social maladjustment.

Self-esteem and Social Acceptance

One of the earliest studies in the series examined the frequently hypothesized relationship between acceptance of self and acceptance by others (Mann, 1959; Wylie, 1961). In one of the reported studies, Coopersmith (1959) found that fourth, fifth, and sixth graders showed a significant positive correlation (0.34) between self-esteem and popularity. The rationale for the relationship is often tautological (*see* Rogers, 1951, p. 520) but the findings are nevertheless consistent. Within the present framework, self-acceptance and the acceptance by others are perceived as inextricable components of social self-esteem.

The subjects in this study (Ziller, Alexander, & Long, 1964) were 321 sixth grade students in eleven classrooms from four elementary schools. The subjects were all white, and the composition of the classes remained unchanged throughout the school day. All subjects completed a sociometric item asking them to name the five children with whom they would most like to play. Twenty-five children (17 boys and 8 girls) who were unchosen and 25 children (17 boys and 8 girls) who were most highly chosen from the same classes as the unchosen were administered one item of the social self-esteem measure. The social set included "doctor," "father," "friend," "the person with whom you are most happy," "mother," "yourself," "the most successful person you know," and "the person with whom you are most comfortable." The directions were read to the subjects. The mean position of the popular children (1 being the left position) was 3.8 and of the unpopular 5.7 ($t = 3.87, p < 0.005$).

Success and Failure of Political Candidacy and Self-esteem

One of the difficulties of studying changes in the self concept is that conditions associated with changes in the self concept are not readily generated and are rarely encountered under circumstances amenable to statistical analysis. A political election, however, provides an exceptional opportunity to study changes in the self concept associated with winning as opposed to losing the election. It also affords an opportunity to test directly the effects of social support on self-evaluation.

One month prior to the 1967 state election in Oregon, 44 candidates for the state legislature were administered the first four items of the adult Form II of the SSE. The same items were again administered to the same candidates approximately one month after the election. Each candidate was approached individually and completed the form in the presence of the data collector. The results are provided in Table 1.4. Fifteen of the 23

Table 1.4   Changes in Self-esteem of Winning and Losing Political Candidates.

Candidates	Direction of Change in Self-esteem		
	Increased	Decreased	No Change
Winners	15	4	4
Losers	8	11	2

$X^2 = 6.01 \ (p < 0.05)$

winning candidates increased in self-esteem as opposed to 8 of the 21 losing candidates. Moreover, 11 of the 21 losing candidates decreased in self-esteem as opposed to 4 of the 23 winners. The results are significant at the 0.05 level of confidence ($X^2 = 5.99$).

Self-esteem and Socioeconomic Status

Although Wylie's review of the literature contains no reference to an analysis of a relationship between socioeconomic status and self-esteem, more recently two studies (Rosenberg, 1965; Coopersmith, 1967) indicate a positive relationship, although only the results of the first are statistically significant. The rationale for the relationship is that social status is one of the most striking indexes of prestige and success. Persons higher in the social system have more prestigious occupations, have higher incomes, and tend to live in larger and more luxurious houses located in more desirable neighborhoods. These persons are perceived as more successful and tend to receive material and cultural benefits that might lead them to believe that they are generally more worthy than others.

Coopersmith (1967) points out, however, that children's social position emanates from experiences in school and the neighborhood, rather than in an occupational context. These attenuating considerations notwithstanding, it is proposed that children from higher status families are more apt to have ego enhancing material reinforcements and social reinforcements. Social self-esteem, then, is presumed to be a general evaluation of the self in relation to significant others, and socioeconomic status is but one component of social self-esteem.

A reanalysis of the results of a study by Long, Ziller, and Henderson (1968) involved an equal number of boys and girls of normative age for grade in each grade 6 to 12 in four schools in Queen Anne's County, Maryland. The subjects were white and lived in a rural area on the Eastern Shore of Maryland. The subjects had completed six items of the student form of the SSE. Hollingshead's Occupational Scale based upon head of household's occupation (Hollingshead & Redlich, 1953) was used. Four classifications evolved which provided classes with maximally equivalent numbers of subjects per class. Thus, 83 subjects whose fathers' occupation was professional, business, office worker, or salesman constituted class 1; 66 subjects whose fathers were classified as skilled labor constituted class 2; 77 subjects whose fathers were farmers constituted class 3; and 69 subjects whose fathers were semi-skilled or unskilled labor constituted class 4. The mean self-esteem scores of these subjects were 23.0, 22.4, 20.4, and 20.5, respectively ($F = 2.54$, d.f. $= 3$ and 292, p about 0.05). Self-esteem and socioeconomic status are positively associated in this American sample of subjects. The children of fathers with lower socioeconomic status reveal lower self-esteem.

Self-esteem and Culture

In an analysis of cultural shaping of conception of the self, Hallowell (1955) assumes that the individual's self-image and his interpretations of his own experience cannot be separated from the concept of the self that is normative in his society.

A similar analysis to the foregoing was made possible by the availability of the caste of Indian subjects in reanalysis of a cross-cultural study (Ziller, Long, Ramana, & Reddy, 1968). The subjects consisted of 50 boys and 50 girls from Form I of the M.V.D.M. High School in Vesakapatnam, Andhra, South India. The children ranged in age from 10 to 14 with a median age of 12. Six items of the student form of the SSE were used. The instructions were read aloud in Telugu, the native language of the children, by one of the Indian experimenters.

The subjects were found to be members of four castes: (a) Caste 1 (Brahmin), $N = 39$, self-esteem $= 27.1$; (b) Caste 3 (Visya), $N = 9$, self-esteem $= 25.1$; (c) Caste 4 (included 18 types such as Satani and Najara which are all associated with crafts), $N = 48$, self-esteem $= 29.3$; (d) Caste 5 (Harijan and Relly), $N = 4$, self-esteem $= 30.3$. Because of the extremely small number of subjects in two of the castes, Castes 1 and 3 were combined and compared with Castes 4 and 5. The results were statistically significant at the 0.05 level of confidence ($F = 5.6$, d.f. $= 1$ and 98).

The results were in opposition to expectations based upon the results of the previous study. In this sample of Indian subjects, the highest self-esteem was expressed by students in the lowest caste (in the results above, the self-esteem scores were simply reversed; high scores represent high self-esteem). However, school was attended within this age group and in the region by only 14% of the population. The children from the lowest castes, then, may be using other children of their caste who do not attend school as points of reference, and within this frame of reference, their own status appears extremely high. Thus, as indicated in the initial self-esteem framework, the field of comparison becomes crucial. Self-esteem is defined with regard to significant others.

In this same study of Indian children, it was possible to compare the self-esteem of a comparable sample of boys and girls from the Queen Anne's County sample mentioned earlier. Here again, the high score represents high self-esteem. The Indian and American means were 28.1 and 20.6 respectively ($F = 65.6$, d.f. $= 1$ and 196, $p < 0.005$). Again, however, the privilege of school attendance may be the crucial variable. The Indian student who perceives himself as being a member of a select group by virtue of school attendance may have higher self-esteem than American children who attend school as a matter of course. In terms of the discussion of the association between self-esteem and socioeconomic status, it is proffered that the school environment is the most salient status variable for the Indian children.

Self-esteem and Conformity

In a summary of the research concerning self-esteem and conformity, Wylie (1961) acknowledges that there is a trend indicating an inverse relationship; individuals with low self-esteem tend to be more persuasible. In the present study, 41 high school seniors were administered the six-item student form of the SSE and then were placed in the classic Asch conformity situation (Asch, 1956). Under the nine extreme conditions where the unanimous majority (of four in this study) chose the line which deviated most from the standard line, the biserial correlation between conformity and the SSE was 0.32, $p < 0.05$. *Higher* self-esteem was associated with *higher* conformity.

As stated at the outset, previous research was equivocal. Nevertheless, it is compelling to view these results as negative. In view of the strong social component inherent in the present measure of self-esteem, however, it is still possible to interpret the results as indicating that the person with high self-esteem within a social context may not perceive conforming behavior under low cost conditions as damaging to the self system.

Self-esteem and the Neurotic Personality

Ausubel (1952) regards self-esteem as the outcome of achieving a status commensurate with one's conception of self-importance. He proposes that a devaluation of the self concept is necessary in the face of reality and in order to avoid severe injury to self-esteem. Trauma to self-esteem may result if ego importance is devalued extremely. On the other hand, personality disorders may evolve from untenable notions of omnipotence to which the child is subject.

Results of experiments which have investigated the relationship between adjustment and self-regard (Wylie, 1961) are equivocal. Again, however, the results may simply reflect the shortcomings of verbal self-report measures of self-esteem, particularly when used with neuropsychiatric patients.

In the first and second of three studies involving the SSE (Ziller, Megas, & DeCencio, 1964), the felt circle approach described earlier was employed. In the first study involving a set of significant other members of an acute neuropsychiatric treatment ward (psychiatrist, psychologist, social worker, nurse, nurse's aide, other patients in the ward, and yourself), patients who had been administered electroconvulsive shock therapy ($N = 10$) from one to six weeks prior to completing the SSE, as compared with those patients who had not received this treatment ($N = 35$), placed the circle representing themselves in the last position to the right more frequently ($X^2 = 12.34$, $p < 0.01$). These results appear to validate the psychiatric screening techniques for depression, since electroconvulsive shock treatment was only recommended for acutely depressed patients.

In the second experiment in the series (Ziller, Megas, & DeCencio, 1964), 25 patients from the neuropsychiatric ward of an acute treatment center and 23 volunteers from the hospital staff, including personnel from several levels of the occupational hierarchy, arranged in a horizontal straight line on a black felt field 10 significant social elements represented by symbols on a piece of felt two inches in diameter. The elements included "mother," "father," "your wife or girlfriend," "the most successful person you know," "the happiest person you know," "the person with whom you are most uncomfortable," "employer," "your doctor," and "your friend." The circles were placed in a random order on a table in front of the black felt field. On each circle there was a one-word description of the person whom the circle represented. A list of the social elements that the circles represented was presented in alphabetical order on the same table. The subjects were asked to "place them all on the board in a straight line according to some relationship that you decide upon." Normals were found to have placed the "self" in a higher position than the patients in the assumed left-right hierarchy ($t = 4.57, p < 0.001$).

In the third study in the series (Ziller & Grossman, 1967), 90 male, acute neuropsychiatric patients and 87 male employees of the same hospital served as subjects. Two self-esteem items were administered to the patients during the first week of admission to the hospital. In the first item, the subject was asked to choose a circle to represent himself from the circles arranged in a vertical column. Circles were weighted from 1 to 10, with a higher score associated with a higher position.

The second measure of self-esteem presented a horizontal array of circles. Subjects were also presented with the same list of ten significant other persons (including the self) used in the preceding study. Here the usual left-right hierarchy was assumed.

The results corroborate earlier findings in the series. Neuropsychiatric patients in comparison with normals show lower self-esteem on both measures (horizontal, $p < 0.10$; vertical, $p < 0.05$).

OVERVIEW

The series of studies described here represents the first phase in a program of research concerning self–other orientation. The program of research involves the integration of a theory of personality involving self–other perceptions and an instrument designed to measure the evaluation of the self in relation to significant others using topological representations of self and others. The outcome of the present approach, although balanced with regard to the emphasis on theory, instruments, and research, rests largely upon the utility of the measures involved. Measurement remains the missing link in personality research. With regard to self-social constructs, measurement is dependent upon the method of communicating between the subject and the scientist. Here we have proposed that there are some distinct advantages to avoiding the usual self-report approach and substituting for it a topological approach with limited verbal demands.

The results tend to support the validity and utility of the approach to the measure of self-esteem. Social objects with greater value tend to be placed to the left in the horizontal display; the absolute difference between location of self and a low status social object is significantly associated with the left to right location of the self; left-right location of the self is significantly associated with the up-down location of the self.

The underlying framework of self-esteem was also supported. Persons with high self-esteem were found to be more consistent in their social participation across tasks. In addition, the evidence supports the proposition that persons with high self-esteem enjoy social support. It was found that higher self-esteem was associated with social acceptance, socioeconomic status, identification with parents, and the normal as opposed to the neurotic personality.

The social context of self-esteem has been emphasized in the present approach, and, indeed, the results of most of the studies are concerned with social behavior (i.e., popularity, frequency of participation in group discussions, parent-child relationships). An attempt was made to describe the concept used here in terms of its social correlates. Thus, the term "social self-esteem" was used. The meaning of social self-esteem, as it evolves against the background of its social correlates, suggests social acceptance or perhaps self–other confidence. The individual who is assured of his high self-evaluation within a social context is more consistent in social behavior and more accepted by others. Self-acceptance and social acceptance are interdependent.

If, then, the traditional self-report measure of self-esteem is unrelated to social self-esteem, a reanalysis of the meaning of the traditional measures is indicated. It is now suggested that the self-report measures indicate a socially desirable self-esteem, an evaluation of the self that the reporter is willing to reveal, or that he desires the other to accept.

Aside from the question of the social context of self-esteem, the limited verbal demands of the present approach recommends it as a most useful measure in cross-cultural research, developmental research, and research in general where there may be some question of the comparable verbal ability of the subjects in relation to the experimental tasks.

A great number of descriptive studies are readily generated by the development of an instrument and framework. For example, it is possible to examine the change in self-esteem following plastic surgery, finding a position, or giving birth to a child. More significant, however, are studies which test the underlying framework, such as the study of consistency of behavior reported here. Perhaps, the single most important area of inquiry is the etiology of self-esteem. It is necessary to examine how different reinforcing behavior of parents toward children within the same family is associated with differential self-esteem (see Chapter 6).

The fundamental assumption of the proposed measure of self-esteem is the proclivity, in the Western culture, for left to right linear ordering of objects. The findings of the present series of studies along with a long history of research appears to support this assumption. As has already been noted, the tendency to attribute greater importance to the object placed at the extreme left position in a horizontal display was recorded by Morgan in 1944. Introspectionists such as Lashley (1961) and Inhelder and Piaget (1958, p. 252) have also noted the use of spatial imagery in thinking about non-spatial orderings.

The most systematic work in this area has been conducted by DeSoto (DeSoto, 1960; DeSoto, London, & Handel, 1965). For example, in spatial imagery associated with syllogisms, the results suggest that the left end is the preferred starting point for a horizontal ordering (DeSoto, London, & Handel, 1965).

One further question remains. How stable is self-esteem? Does self-esteem fluctuate in response to daily events, salient characteristics of the situation, or the demands of the social situation? To answer this it would be necessary to monitor the self-esteem of the individual over a period of time and to chronicle the events preceding the self-esteem probe. For example, what is the effect of obtaining a job on the self-esteem of a young adult? Such a study has much to recommend it. Until the data are in, however, it can only be proposed that variation in self-esteem is to be expected along some continuum above and below some model position toward which the individual's representations are presumed to egress and regress. A study of the variation in self-esteem over time should also include a measure of the resiliency of self-esteem. Following some demeaning social event or act, such as rejection by a spouse or lover, how much time elapses before the reported level of self-esteem reverts to the model level?

The studies presented here have attempted to extend this work to the development of a universal communication system – a sign language, if you will, for describing self–other orientations. On this assumption, a number of self–other configurations have been developed using other spatial arrangements of symbols representing self and significant others which are designed to measure self–other power orientation, marginality, social interest, identification, identification with the majority, self-centeredness, social inclusion, and openness. One of these, social interest, is described in detail in the next chapter.

CHAPTER 2

Social Interest

Although the preceding section sought to emphasize the social basis of self-esteem, the self rather than the other was of central concern. Persons with high self-esteem were seen to impose structure on the situation, thereby maintaining a stable self system. In the present section, significant others become a more central concern. It will be shown that a stable self system may also be achieved by guiding personal behavior on the basis of other's expectations, group norms, identification with others, and social trust.

Again, the interaction of theory, measurement, and research will be apparent. In the previous chapter, the measurement aspect of the tripartite interaction was emphasized because it was the most wanting. In the present chapter, the theory assumes greatest emphasis because by restructuring the underlying frameworks of several separate areas of measurement and research a more simplex and general framework evolves. The underlying framework proposes that a crucial consideration in self–other orientation is the individual's expectation of support from another person. It will be seen that this concept is the basis of a number of other concepts, such as fear of being rejected, extraversion-introversion, social desirability, need-affiliation, and social trust. Again, the focus is upon self–other orientation and the topographical approach to measurement.

THEORY

The conflux of the individual and the group is attended by an inherent potential for conflict. In becoming a member of the group, the individual must be willing at times to surrender some degree of autonomy. Group guidance systems must sometimes take precedence over individual guidance systems. Indeed, acceptance of this tenet is the basis of the socialization process. We may begin with a concern with the self, but inevitably there is an accounting with the other. The development of Adler's theory of personality demonstrates this principle (Ansbacher & Ansbacher, 1956).

Early Theoretical Approaches

In his early writings, Adler stressed the individual's striving for personal superiority. Power and domination of others were emphasized and were presumed to emerge as compensatory behaviors for deep seated feelings of inferiority.

In later writings, Adler shifted his emphasis toward social attachments. The term used by Adler was "social interest." Social interest includes such behaviors as cooperation, other directedness, group identification, empathy, and in general a concern for others in order to compensate for personal weaknesses, but also to contribute to public welfare. The individual's thoughts and judgments take into account the characteristics and aspirations of others as well as of oneself. The common view is differentiated from the private view. Thus, Adler's initial concern with the individual, followed in later years by his concern for the group, depicts the inherent conflict between self and other which social psychological theories of personality must confront.

For Adler, social interest referred to the range of a person's affectionate interest and concern. A disruption in a person's affectionate ties was assumed to be related to his perception of the self as "different" and to the eventual isolation of the individual and the development of a "private view of the world." The private view of the world may develop from striving for personal superiority but disregarding the needs of others and thereby eventually alienating others.

Freud (1914) had previously discussed the conflict between the self and other in terms of id and superego, but he was inclined to emphasize the self as opposed to the other. In Freud's terms, "the id" represents the instinctual responses of primordial man. It is closely associated with body processes from which its energy is derived. The id tends to represent the individual's inner world and subjective experience. The id operates by the "pleasure principle." Behavior guided by the id moves toward immediate gratification usually associated with the satisfaction of body needs. In terms of self–other orientation, the id represents self-orientation as opposed to a social orientation.

The superego represents the expectations of traditional society as communicated to the child by the parents. In contrast to the id, the superego is associated with external and social concerns as opposed to internal, body, and self concerns. The superego represents the ideal rather than the real, and it is directed toward perfection rather than pleasure. In terms of self–other orientation, the superego represents other orientation. The other rather than the self is the point of reference.

The direction of attention and interest inward upon the self or outward upon the environment was one of the central concerns of Jung (1923) in his theory of introversion-extroversion. According to Jung, one of the most fundamental distinctions in personality is orientation toward objective reality or toward subjective determinants. For Jung, extroversion referred to the tendency of an individual to expect important determinants of his behavior to come to him from his immediate environment. As a consequence, the extrovert attends and is interested in objective relations and he is conscious of the outside world. The introvert, on the other hand, views the external conditions and selects the subjective determinants as the decisive ones. The introvert is more subjective or self-oriented. The potential conflict between inner- and outer-directedness was not confronted by Jung.

Self–Other Orientation

The classic conflict between self and other may be resolved in part by forming a coalition with the other, that is, by perceiving oneself as included within a group of significant other persons. By forming a coalition of the self and the other, the rules of conduct of the group provide a stable guide and lead to regularity of individual behavior in social situations.

The consistency of social behavior of the individual is itself a method of conflict resolution between self and other. Adherence to group normative behavior makes for predictability of individual behavior. Predictability, in turn, makes it possible for other members to adapt to the individual's behavior. Moreover, surprising behavior by the individual will not compel the group members to examine frequently their own mode of behavior.

Consistency of individual behavior also makes studied change by the group more possible. If every social event presents a social problem (conflict), the efforts of the group to solve the moment to moment problems will leave the group more vulnerable to a major intragroup conflict.

Without group norms as a theory of social behavior, individual behavior would be fortuitous and vulnerable to the contingencies of daily events. Shared expectations of group members regarding the social behavior of the members of the group (group norms) serve as conflict control mechanisms. Thus, the perception of the self as included within a group of significant other persons will also serve as a conflict control mechanism. Group norms offer a ready guide for social behavior.

In terms of self–other orientation, social interest is assumed to involve inclusion of the self with others as opposed to being apart from others. To desire inclusion involves a willingness to be subject to the field of forces generated among others and the self. This latter component suggests an association with social trust. The person with high social interest is willing to place his fate in the hands of others. The other is perceived as a source of social support.

High social interest is also assumed to be associated with a knowledge and acceptance of the norms of a primary group. Social trust and normative behavior within the construct of social interest is presumed to operate as stimulus control. By placing one's fate in the hands of another, it is possible to eliminate concern about a wide variety of social stimuli. Under conditions of social trust, the other is a source of support or positive reinforcement. Social trust renders unnecessary the constant monitoring of the others' behavior, thereby facilitating focus on a problem of key concern. In so doing, greater control of the social environment is achieved since the task is less complex.

Normative behavior serves a similar control function. Group norms provide guides for social behavior, thereby again rendering the potentially impinging field of social stimuli less complex by narrowing the range of areas to be monitored. Areas of concern are indicated by the group guidance system and decision making in social situations is facilitated by group norms and values. Social norms act as screening and control mechanisms. Social stimuli and social responses are mediated by social interest. Still, willingness to place one's fate in the hands of others is achieved at some cost to autonomy. It is usually proposed, however, that a conflict between the needs for autonomy and mutuality is inherent.

The underlying assumption in a variety of social psychological theories of personality is the conflict between the need for dependence and the need for independence (Rank, 1936; Ausubel, 1952; Levy, 1955; Harvey, Hunt, & Schroder, 1961). Inherently, the socialization process involves conflict between the satisfaction of individual and the satisfaction of group needs. More recently, Ziller (1964) has examined this conflict in terms of Erikson's (1959) ego identity and group identity.

Most personality theorists propose, in one form or another, that most children experience a period of dependent identification with their parents. In this stage the child is submissive to external control almost to the point where there exists a lack of differentiation between parents and the self.

The second stage of development is usually described as independence (Levy, 1955) or "negative independence" (Harvey, Hunt, & Schroder, 1961). Here is witnessed the growth of the "self will." Parental control is resisted.

Exclusive reliance upon external cues for behavior controls proves unreliable as the life space of the child is enlarged to include other individuals or to include the alone condition. With the enlargement of the social field, the absolutistic rules established with a single individual prove too rigid to operate effectively under a wide variety of situations. For example, behavior acceptable to parents may not be acceptable to teachers or peers.

Reduced exclusive interaction with parents also demands and necessarily creates a more differentiated self concept. At this developmental stage, information concerning the consequences of personal behavior is frequently transmitted solely and directly to the individual, rather than to the parent-child complex. Emerging from the dependent developmental period, the child begins to distinguish himself from other group members, is recognized by other members, and enables other members to distinguish or locate him among the members. Thus, in this period, the child begins to establish an identity as a separate, unique individual.

The process of socialization with reference to the parents is repeated in turn with peer groups and school authority groups. Integration with the other is followed by differentiation. The conflict between dependence and independence is a concomitant of socialization. The hypothesized resolution of the conflict is an ego identity and group identity duality.

Definition of the self in terms of others is necessary. But definition of the self exclusively in terms of significant and powerful others may lead to ego diffusion. The self fuses with the other. Stability of the self definition and other definition may be achieved by a definition of the self in terms of others but apart from others. This duality preserves a degree of objectivity within self–other perception. Ego identity and group identity are proposed as the two primary foci around which the life space of the individual is described. The two foci act as points of reference for each other and as correcting or guidance mechanisms. Social stimuli may be viewed from either or both foci, thereby providing stereoscopic perception, if you will, of the self-social complex. (A similar bipolar effect may be achieved by alternately assuming high and low social interest orientation. To avoid being constantly under the control of the field of forces of others, the individual may adopt periodically an independent position, low social interest.)

Translating these concepts in terms of the self–other orientation, self-esteem and ego identity are assumed to be similar, as are social interest and group identity. Thus, self-esteem and social interest provide the foci from which the life space of the individual is defined. The duality of self-esteem and social interest permits the individual to define the self in terms of others, yet apart from others. These dual constructs provide correcting and control mechanisms for each other. A person with high self-esteem has recourse to self supports. A person with high social interest has recourse to social supports. Together high self-esteem and high social interest provide the basis for dual sources of satisfaction and dual control mechanisms, the inherent conflict between the self and other notwithstanding.

Social interest is defined as the individual's perception of himself as included within a field of significant others. It will be shown that social interest is maintained by an expectation of positive reinforcements from others. The concept is derived from the work of Adler who was perhaps responsible for emphasizing the salience of the other for theories of personality. But social interest as used here departs dramatically from earlier concerns with the significance of the other as proposed by Adler, Freud, and Jung. The theory of self–other orientation developed here is based upon a cognitive framework, thereby managing to avoid or to minimize the generation of concepts which defy experimental verification. Again, too, it must be stressed that the concept of social interest is best viewed within a matrix of self–other orientation including self-esteem, self-centrality and other components of the framework as well as within the still larger personal-social system. Yet, the present framework is seen to emanate from earlier theories of personality which sought to include a consideration of the other.

An attempt was also made here to show the development of the concern for the other. The concepts of independence and dependence were assimilated within the concepts of self-esteem and social interest. In contrast to earlier frameworks, no final resolution is proposed for the inherent conflict between the self and the other. The individual constantly strives for control of his fate within a social environment. Adaptations rather than solutions are worked out through recourse to the guidelines provided by a group of significant others (social interest) as well as by a personal guidance system (self-esteem).

MEASUREMENT

The measure of social interest is derived from the cognitive approach to self–other orientation described in the preceding chapter. The measure incorporates the central features of the theoretical framework including expectation of social support, identification with significant others, and the perception of the self as included within a group of significant others.

The measure of social interest required the subject to draw a circle representing the self anywhere within a rectangular field in which three circles are already included which represent "parents," "friends," and "teachers." (In the adult form these circles represent "family," "friends," and "work group.") (*See* Item 2 in Appendix A.) Location of a circle representing the self within, rather than without, the imaginary societal triangle is presumed to be related to social interest. In the five other items comprising the measure, the apexes are rotated and the imaginary triangle is located either to the right or left side of the enclosing rectangular field. A score of one is given when the self circle is located anywhere within the imaginary triangle of significant others, and a score of zero is given when the self circle is located anywhere else. The sum of the scores of the six items represents the social interest score. The split-half reliability corrected for length was 0.90 for 207 ninth grade students and 0.92 for 81 fifth grade students. As is readily seen, the concept of social interest involved here incorporates the concept of identification with significant others.

The concept of identification has had a long and troublesome history. Indeed, it has been suggested frequently that the concept could be eliminated without any loss in explanatory or productive power of social psychological approaches to personality (Sarason, 1966). Again, however, the lack of adequate measures may be partially responsible for the criticism of the concept.

Psychoanalytically oriented theories of personality propose that the introjection of the generalized other is the basis of social development as well as the development of a functional self concept. Introjection refers to the capacity of the organism to take up into itself as a perception, and later a memory trace, its own activities and the acts of others toward its own responses. In the evaluation of the self, the process of introjection consists of taking the responses of others into ourselves and associating them with our own responses. We learn to react to ourselves as others have reacted toward us (Mead, 1934). Identification with others is assumed to involve introjection.

More directly, however, identification may be understood as modeling behavior. Through the selection of an appropriate model of human behavior and through the process of imitation, socialization is facilitated. Appropriate or adaptive behaviors and attitudes for given situations may not be within the given repertoire of the individual. A convenient way to learn the appropriate behaviors and attitudes is to observe the behavior of a selected or available model, a person or group of persons who may be observed emitting the crucial responses. If the other person is similar to the self or a person whom one is pleased to imitate, a minimum of adaptation for differences between self and other (the model) is required.

By modeling others or identifying with others, the individual can expect with high reliability that his behavior will be supported by others. Thus, social interest and expectation of social support are allied concepts.

The parents serve as convenient models in the process of socialization, and retardation of identification with parent is usually assumed to retard the socialization process. The expanding social environment, however, presents an array of individuals who may serve as models such as friends and teachers. The ability to identify with more than one group of significant others including parents, friends, and teachers is assumed to be associated with higher expectancy of social reinforcement.

RESEARCH

It is proposed that persons high in social interest have learned to expect positive reinforcement from significant others. High social interest persons have been supported by significant others, such as parents, teachers, and friends (or family, friends, and work group) leading to an expectation of continuing support. This expectation of support establishes the positive social set which is referred to here as social interest.

Partial support for this proposition was found in a series of studies. In the first of these (Long, Ziller, & Bankes, 1970), it was found that behavior problem children in a state institution showed less social interest on the Self-Other Orientation Tasks than a control group of children matched for age from the public schools. The group studied included a wide range of children of whom the parents and school officials had decided that a more controlled environment away from home would be therapeutic. In terms of social learning, it might be said that the rates of negative to positive reinforcements experienced by the children were extremely high. These children could not expect support from significant others, and this was coded as low social interest in terms of the cognitive mapping used here. Perhaps even more significantly, however, the low expectation of social reinforcement precludes the socialization process and perpetuates social exclusion.

In a more direct analysis of the hypothesis relating social support and social interest, a comparison was made of differences in social interest scores between Asian Indian adolescents and a sample of American adolescents matched for age (Ziller, Long, Ramana, & Reddy, 1968). A detailed analysis of this study is presented in Chapter 7, so it is sufficient to say that Asian Indian children are extremely prized by their parents. They are "the parents' reason for being" (Murphy, 1953). Observations of Indian family life seem to indicate that the children are unusually and warmly supported by the members of an extended family. Consistent with the hypotheses of this section, Indian adolescents showed higher social interest in terms of self–other orientation.

A crucial test of the hypotheses linking social interest and expectation of positive reinforcement was conducted in a minimal social situation. Male college students answering an advertisement for subjects for an experiment were first asked to complete a form of the Self–Other Orientation Tasks which included the measure of social interest. The subjects were then required to prepare a three-minute speech on the topic of population control. An article on the topic was presented to the subject, and he was instructed to prepare the speech using notes to aid in the presentation. Each subject was given about twenty minutes to prepare the speech.

The subject was then led into another room and placed before a podium. He faced an array of three television monitors arranged in an arc twelve feet in front of him. The monitors were five feet apart from each other.

The monitor directly in front of the subject portrayed the subject as he spoke. A television camera was located directly above the monitor.

The monitor to the left portrayed a college-age girl who negatively reinforced the subject, whereas the monitor on the right portrayed a positively reinforcing college-age girl. The positive reinforcer nodded her head up and down, smiled, and looked directly at the subject at all times. The other girl looked at the subject only rarely, never smiled, yawned, moved her head from side to side in a gesture of disagreement, and other gestures of mild disagreement. The girls, of course, were taped, thereby presenting the same social environment (with the exception of the self) to each subject.

In yet another room, two observers recorded the frequency with which the subject oriented himself to each of the monitors by observing the subject on a fourth monitor which presented the same image as that on the monitor directly before the subject.

Since the social interest measure consisted of a single item, only a small number of low social interest subjects were found. Nevertheless, the results support the hypothesis. Low social interest subjects, in contrast to the high social interest subjects, oriented themselves toward the positive reinforcer less frequently. The mean was 6.57 for low social interest subjects, and 19.29 for high social interest subjects. The difference between these means was statistically significant ($p < 0.05$). The psychological significance of this finding should be underscored. Persons with low social interest do not observe as much positive reinforcement as persons with high social interest even under conditions where both are receiving equal amounts of positive reinforcement. This difference in social orientation or social monitoring behavior thereby tends to perpetuate the expectation of a lower rate of positive reinforcement. This principle is the basis of the alienation phenomenon discussed in Chapter 4.

The evidence tends to support the social interest-social support hypothesis. Persons with high social interest tend to expect support from significant others because they have experienced support from significant others.

It would seem consistent with this hypothesis to expect that persons with high social interest also tend to support others more frequently. Persons with high social interest have been presented with models who have emitted supports frequently, and they may be expected to imitate these models (Bandura & Walters, 1963). Indeed, persons who have been supported frequently may simply have a different frame of reference for supports. High reinforcements (smiling, approving, head nodding, pats on the back) may be normative behavior within their social sphere and they merely carry these norms to new social situations. Thus it is hypothesized that persons with high social interest tend to reinforce others more frequently.

This hypothesis was tested by Terbovic (1970) in a laboratory setting. Two persons (female) participate in a training exercise. One, the subject, is asked to follow directions from another person in order to reproduce a design. The other person is in an adjoining room and has a copy of the design. This latter person describes the drawing over an intercom system. The subject can only communicate to the direction sender by means of a red and a green button located in the booth. When the red or green button is pressed, a corresponding light flashes on the panel before the person in the other room. It was explained that the other person was located in the next room in order to eliminate other communication such as sounds, gestures, or facial expressions.

Every thirty seconds during the direction-giving exercise a buzzer was sounded. The buzzer was a signal to the subject to communicate her reactions to the partner's instructions. If she was dissatisfied in any way with the explanation being given, she was instructed to press the red button. If, for instance, she did not understand or felt that the instructions were too fast or too slow, she could communicate this to the partner by pressing the red button. On the other hand, if the subject was satisfied and felt she had no problems understanding the directions, she could indicate this by pressing the green button. This would indicate that she wanted the partner to continue in the same manner.

Once the subject had responded by pressing a button, the directions from the partner were continued. The sequence continued until the partner had completed her explanation to the satisfaction of the subject or until a ten-minute time limit was exceeded.

The partner, of course, was a confederate of the experimenter and presented the same directions for every subject. The subject had previously completed the six items of the social interest scale.

The social interest scores were related to the frequency with which the subjects pressed the red button. Pearson correlation between the two scores was 0.24 for 37 subjects. The results approach statistical significance and suggest that subjects with high social interest tend to support their partner more frequently in a training situation. Together with the earlier findings, the results suggest that persons with high social interest expect support from significant others and also tend to support others more frequently than persons with low social interest. If it can be assumed that social interest derives from experiencing social support, then these results indicate that those who have been supported by significant others tend to support others in turn. It is also possible, however, that persons who support others frequently are, in fact, seeking approval from others or are attempting to ingratiate themselves.

RELATED CONCEPTS

In this section, an attempt will be made to show that earlier concepts, such as fear of rejection, inclusion, extroversion-introversion, need affiliation, and social trust may be subsumed under the more inclusive concept of social interest interpreted in terms of expectation of positive reinforcement from significant others. The goal is an economy of concepts.

Early efforts to measure social interest include Schutz's (1958) measure of inclusion and Shipley and Veroff's (1952) measure of need-affiliation. Schutz associates inclusion behavior with such terms as "join," "member," "communicate," and "belong." Some of the items included in his self-report device were: "I try to be with other people." "I try to avoid being alone." In the measure developed by Shipley and Veroff, responses to TAT pictures were coded in terms of indications of the individual's fear of being rejected.

Schutz's approach relies on a self-report medium which, in terms of the preceding section, raises serious doubts about its utility. The approach by Shipley and Veroff emphasizes the avoidance of a painful stimulus and is concerned only minimally with affiliation as a pleasant stimulus. Nevertheless, both measures suggest that they may be related to social interest as defined here.

An examination of the association between Schutz's measure of expressed inclusion and social interest resulted in a correlation coefficient of 0.22 for 20 summer school students. High social interest is associated with high expressed inclusion, but the results are not statistically significant. No data are available associating social interest and Shipley and Veroff's measure of need-affiliation.

Eysenck's Extroversion-Introversion Scale

The first extensive systematic approach to the area of social interest was taken by Eysenck (1957). Unfortunately, his framework is concerned largely with abnormal behavior or with failures in the socialization process. Consistent with Jung's earlier observation, Eysenck found that extroversion-introversion is one of the main dimensions of personality.

Eysenck associates extroversion with hysteria and introversion with anxiety neurosis or dysthymia. The extrovert is very excitable and his inhibitions are poorly developed. As a result, the extrovert tends to be overly responsive to environmental elements leading to criminal activities, antisocial acts, and generally unethical behavior.

Dysthymias, on the other hand, are reported to display over-socialized reactions. They show guilt and worry over relatively slight and unimportant actions whose unethical character is more apparent than real. Their main characteristic is fear of anxiety reactions.

The extrovert tends to *monitor his own needs rather than the needs of others*. When he is involved with others, it is largely for the purpose of self-stimulation and social stimulation is readily available.

Some of the questions used by Eysenck to measure extroversion-introversion include: "Generally, do you prefer reading to meeting people?" "Do you like going out a lot?" "Would you do almost anything for a dare?"

Consistent with his framework, Eysenck found that extroverts condition poorly, whereas introverts condition particularly well. He concludes that under conditions of equal environmental pressure, extroverts would be expected to be under-socialized and introverts would be over-socialized.

Within the self–other orientation framework described here, Eysenck's ideas may be translated as indicating that in the inherent conflict between self and others, the extrovert is self-centered, whereas the introvert is other centered. Indeed, one of the most frequently mentioned characteristics of the extrovert or hysteric is egocentrism. In the present context, the extrovert does not have recourse to social norms. His behavior is guided largely by a personal frame of reference designed to gratify immediate personal needs.

In a study involving 20 summer college students, social interest and introversion as measured by Eysenck's instrument were found to be negatively correlated ($r = -0.34$, p about 0.10). High social interest is associated with low introversion or low anxiety.

Schachter's Psychology of Affiliation

A more behavioral approach to the problem of social interest was undertaken by Schachter (1959) using normal female subjects. In these studies, rather than using a questionnaire to determine the subject's social interest, the subject was placed in a threatening situation (for example, participating in a drug experiment), then just prior to the occurrence of the situation the subject was asked if she wished to wait in a room with someone else or in a room by herself. The choice of a companion was used as an indication of affiliation or social interest.

Schachter proposed that affiliative behavior is motivated largely by the arousal of a variety of drive states, and that social interaction is instrumental in that others provide a basis for determining appropriate behavior under ambiguous conditions or conditions which are uninterpretable in terms of past experience.

In one of the studies, female college students who were given extra grade credit for participating in the experiment were divided into two groups. One group (high anxiety) was met by a serious looking gentleman wearing a white laboratory coat and surrounded by complicated electrical equipment. He introduced himself as Dr. Zilstein of the Medical School's Department of Neurology and Psychiatry. He told the subjects that they were to take part in an experiment concerning electroshock therapy and that the shock would be painful but would not be a permanently damaging experience. A second group (low anxiety) entered a similar situation, but were introduced to Dr. Zilstein without the array of equipment and without identification of his purpose. They were told that the experiment would be enjoyable with no painful effects. Subjects in each group were then told that a ten-minute wait would be necessary and that they had the choice of waiting either alone or with a group of other girls.

In the high anxiety situation 63% of the subjects chose to wait together, compared with only 33% in the low anxiety situation. Affiliative preferences were higher under conditions of anticipation of a painful and unpleasant experience. Schachter proposed that just as evaluations of abilities and opinions are aided by a social comparison process, so are evaluations of the appropriate emotional states.

In the same series of studies, Schachter also found that the first born or the only child as opposed to later born children chose the together situation more frequently. Various interpretations of these results are possible. Schachter proposed that since the situation is ambiguous, a companion may provide cues to the subject for expected and acceptable or normative behavior. Presumably first borns are more concerned about these norms. Another interpretation is that the first born or only child seeks social settings when under stress because in early stress situations he had greater recourse to parental support. Thus, it is proposed here that the first born or only child tends to anticipate positive reinforcement from others to a greater degree than do later borns. Social interest, then, may be equated with expectations of positive reinforcement from others.

Social Trust

Social psychologists, it would seem, were the last persons to discover the concept of social trust. In a review of leading social psychology texts before 1958, Deutsch (1958) found that the word trust did not appear in any of the indexes. On the other hand, it is a concept frequently employed by persons, including psychologists, to express a perceived relationship between the self and a significant other person or persons. The concept cannot be dismissed as a meaningless, intervening variable because persons act on the basis of these perceptions. Persons behave differently with regard to persons trusted and persons distrusted. It remains to be shown more systematically how and why persons behave differently under conditions of trust and distrust. Again, however, the measurement of social trust is crucial. Indeed, the delay in developing research in this area may be attributable largely to problems of measurement.

Deutsch's Studies of Social Trust

In his pioneering study in the area of trust, Deutsch (1958, p. 266) defined trust as occurring in a situation where the individual is dependent upon the behavior of another person in order to realize an outcome. He trusts the other person if he behaves in a way which renders him vulnerable to exploitation by the other, yet permits the other to act in such a way that both parties will benefit equally.

Consistent with the earlier discussion of social interest, Deutsch is defining an interpersonal setting in which one person expects benevolence from the other or others, that is, the trusting individual anticipates positive reinforcement from others.

The game from which Deutsch derived his measure of trust is illustrated in Fig. 2.1. Person I must choose between Rows "X" and "Y," Person II must choose between Columns "A" and "B." The amount of (imaginary) money each person wins or loses is determined by the box they get into as a result of their respective choices. For example, if Person I chooses Row "X" and Person II chooses Column "A," Box "AX" is the result and

Person I chooses between Rows X and Y, Person II between Columns A and B. Person I's payoffs are the first numbers in the parentheses, Person II's are the second numbers.

	A	B
X	(+9, +9)	(−10, +10)
Y	(+10, −10)	(−9, −9)

Fig. 2.1   Deutsch's (1960) version of the Prisoner's Dilemma Game. (From Deutsch, M. Trust, trustworthiness and the F-Scale. *Journal of Abnormal and Social Psychology*, 1960, **61**, 138–140.

each person wins $9. The response by Person I which indicates trust is Row "X." If Person II is not trustworthy (chooses Column B), Person I loses $10.

In the first study in the series, Deutsch (1958) demonstrated that under conditions where each subject was led to feel that he wanted to do as well as he could for himself and he also wanted to do better than the other person and that the other person felt the same way (competitive) as opposed to conditions where each subject was led to feel that the welfare of the other person as well as his own welfare was of concern to him and that the other person felt the same way (cooperative), the subject tends to make the non-trusting choice, that is, Column "B" or Row "Y." This study is clearly a test of the hypothesis that trust is associated with positive reinforcement from others.

In a second study (1960), Deutsch found that subjects who scored high on the Authoritarian Scale (Adorno et al., 1950) made fewer trusting responses. Extensive surveys of research on the F-Scale (Christie & Jahoda, 1954) indicates that persons with high F-Scale scores tend to make extreme responses, and experienced and favor stricter child rearing practices. This may suggest that high F-Scale responders tend to use negative reinforcement to control the behavior of others. In the game used by Deutsch, then, the competitive response is translated as indicating a bid for control of the game by his willingness to make the punitive response. Elsewhere Deutsch (1958) has suggested that low trust persons are inclined to be punitive of deviant behavior and to be less interested in "feeling."

In another set of studies, Litzker (1960) used a measure of attitudes toward other nations and found that those who were favorable toward other nations made significantly more trusting responses in the game situation than those unfavorable. The results of McClintock et al. (1963) supported these findings.

Rotter's Measure of Social Trust

A scale of interpersonal trust was also developed by Rotter (1967). The scale contains 25 trust items and 15 filler items. It was designed to measure a person's generalized expectancy that the promises of other individuals or of groups with regard to future behavior can be relied on. Most items deal with the believability of social agents, but some items tap optimism about the future of society here and elsewhere in the world.

Some of the items include: "In dealing with strangers one is better off to be cautious until they have provided evidence that they are trustworthy."

"The future seems promising." "In these competitive times one has to be alert or someone is likely to take advantage of you."

Again, the reluctance of the individual to place himself within a field of significant others is clearly depicted in the measure of trust. Again, too, however, one worries about the meaning of the construct in this context since the items involve verbal self reports.

Ziller's Measure of Social Trust

A mechanical-perceptual apparatus for measuring an individual's trust in a group has been constructed by the author. In one sense, it attempts to create a situation which the social interest item represents symbolically in the self–other orientation tasks. The apparatus involves a platform which elevates the subject in a dark room by means of a hydraulic lift. The platform is unstable and requires three persons to maintain the horizontal attitude of the platform in its ascent. Unknown to the subject, the platform is locked into a stable horizontal position at the height of its ascent (1.14 meters). While in this position, an autokinetic light is turned on directly in front of the subject. The small light source is stationary, nevertheless the subject will perceive movement of the light even when he is standing on a stable surface (the autokinetic effect).

Suspended as he is and requiring support from three other persons in order to maintain the stability of the platform, the subject can attribute the perceived movement of the light either to the light itself or to movement from the platform, that is, to instability caused by the poor performance of the persons whose task it is to maintain the stability of the platform. If the subject attributes the perceived movement of the light to the persons with the support task, then he will be delayed in reporting the autokinetic effect. He is not willing to place his fate in the hands of others. He distrusts others. On the other hand, the person who perceives the autokinetic effect more quickly, assumes that the platform stabilizers are performing adequately or better (he trusts them) and consequently, reports the autokinetic effect sooner.

The problem facing the subject is similar to that of a person who is sitting in one train in a railroad station looking out at another train. Suddenly he senses motion. Before he can attribute motion to the other train he must first eliminate the possibility of movement by the train in which he is a passenger.

In the first of the experiments with the apparatus, subjects guided by fraternity brothers (but confederates who were uniform in this behavior) who were told that the guides would assume the platform position in their turn, while the subject assumes the support position (the trust condition) reported perceiving the autokinetic effect in *less* time over 25 trials ($p <$ 0.05) than subjects under the low trust condition in which the guides were strangers (the same confederates as in the trust condition but they had not been introduced to the subjects prior to the platform trials in the dark room). It was also found that under the conditions of support by fraternity brothers (the trust condition), the persons suspended on the platform required decreasingly less time over trials to report viewing the light movement, whereas under the low trust conditions, the subjects required increasingly more time over trials to report viewing the light movement. The results were interpreted as supporting the validity of the measure of trust. Furthermore, the results suggest that trust escalates as does distrust.

In general, these studies suggest that social trust is a facet of self–other orientation which is associated with a set for expectation of positive reinforcement from others. In this sense, it seems justified to include the concept within the subset of social interest.

SUMMARY

Social interest is associated with the perception of the self as being included within a field of significant other persons. The self is defined in association with significant others, such as parents, friends, and teachers. The concept was also associated with the concept of social trust or the willingness to place one's fate in the hands of another. Self-esteem and social interest were assumed to be the basis for consistency of social behavior. Persons with high self-esteem and high social interest have recourse to self-reinforcement and social reinforcement leading to stability of behavior. Social interest is the social component of stability. Self-esteem is the personal component of stability.

Although the concept dates to the early writings of Adler, its development within a social psychological theory of personality has been truncated by the inadequacies of available measures. A wide variety of measures were reviewed including the limited verbal approach of self–other orientation. Using the latter approach, social interest was found to be associated with expectations of positive reinforcement from significant others and with positive reinforcement of others.

Whereas those with an existential orientation tend to be concerned almost exclusively with the self accompanied by an appreciation of the absurdity of the human ordeal, the present framework emphasizes the dual foci of the self and the other. A mode of adaptation is suggested in which self-orientation is accompanied by an appreciation of and dependence upon the other with, perhaps, an appreciation for the limitations of both the self and the other. Indeed, social adaptation will be shown to emerge from the dual orientation of self-esteem and social interest (*see* Chapter 4).

CHAPTER 3*

The Marginal Man

In the preceding chapter the individual's perception of the self *within* a group of significant others was studied. In the present chapter the individual's perception of the self *between* two groups of significant others is examined. By placing the person in a position of a forced choice between the perception of the self *inside one of the two groups* or *outside of both groups*, the concept of the marginal man (the man in the middle) is introduced. A brief history of the concept is presented here, along with a new measure of the concept using the topographical approach to self–other orientation. A reconsideration of the concept along with the development of a new measure and subsequent research indicates that there may be some advantages to perceiving the self as being outside two opposing groups rather than inside one of the opposing groups.

In the classic study by Stonequist (1937), the marginal man was described as "one whom fate has condemned to live in two societies and in two, not merely different, but antagonistic cultures." Some of the sources of marginality include ethnic origins (Italian–American), membership in distinctive racial groups (the American Negro), adolescents, and first line supervisors.

The marginal individual finds himself within the field of forces of two opposing groups (Lewin, 1935). He is unable or unwilling to relinquish membership in either, and finds it impossible to be regarded, or to regard himself, as a full-fledged member of either group. The situation is similar

*This chapter is based on a series of studies conducted by the author, B. J. Stark, and H. Pruden, University of Oregon.

to that of classic conflict. If, as is often the case, one of the groups is higher than the other, in the societal hierarchy of status, the conflict is only intensified. In the higher status group he may be regarded as an intruder, in the lower status group he may be seen as disloyal.

The problems of the marginal man are usually described in terms of role conflict. The two incompatable groups with which he may identify present simultaneously incompatible expectations. The foreman is a case in point. As a former member of the basic work force he tends to identify with the work force and emphasize conditions favorable to the employee. Yet as a member of management he is expected to emphasize productivity.

The foreman's method of coping with this conflict is assumed here to be reflected in his self–other orientations. The alternatives of self–other orientation include identification with one or the other of the opposing parties or assuming a pendulous position somewhere between the two (or more) parties. The non-marginal man perceives himself as included within the boundaries of one of two separated groups. In so doing, he necessarily excludes himself from the second group.

Within the self–other orientation framework, marginality refers to the subject's view of himself as outside the boundaries of both of the separated groups. Although the marginal man may not perceive himself as included in either group, it is important to note that he may not perceive himself as entirely excluded from either group. Marginality in this sense suggests non-commitment, neutrality, non-alignment, avoidance of categorization, or even disinterest. It is also possible, however, that marginality represents an intense conflict stemming from a strong desire to belong to both groups.

In contrast to traditional discussions of marginality, the concept as presented here is phenomenological in orientation. The individual's orientation to the groups is central rather than the group's orientation to the individual. When a group perceives an individual as marginal, alienation is suggested. When the individual perceives himself as marginal, however, a more positive meaning may evolve. For example, the person who adopts a marginal role may wish to remain neutral in a conflict between opposing groups in which he may claim membership. Or the individual may select the alternative of separateness in an effort to avoid pressures toward uniformity associated with membership in one of two opposing groups. Labor relations representatives of an organization have been described as occupying boundary roles (Blau & Scott, 1962). Hired as staff experts to work with the union, they soon become viewed by management as representative of the union's point of view. They are also regarded with suspicion by the union. But their marginal position is an asset to the labor-relations men in performing their duties. A certain amount of marginality appears to be functional for discharging the responsibility of boundary roles (Blau & Scott, 1962, p. 197).

In terms of conflict resolution, marginality may be associated with indecision or with a state of information search prior to decision making. Since the marginal man does not perceive himself as bound by the norms of either group, he may be more open to new information in the period prior to decision making.

These advantages are not assumed without some counterbalancing disadvantages. The marginal individual lacks the assurance of group norms for guiding individual behavior. Moreover, the bi-separated person may be expected to have a lower base rate of reinforcement from others since he is not identified with a given group. Thus, Lewin (1951) describes the uncertainty of the adolescent "about the ground on which he stands, and the groups to which he belongs, often making him loud, restless, at once timid and aggressive, over-sensitive and tending to go to extremes, over-critical of others and himself" (p. 121). According to Lewin, the real danger of marginality lies in standing "nowhere," in being an eternal adolescent. Nevertheless, an exploration of the positive as well as the negative associations of the perception of marginality is suggested here.

COMMUNICATION OF MARGINALITY

Although the concept of marginality has been used for at least 34 years, no measure of the concept is known to the author. The measure used here derives from the theory of self–other orientation. A representative item appears in Appendix A, Item 3. The item presents two representational groups of people separated within a social field. The subject is required to draw a circle which stands for himself anywhere in the demarked space including the two groups. Placement of the self inside of neither of the groups is assumed to represent marginality and is given a score of one. If the circle representing the self is included in any one of the two subgroups or if the outer limits of the self circle and a group circle coincide in any way, a score of zero is ascribed. Placement of a circle in each of the two subgroups also receives a zero score as does placement of the self outside the entire rectangle field.

Four similar items comprise the measure. The four items are interspersed among different items measuring different components of self–other orientation in order to mask the focus of the series of tasks and to maintain interest. The sum of the scores for the four items represents the marginality index.*

The concept and measure of marginality as used here represents the subject's organization of his life space including himself and two sub-groups. Essentially the measurement of the approach is consistent with that described with regard to self-esteem and social interest. The orientation is from the person to other persons. The data concerning self–other orientation are subjective and are communicated by means of a pre-verbal language in the hope of preserving the subject's point of view, rather than imposing the investigator's orientation on the subject.

Again, the method of communication between the subject and the investigator employs the medium of a structured projective technique involving no verbal response on the part of the subject. The outcome of the communication is a cognitive sociometric of self and two groups of others, that is, the subject is asked to arrange symbols representing the self and significant other persons, and the resulting array is presumed to reflect some important aspect of the individual's life space.

The cognitive mapping assumed to underlie the concept of marginality has not been experimentally established. Lewin's (1951) description of the marginal man in terms of "topological psychology" comes very near to the marginal configuration of self and other used here.

> The marginal man is a person who stands on the boundary between two groups, A and B. He does not belong to either of them, or at least he is not certain about his belonging-ness. Not infrequently this situation occurs for members of an underprivileged minority group, particularly for the more privileged members within this group . . . The fact of being located in a social "no man's land" can be observed in very different types of minority groups – for instance, racial groups of the hard-of-hearing, which is a marginal group between the deaf and the normal group. (p. 144)

VALIDATION

The validity of the measure of marginality was examined in three ways. The first was a study of the relationship of the measure with other well-established instruments designed to measure similar constructs (concurrent validity). Marginality was examined in relation to Rokeach's (1960) Dogmatism Scale, social interest, extroversion-introversion (Eysenck, 1957), and expressed inclusion (Schutz, 1958). The second was a study of the association between marginality and balance of reinforce-

---

*The split-half reliability of this measure corrected for length was 0.83 for 61 high school students and 0.87 for 61 high school students with speech handicaps.

ment of pro and con arguments on a controversial issue (construct validity). Finally, the marginality scores of first line supervisors, whose role has frequently been described as the model of marginality, were compared with a control group who were presumed to be less marginal (predictive validity).

Marginality and Related Concepts

In defining the concept of marginality as used here, the marginal man was described as one who avoids categorization or who will take a neutral position between opposing groups. Marginality was also assumed to be associated with a state of information search prior to decision making.

In contrast, Rokeach's (1960) extensive analysis of dogmatism includes descriptions of rigid categorization behavior, a leveling tendency in forming categories where details are overlooked and grossly dissimilar objects are categorized. These information processing and coding behaviors devolve from control mechanisms which permit the dogmatic individual to maintain his belief-disbelief system intact. In this sense, the dogmatic person is closed to new information — his convictions are inviolable.

The first study in the series examined the relationship between marginality and dogmatism. On the basis of the aforementioned frameworks, a negative correlation was proposed.

Ninety-one male students from a marketing class in the School of Business, University of Oregon, completed the two instruments during the first fifteen minutes of a regular class period. The four marginality items were interspersed in a series of 20 items from the Self–Other Orientation Tasks. A short-form of Rokeach's Dogmatism Scale developed by Troldahl and Powell (1964) was used. The product-moment correlation between the two measures was -0.433 ($p < 0.001$). The marginal man was found to be less dogmatic, as the initial framework indicated.

In a second validation study involving 20 students in an introductory psychology class held during a summer session, marginality was found to be correlated negatively with social interest as measured with the Self–Other Orientation Tasks ($r = -0.46$, $p < 0.05$), negatively with extraversion ($r = -0.35$, not statistically significant), negatively with expressed inclusion ($r = -0.21$, not statistically significant, example of an item: "I try to be with other people") and negatively with age ($r = -0.55$, $p < 0.01$). It is apparent that marginality is associated with the concept of social interest. The marginal person does not perceive himself as included within a group of others.

Most interestingly, however, marginality is found to be negatively correlated with age. This suggests that persons become less marginal, less neutral, and perceive themselves as more included within one group as opposed to another as they become older. A similar phenomenon was observed by Snyder with regard to the assimilation of new Supreme Court Justices (1958). She noted that the newcomers assumed neutral positions between the liberals and conservatives during the early years of their tenure, but in later years became identified with one or the other of the polar groups.

Marginality and Neutrality

Consistent with the definition of marginality within the self–other orientation framework, it was proposed that under conditions of controversy, persons with high as opposed to low marginality scores tend to take a more neutral position. From the original 91 male subjects in the first study, 32 subjects were selected for the second study in the series, so that 16 of the subjects had high marginality scores (they located the self in a marginal position on each of the four items), and 16 had low marginality scores (they never located the self in a marginal position).

The experimental situation required each subject individually to view two five-minute presentations on a television monitor. A controversial topic (guaranteed annual income) was debated by two male members of the University of Oregon debate team. Each speaker gave a five-minute pro presentation and a five-minute con presentation. The speakers were instructed to rely on facts and to try to present equally good arguments for both positions.

The experimental design included 4 marginals and 4 non-marginals under each of 4 conditions: Speaker A giving a pro presentation followed by B giving a con presentation (A-Pro and B-Con), A-Con and B-Pro, B-Pro and A-Con, and B-Con and A-Pro (see Table 3.1).

The subjects (paid volunteers) arrived at the laboratory knowing that they would watch two five-minute presentations and that about fifteen minutes of their time would be required.

Each subject held a push button in his hand while viewing the television monitor. His instructions were to press the button each time the speaker said something with which he agreed. When the button was depressed there was no audible sound, but the response was recorded on a tape recorder. In this way, the subject was not communicating his responses directly to the experimenter.

The instructions which the subject read upon his arrival at the laboratory were as follows:

"You are not being evaluated in any way. You are simply helping us to learn how people in general behave in this situation. The task requires you to view two five-minute video tapes concerning a controversial subject — Guaranteed Annual Income. One of the speakers will advocate a guaranteed annual income, and the other speaker will take the opposite position.

"All you are asked to do is listen attentively to each speaker and press the button in your hand each time you agree with something either speaker says. Your responses will be recorded on tape, and no one will know when you respond during the experiment itself since the clicker is silent.

"Remember, there are no correct responses. Now please listen carefully and press the button whenever you agree with the speaker."

The subject was seated ten feet directly in front of the twenty-four inch television monitor. Only the subject and the investigator were present during the data collection period. The subject was not told which argument would be presented first.

The dependent measure was a majority response ratio. This ratio is obtained by placing in the numerator the greater number of responses made by the subject to either presentation and placing in the denominator the total number of responses. The more neutral subject is assumed to be the one whose ratio approaches 0.50, that is, the neutral is assumed to agree with both presentations about equally. The less neutral person's support of the two positions is more one-sided. The results are presented in Table 3.1.

Differences in supporting behavior between persons high and low in marginality were statistically significant ($p < 0.01$). Marginal persons tended to support the pro and con arguments about equally, while the non-marginal persons were more one-sided in their support. The latter tended to support one or the other of the arguments more frequently. The results support the proposed meaning of the marginality measure.

Role and Marginality

Perhaps the role which has been most frequently cited as an example of marginality is the foreman (Roethlisberger, 1945; Gardner & Whyte, 1945; Etzioni, 1958; Caplow, 1964). Most writers, however, say little more than that the foreman is the "man-in-the-middle" and therefore marginal.

Table 3.1   Frequency and Ratio of Supporting Responses to Pro and Con Arguments by Two Speakers (A and B) Under Four Conditions of Presentation.

Non-marginal Subjects

Presentation 1			Presentation 3		
A-Pro	B-Con	Ratio of Pro or Con	B-Pro	A-Con	Ratio of Pro or Con
0	12	100%	6	11	65%
7	2	78%	9	15	62%
12	6	67%	5	10	67%
10	14	59%	4	9	69%

Presentation 2			Presentation 4		
A-Con	B-Pro	Ratio of Pro or Con	B-Con	A-Pro	Ratio of Pro or Con
24	4	86%	17	20	54%
15	5	75%	11	6	65%
17	7	71%	10	7	59%
11	5	69%	10	14	58%

Marginal Subjects

Presentation 1			Presentation 3		
A-Pro	B-Con	Ratio of Pro or Con	B-Pro	A-Con	Ratio of Pro or Con
14	16	53%	7	9	56%
4	5	56%	8	7	53%
11	7	61%	9	10	53%
22	26	54%	9	23	72%

Presentation 2			Presentation 4		
A-Con	B-Pro	Ratio of Pro or Con	B-Con	A-Pro	Ratio of Pro or Con
17	14	55%	15	15	50%
9	9	50%	9	7	56%
13	10	57%	6	7	54%
10	8	56%	12	10	100%

F (Marginality) = 28.0 ($p < 0.001$)
F (Interaction of Marginality and Presentation) = 6.0 ($p < 0.01$)
(From Stark, 1969 with permission.)

Roethlisberger was among the first who described the foreman as the "man-in-the-middle" — looked upon by the workers as a part of management, responsible to management and yet not really feeling that he is a part of management. He is expected to gain the loyalty of the workers, but at the same time remain loyal to management and ensure that whatever his supervisor decides needs to be done is done. Davis (1967, p. 115) maintains that the man-in-the-middle viewpoint still prevails and that in this position the foreman is merely a mediator and buffer between opposing pressures. Unfortunately, only observations by individuals are cited in support of the man-in-the-middle proposition.

In the present study, the marginality scores of a group of first line supervisors were compared with those of a class of business administration students and with those of a large sample of teachers. The critical subjects were 30 first line supervisors who attended a supervisory training class conducted by the Oregon State System of Higher Education, Division of Continuing Education. The subjects held positions in a wide variety of local industries and business organizations. They completed the Self–Other Orientation Tasks during the first fifteen minutes of a class period.

The sample of business administration students were the same as those in the first study. The second comparison group was 108 elementary and high school teachers from as many schools from the states of Oregon, Nevada, Washington, and Idaho. These data had been collected in connection with an earlier study (Ziller & Golding, 1969).

Supervisors were found to have higher marginality scores than teachers ($r = 3.57$, $p < 0.01$) and higher marginality scores than business administration students ($r = 4.55$, $p < 0.01$). The results support earlier observations describing the first line supervisor as the man-in-the-middle. The present results, however, indicate that the first line supervisor perceives himself as the man-in-the-middle. The approach is phenomenological. The results would be more convincing, of course, if control groups had been available within the same organizations as the first line supervisors. A study of salesmen as marginal men supports these findings, however (Stark, 1969).

Salesmen have been described by Ditz (1964) as occupying a marginal position somewhere between their customers and their employer. In a study similar to the preceding study and using the same booklet to measure marginality, Stark (1969) demonstrated that salesmen located the self in a marginal position more frequently than several control groups.

OVERVIEW

In the definition of the concept of marginality given here, the positive potential of the orientation of the self as separate from both of two antipodal groups was stressed, although possible negative consequences of a marginal orientation were not ignored. The marginal person will become a convenient target for criticism from the opposing groups. He is associated with both groups, but not totally committed to either one.

In addition, a non-verbal phenomenological measure of marginality was presented and validated in a series of studies. In the first analysis, the marginal man was found to be less dogmatic. Also, first line supervisors as well as salesmen, examples of occupational roles in which marginality may be functional, were found to score higher on the measure of marginality in comparison with control groups.

In one of the studies in the series, the marginal in contrast to the less marginal men tended to support about equally two opposing statements on a given issue. In a sense, the marginal person was shown to adopt an ambivalent or neutral position under conditions of conflict. The measure of neutrality in this latter study was the higher frequency of support of either position in relation to the total frequency of support of both positives. This latter measure itself may be a more valid indicator of marginality than that derived from the Self–Other Orientation Tasks, and its utility should be explored further.

Most significantly perhaps, the study demonstrates the utility of the Lewinean concept of marginality particularly when accompanied by suitable phenomenological measures of the concepts. The measure requiring the subject to locate himself within a social field of significant groups of people presents a geometric model of the individual's view of the social field. Moreover, this representation is found to be related to social behavior. In a sense, the self–other orientation approach helps to instrument field theory which has previously been truncated in its development by lack of objective phenomenological measures.

Again, as in the two previous sections, the cognitive mapping of self and other was found to be associated with social behavior. The behavior central to the present study was the support given to another person's arguments on a given issue, specifically, the frequency with which the person pressed a button indicating approval of the point of view expressed. In terms of behaviorism, the frequency of button pressing is a measure of reinforcing behavior.

In the previous chapter dealing with social interest, the central study concerned the expectation of support (smiles, head nods, and general approval) when presenting a speech to an audience of two other persons, one of whom was approving and one of whom was disapproving. The reinforcing behavior of the other rather than the reinforcing behavior of the self was emphasized.

In the section concerning self-esteem, it was proposed that persons with high self-esteem have recourse to self-reinforcements or self-approval and are not as dependent as persons with low self-esteem on approval or reinforcement from others from moment to moment.

Most certainly, reinforcement of others is a critical behavior in interpersonal relations. This is recognized in Bales' analyses of communication where six of the twelve original categories for coding human interaction refers to approval or disapproval of the other (Bales, 1950). Approval categories include showing solidarity, showing tension release (such as satisfaction), and agreeing. Disapproval categories include disagreeing, showing tension, and showing antagonism. By linking self–other orientations to positive and aversive reinforcement as defined by the categories of communication described above, a basic approach to developing a link between personality and social psychology evolves. The link derives from a cognitive learning theory.

It has been proposed here that the self–other orientations evolve from the social supports or social reinforcement of certain social behaviors. Self-esteem, for example, was presumed to derive from parental support of the child when he behaved in accordance with certain parental expectations. In a sense, then, these behaviors have been coded and stored by the individual by means of these simple mappings of himself in relation to significant other people such as the parents. These cognitive mappings such as self-esteem, social interest, and marginality, in turn, lead to certain behavior in other social situations making for a degree of continuity and consistency of social behavior. Self-esteem, social interest, and marginality are mediating constructs by means of which the individual influences the relationship between the social stimulus and the social response. Marginality is the construct which is presumed to mediate the individual's social behavior under circumstances where the social field includes himself and two other groups where the three elements are somehow interrelated. An example might include a social psychologist in relation to a psychology department and a sociology department.

The three cognitive mappings discussed thus far (self-esteem, social interest, and marginality) do not exhaust the system. Others, such as self-centrality, will be briefly discussed as they become pertinent in subsequent sections. More significant than the discovery of additional self–other orientations, however, is the demonstration of the utility of cognitive constructs in a theory of social behavior. The research indicates that at least some forms of human behavior are mediated by self–other orientations and that these social orientations can be measured objectively.

Heretofore, many social scientists have avoided the use of a phenomenological approach to social behavior because of its subjectivity, difficulty of
measurement, and because the intervening variables could be avoided
without great loss in predictability.

Part II Patterns of Self–Other Orientation

Until very recently, the difficulties presented by measurement of the self concept have retarded the development of the theory. For the most part, research has usually been concerned with a single component of the self concept, and that component was self-esteem. With the advent of a multi-component approach, however, an analysis of patterns of self–other orientations is possible. In the following two chapters, alienated persons are discussed in terms of self-esteem, social interest, and self-centrality; and the political personality is discussed in terms of self-esteem and complexity of the self concept.

CHAPTER 4

The Alienation Syndrome: A Triadic Pattern of Self–Other Orientation

Alienation is a much used and much disputed concept (Seeman, 1959; Josephson & Josephson, 1962; Scott, 1963; Feuer, 1963; Horton, 1964; Neal & Rettig, 1967). The concept is attributed to Marx (Bendix & Lipset, 1953), and evolved in his theory of the relationship between social class and political action. Erich Fromm (1955) describes alienation as "a mode of experience in which the person experiences himself as an alien. He has become, one might say, estranged from himself."

Seeman (1959) attempted to clarify the concept through qualifications in terms of five major components: powerlessness, meaninglessness, normlessness, isolation, and self-estrangement. Yet, this definition is hardly enlightening and certainly does not readily suggest any measures of the concept. Thus, again, speculation about the concept has outrun measurement and research, and the theory of alienation remains in an incunabular state. The problem is more severe than that described earlier with regard to the development of the concept of self-esteem, because alienation is an omnibus concept whose complexities tend to proliferate unchecked by benefit of data.

Powerlessness as a variant of alienation is conceived as "the expectancy or probability held by the individual that his own behavior cannot determine the occurrence of the outcomes, or reinforcements that he seeks" (p. 784). The reference to expectation of reinforcement is underscored here because it suggests a relationship to social interest described earlier.

*An earlier version of this chapter was published by the author in *Sociometry*, September 1969, pp. 287–300.

The person who perceives himself as powerless is not oriented toward positive reinforcement.

Meaninglessness is described as the condition when "the individual is unclear as to what he ought to believe — when the individual's minimal standards for clarity in decision making are not met" (p. 786). Seeman also suggests that meaninglessness is related to the person's inability to control his own destiny. Again, the expectancy of negative reinforcement in the social environment would seem to be associated with this concept.

Normlessness, as used by Seeman, is again associated with low predictability of behavior because of the absence of rules of behavior for regulating individual conduct. Isolation as used by Seeman seems to suggest the inutility for the individual of the usual reinforcements available or offered. In this sense, he feels estranged from his environment. Finally, "estrangement" is defined in social learning terms by Seeman as a condition in which the individual is engaged in activities which are not self-rewarding. For example, the housewife who cooks merely to get it over with is described as estranged from herself.

Throughout, it is possible to translate Seeman's concepts into concepts associated with social reinforcement. The alienated persons do not expect reinforcements from others and are not capable of self-reinforcement.

More recently, Feuer (1963) proposed that the term alienation "is used to convey the emotional tone which accompanies any behavior in which the person is compelled to act self-destructively." Again, this may be associated with the search for negative reinforcement or negative identity (Erikson, 1959). The latter definition and other recent uses of "alienation" (Meier and Bell, 1959; McDill, 1961) suggest that a search for similarities between alienation and maladjustment may be fruitful.*

The central concern of the concepts of alienation and maladjustment is the inherent conflict between the interests of the single individual and the common interests of all individuals. In the latter sense, studies of alienation may provide the basis for synthesizing sociological and psychological concerns with the individual in his social environment (Neal & Rettig, 1967). It is now proposed that this synthesis may evolve from the theory of self–other orientation.

SELF–OTHER ORIENTATION AND ALIENATION

Social psychological theories of personality and the concept of alienation are essentially concerned with the interrelationship of the self and significant others. The self concept is presumed to be an "apperceptive

---

*An opposing viewpoint has been outlined by Nettler (1957).

mass," an abstraction of serial events which facilitates prediction of future events involving the self. The other is a generalization of selected significant persons in the individual's life space. The apperception of others in relation to the self and the apperception of the self in relation to others provide the foci of the self–other orientation theory of personality.

Three self–other configurations are deemed definitive with regard to social adaptation. These are self-esteem, social interest, and self-centrality. These same three self–other concepts constitute the central personality variables of Adler's (1927) individual psychology. Two of these components, self-centrality and social interest, are similar to Cameron's (1943) precursors of paranoid delusional development, loss of social reality and increased self-reference, and to Eysenck's (1957) core traits of introversion-extroversion and sociability. The same three self–other orientations are also related to the five components of alienation described by Seeman (1959).

Self-esteem

Self-esteem as used here is concerned with the individual's stability of behavior stemming from his recourse to self-reinforcement under conditions of stress. The person with high self-esteem is somewhat insulated from moment to moment changes in the environment or lack of reinforcement from the environment, whereas the person with low self-esteem is particularly subject to environmental contingencies, either positive or negative and is inclined toward inconsistency.

In terms of alienation, Faunce (1968) has suggested that alienation is an incongruence in self-evaluation and the evaluation by others. In terms of self-esteem, this suggests that persons with low self-esteem will feel alienated because they are more dependent upon external reinforcements.

Seeman's (1959) component of alienation referred to as "meaninglessness" is similar to the concept of low self-esteem as used here. Meaninglessness is defined as a mode of alienation characterized "by a low expectancy that satisfactory predictions about future outcomes of behavior can be made." Similarly, Merton (1957) describes the low predictability of behavior under conditions of anomie. Again, with regard to self-esteem, this meaninglessness is assumed to derive from a lack of consistency in the behavior of persons with low self-esteem.

Social Interest

Social interest is used here to represent the perception of inclusion of self and other, and the expectation of positive reinforcement from the other. Social interest is associated with knowledge and acceptance of the norms of a primary group.

In terms of alienation, Seeman's (1959) component of "isolation" may be similar to the concept of social interest. Isolation refers to the detachment of the individual from common cultural standards.

To measure the extent of the social isolation factor in alienation (low social interest in our terms), Dean (1961) proposes such items as: "Sometimes, I feel all alone in the world."

Self-centrality

Self-centrality as used here concerns the use of the self as opposed to others as the key point of reference. Inner as opposed to outer orientation of the self has been a perenially controversial personality construct. A review of the literature (Carrigan, 1960) indicates that the evidence concerning the correlates of the construct are unclear. In the present approach, the question of inward-outward directionality of the self is recast in terms of whether the individual defines the self in terms of others or defines others in terms of the self. Either the self or significant others may be perceived as the figure or ground. Thus, self-centrality is defined as the perception of the social environment largely from the point of view of the perceiver, rather than from the point of view of significant others. Similarly, Ausubel (1952) speaks about the relative distribution of interest in self and others as egocentrism and sociocentrism, respectively.

Essentially, the concept is associated with withdrawal from social situations. The high self-centrality individual disengages himself from others or from social norms and develops a private frame of reference. Adler (1927) refers to the egocentric idealism processes of persons with neurotic dispositions. The neurotic thinks with idiosyncratic ideas, assumptions, and values which do not correspond with the ideas of other people.

Similarly, psychoanalysts emphasize the pathological features in narcissism (Federn, 1959). Excessive narcissism is said to interfere with any interest but particularly makes it more difficult or impossible to develop social relationships (transference). Cameron's (1943) concept of the paranoid's tendency to develop a pseudo-community which has little relation to reality may be attributed to extreme self-centrality.

As already stated, inherently, the socialization process involves conflict between the satisfaction of individual and group needs. The inability to maintain a workable degree of stability under conditions of self–other conflict is assumed to stem from inadequate guides for behavior (low self-esteem and low social interest) which are assumed to lead to withdrawal (high self-centrality). An individual with low self-esteem prematurely withdraws from an exchange of views when his own beliefs and those of a group which he is a member are in conflict. Similarly, an individual with low social interest may prematurely dismiss the arguments associated with a group's belief system, he remains outside the group's power field.

The inability to reconcile opposing guidance systems is assumed to lead to reduced social interest or "disengagement." Since self-esteem is socially derived and reinforced, reduced social interest also is associated, in turn, with a reduced self-estimate, which, in turn, is associated with increased self-centrality and reduced social interest. The process is cyclical and degenerative. Increased self-centrality tends to lead to further reduction in social interest and so on, as a function of the situation. The cycling and interaction effects of low self-esteem, low social interest, and high self-centrality is assumed, here, to be the essence of the concept of alienation.*

Thus, Seeman's (1959) components of self-estrangement and normlessness may be associated with self-esteem and social interest, and isolation may be associated with self-centrality.

The widespread interest in the omnibus concept of alienation attests to its significance. The present approach to alienation attempts to clarify the protean term by defining it in terms of the individual's perceptions mediated by self-esteem and social interest and self-centrality in interaction. Against the background already presented here, alienation is defined as an attitude of hopelessness resulting from an inability to structure the environment in terms of either a stable self-orientation or a stable other orientation, and a cessation in the individual's attempts to confront the social environment. Having no guidance mechanisms from self or other, the sense of meaninglessness, powerlessness, and normlessness is generated. The alienated individual does not mediate environmental stimuli through the concept of self or the concept of other. The alienated are not accepted as members within a significant subgroup and they perceive themselves as unguided persons in an uncharted environment. Against this theoretical background, it is proposed that alienation evolves under conditions which generate low self-esteem and low social interest leading to isolation.

Three studies will be described which demonstrate the relationship between alienation and a recurring triadic pattern of self–other orientation.

*A similar cyclical process of increasing separation has been proposed by Feuer with reference to alienation in a *kibbutz* (1950).

The subjects assumed to be alienated include behavior problem children, neuropsychiatric patients, the aging, and American Negroes, before 1965. The self–other orientation tasks provided the measures of self-esteem, social interest, and self-centrality.

SELF–OTHER ORIENTATION TASKS

As guidelines for research in the area of alienation Neal & Rettig (1967, p. 61) have suggested "(1) that each alienation construct have a single, identifiable referent; (2) that researchers operationalize their concepts and assume responsibility for showing the congruence of their concepts with their empirical referents; and (3) that the alienation constructs be related empirically to either their generative social conditions or their social consequences." The Self–Other Orientation Tasks concerning self-esteem, social interest, and self-centrality are presumed to meet these criteria.

The measures of self-esteem and social interest were the same as those described in previous sections. The measure of self-centrality is another in the series of Self–Other Orientation Tasks. The six items designed to measure self-centrality were interspersed among the other items throughout the booklet. The six items were identical and required the subject to draw a circle to represent the self and another circle to represent a friend within a large circular field (*see* Appendix A, Item 4). Again, a one-zero scoring method is used. Location of the self circle nearer the center of the circular field is given a weight of one. Location of the other person nearer the center is given a weight of zero. The sum of the individual scores represents the self-centrality score.

The placement of the self rather than other closer to the center of the circle was assumed to depict greater self-centrality; the self is perceived as the cynosure of the constellation of self and others. Supporting the validity of this assumption are the findings that sociometric isolates in comparison with sociometric stars placed the self in a central position more frequently (Ziller, Alexander, & Long, 1964), as did children who had moved frequently between communities, than those who had lived in but a single community (Ziller & Long, 1964), as well as Asian Indian adolescents (who are the family's "reason for being") in comparison with a sample of American adolescents (Ziller, Long, Ramana, & Reddy, 1968).

The split-half reliability corrected for length of the measure for a sample of 99 American children in grades 6 to 12 was 0.58. Intercorrelations among measures of self-esteem, social interest, and self-centrality have not shown any significant relationships. These measures contrast with other measures related to alienation (Nettler, 1957) in that they are non-verbal and positive in their orientation. Items used by Nettler, for example, were "Do you think children are generally a nuisance to their parents?" "Do you think most politicians are sincerely interested in the public welfare or are they interested in themselves?"

BEHAVIOR PROBLEM CHILDREN*

Paralleling Adler (1927) in his description of physically handicapped children, it is proposed the institutionalized behavior problem child finds it difficult to feel that the meaning of life is contribution. Unless there is someone who can draw attention away from themselves (self-centrality) and interest them in others (social interest), they are likely to occupy themselves largely with their own sensations. Later on, they may become discouraged (self-esteem) and their feelings of inferiority stressed through ridicule and avoidance on the part of their fellows. "These are all circumstances in which a child may turn in upon themselves, lose hope of playing a useful part in our common life and consider themselves personally humiliated by the world" (p. 80).

Berkowitz (1962), for example, concludes that persistent lawbreakers feel alienated and apart from other people. Consistent with the alienation syndrome framework, Berkowitz (p. 312) describes behavior problem children in terms of parental rejection leading to non-adoption of societal moral standards and lack of development of ego controls. The present study seeks confirmation of these hypotheses in terms of social interest and self-esteem.

Finally, Josephson and Josephson (1962) particularly refer to juvenile delinquents as among the social groups who have been described as alienated in some degree.

A group of 30 boys and 27 girls from the Governor Bacon Health Center, Wilmington, Delaware, constituted the sample (all the subjects available on a given day) of severe behavior problem children. School officials and the child's parents had recommended that the child be institutionalized in order to maintain closer supervision. The institutionalized sample represented a wide variety of behavior disorders including delinquency, neurosis, and psychosis. Their intelligence as measured by

*From an unpublished report by John Bankes, Governor Bacon Health Center, Wilmington, Delaware; Barbara H. Long, Goucher College, Towson, Maryland; and Robert C. Ziller.

the Terman-Binet ranged from 75 to 130. The subjects were matched for sex and age. The age range was 10 to 18. The matched control group was drawn from a sample of 420 adolescents from a neighboring school community. The Self–Other Orientation Tasks were group administered.

The means with regard to the three measures of self–other orientation are reported in Table 4.1. The results are statistically significant at the 0.05 level of confidence or better in each case. Behavior problem children were found to indicate lower self-esteem, lower social interest, and higher self-centrality than the control group.

Table 4.1   Means of Self-esteem, Social Interest, and Self-centrality with Regard to Alienated Subjects and Control Groups.

	Self-esteem		Social Interest		Self-centrality	
	$\bar{X}$	σ	$\bar{X}$	σ	$\bar{X}$	σ
Behavior Problem						
Children ($N = 57$)	2.9*	0.20	0.55	0.05	38%	0.06
Control ($N = 57$)	2.3	0.23	0.70	0.05	20%	0.06
	$t = 2.34$	($p < 0.05$)	$t = 2.37$	($p < 0.02$)	$t = 3.33$	($p < 0.01$)

*A low score indicates high self-esteem. With regard to social interest and self-centrality scores, a high score indicates high social interest or high self-centrality.

A cause and effect relationship between institutionalization and alienation is not suggested. A longitudinal study of institutionalized children is suggested, however. The results strongly support the self–other orientation framework as a basis for describing the alienated under conditions of institutionalization or conditions leading to institutionalization. It remains to be demonstrated, however, that the approach is useful across situations.

NEUROPSYCHIATRIC PATIENTS AND THE AGING

In an earlier study (Ziller & Grossman, 1967), it was stated that two findings with regard to age of the adult subjects, low self-esteem, and low social interest, were similar to findings with regard to the neurotic personality. It was assumed that the results reflected "social isolation deriving from membership in a minority collective (the neurotics and the aging), and the perception of the self by others and the self as different or outside the social frame of reference of the members of the majority collective." In addition, it may be noted that old age and institutionalization because of severe problems of adjustment are associated with social isolation and social stigma, conditions associated with alienation (Cumming & Henry, 1961; Josephson & Josephson, 1962).

The subjects in the study were 90 acute male neuropsychiatric patients from the Veterans Administration Hospital, Elsmere, Delaware, and 87 male employees of the same hospital, the latter served as subjects on a volunteer basis. The patients represent the total population of neuro-psychiatric cases in the hospital over a period of five months. Each of the samples involved 10% Negroes. The average years of education for the neuropsychiatric patients and normals were 11.8 and 11.6 respectively.

All patients were administered the Self–Other Orientation Tasks within the first week of admission to the hospital. The hospital staff (the comparison group) completed the tasks during their monthly staff meetings. All subjects completed the tasks in fifteen to thirty minutes.

The form used in the present study only involved a single item for each self–other construct. The self-esteem task was similar to that used in the previous studies. In this case, however, a vertical array of ten circles (rather than six horizontal circles) was presented which was described as representing important people in their life. In contrast to the earlier form, however, the important people were not listed. The subjects were required to choose any one of the circles to stand for themselves and place an *S* within it. The higher position was assumed to depict higher self-esteem. The circles in the array were weighted from ten to one beginning with the circle at the top. Again the score for self-esteem was the weighted position of the self.

In a subsequent reliability study, the correlations between the left-to-right location of the self and the up-down placement of the self was 0.50 for 82 subjects. The vertical item, however, may be more "visible" than the horizontal item, for adults at least.

The social interest item was the same in form as that used with children but two of the circles of reference were changed for the adults. "Parents" was changed to "family," and "teachers" was changed to "work group." The "friends" reference remained the same. The same rating was used, one for inside the societal triangle and zero for placement outside the triangle of significant others.

The centrality item was identical with the item used in the previous studies. The results are indicated in Table 4.2.

The analysis involved a 2 × 3 analysis of variance design comparing the Self–Other Orientation Tasks responses of neuropsychiatric patients and

Table 4.2 Means and Significance Levels of the Analysis of Variance of the Self–Other Orientation Tasks Responses of Normals (N) and Neuropsychiatric Patients (NP) and with Regard to Age.*

Self–Other Orientation	N (N = 60)	NP (N = 60)	F	d.f.	p	Age 22–39 (N = 40)	40–45 (N = 40)	46–64 (N = 40)	F	d.f.	p
Self-esteem	3.6	4.7	6.04	1/114	< 0.05	3.7	3.8	5.0	3.66	2/114	< 0.05
Social Interest	0.6	0.4	6.00	1/114	< 0.05	0.7	0.3	0.3	8.00	2/114	< 0.01
Self-centrality	0.3	0.6	6.64	1/96	< 0.05	0.4	0.5	0.4	—	—	N.S.

*The results in this table are those reported by Ziller and Grossman (A developmental Study of the Self-social Constructs of Normals. Journal of Clinical Psychology, January 1967, p. 20). Again, a low score indicates high self-esteem, whereas with regard to social interest and self-centrality scores, a high score indicates high social interest or high self-centrality.

normals according to three age categories, 22 to 39, 40 to 45, and 46 to 64. In forming the age categories, it was necessary for purposes of analysis to include an equal number of subjects within each cell but maintaining critical age classifications. A cut-off point of 40 years of age was assumed to be perceived as a significant division of the life span and associated with a deceleration of some aspects of human development (*see* Hurlock, 1968, pp. 672–766). A second cut-off point between 45 and 46 was dictated by the distribution of the subject's ages and the requirement of an equal number of subjects in each cell. A total of 120 subjects comprised the resulting sample and included 20 subjects per cell. The mean age of the subjects in each of the age categories were 33.2, 42.4, and 51.1.

Earlier investigations of the process of aging (Cumming & Henry, 1961; Cumming, Dean, Newell, & McCaffrey, 1960) have proposed the term "disengagement" to indicate tendencies of detachment and depression accompanying increasing age, particularly with regard to persons 60 and older. Cumming, Dean, Newell, and McCaffrey propose that disengagement begins with a shift in self-perception which reflects withdrawal. This shift in perception is accompanied by a reduction of interaction and time spent with others. The result is a "more self-centered and idiosyncratic style of behavior." The results of the present investigation suggest that the term "disengagement" may be subsumed under the concept of alienation and expressed in terms of the triadic pattern of self–other orientation.

It must be noted that two of the findings with regard to age, (self-esteem and social interest) are similar to the findings with regard to the neurotic personality. This suggests, that there may be a common base for the psychological and sociological approaches to deviant behavior, and that the self–other orientation approach offers promise in the search for further commonalities.

The results are presented first with regard to the comparisons between neuropsychiatric patients and normals, followed by the results with regard to the three age categories (Table 4.2). None of the interactors were statistically significant and were eliminated in the earlier report (Ziller & Grossman, 1967).

The results again support the alienation self–other orientation framework. Neuropsychiatric patients in comparison with normals indicate lower self-esteem, lower social interest and higher centrality of the self in relation to friend.

The results with regard to increasing age indicate decreasing social interest and decreasing self-esteem. The results with regard to self-centrality were not statistically significant.

THE AMERICAN NEGRO*

The American Negro, who is often socially stigmatized by virtue of skin color and socially isolated in many ways, provides a unique subgroup to examine the alienation syndrome hypothesis. Those who have investigated the sociological sources of alienation (Meier & Bell, 1959; Bell, 1957; Killian & Grigg, 1963; Mizruchi, 1960; Srole, 1956) have found that alienation is most characteristic of those individuals who are deprived of full and equal participation in American society. Consistent with the social psychological theory of alienation presented here, the low self-esteem, the tendency to withdraw, and the general attitude of hopelessness of the American Negro has been cited frequently (Pettigrew, 1964; Drake & Cayton, 1962; English, 1957; Hammer, 1953; Mussen, 1953). Again, however, the previous approaches to the measurement of the self concept must be seriously questioned. Moreover, no study has previously focused on the three variables which are assumed here to be the crucial components of the alienation syndrome.

The subjects were 43 Negroes and 83 White boys and girls from the sixth grade of 10 schools in Delaware and Maryland. The original sample involved an equal number of boys and girls by race, but due to incomplete forms the ratio varies slightly for each of the three measures. Seventy-four percent of the original Negro sample were students in segregated schools. Seventy-nine percent of the original White sample were in integrated schools. The data were collected in May 1965.

The measures of self-esteem, social interest, and self-centrality were the same as those used in the study of behavior problem children. The tests were group administered.

The results with regard to social interest and self-centrality support the theory. The Negro subjects expressed lower social interest and higher self-centrality than the White subjects, but the results with regard to self-esteem were opposite to those predicted, although they were not statistically significant (see Table 4.3).

Only the results with regard to self-esteem with regard to the Negro and the self-centrality of the aging were inconsistent with the theory and the other results. It is possible, however, that the self-centrality of the aging sample was not *yet* different than the younger sample, and that the Negro

*I am indebted to Dr. Charlotte P. Taylor, University of Delaware, who provided me with the data from her dissertation (1967). The results reported here are based on a re-analysis of the data using *t*-tests rather than the chi-squared technique reported in the original work.

Table 4.3   Means and Significance Levels of the Self–Other Orientation Task Responses of Negro Compared with White Subjects.

Self–Other Orientation	Negro ($N = 43$)	White ($N = 83$)	t	p
Self-esteem	2.3*	2.4	0.25	N.S.
Social Interest	2.6	3.9	0.25	< 0.01
Self-centrality	2.8	1.7	3.44	< 0.01

*Again, a low score indicates high self-esteem, whereas with regard to social interest and self-centrality scores, a high score indicates high social interest or high self-centrality.

formerly possessed a lower self-evaluation. The mean age of the oldest grouping of the aging sample was only 51.1. An older group may reflect lower self-esteem.

The alienation of the Negro may be in the process of change and the data with regard to self-esteem may reflect this change. Unfortunately, longitudinal data are not available.

If these latter two assumptions are permitted, the results suggest that in alienation regress, self-centrality is the last component to change. In alienation redress, however, self-esteem is the first component to change. Self-esteem, then, emerges as the pivotal component of alienation. Self-esteem is the most critical indication of perceived deviation.

I have attempted to deduce a relationship among the concepts of alienation, social psychological theories of personality and self–other orientation. The fundamental unifying framework is the triadic syndrome of low self-esteem, low social interest, and high self-centrality. This pattern emerged with regard to behavior problem children, neuropsychiatric adult patients, and to some extent, with males above 40 years of age and older and with American Negro children. It was proposed that the alienation syndrome emerges as a consequence of inadequately defined systems of behavior stemming from an unstable self-definition (low self-esteem) or lack of acceptance of or by a group which provides social norms for individual behavior (low social interest). It was proposed that the individual without a method of resolving the conflict between self and other guidance systems finds refuge in an involuted environment, that is, he turns to a self-centered orientation. Moreover, withdrawal sets into motion a degenerative cycle. Outside of a social context, self-esteem is difficult to maintain. Reduced self-esteem, in turn, will again adversely affect social interest and lead to further withdrawal. The resolution of self and other orientations toward the social environment is a major consideration of social psychological theories of personality.

Assuming the critical nature of social interest in the etiology of the alienation syndrome, the alienating process may be attributable, in part at least, to exclusion from a significant group. If the significant group also controls the reward system, exclusion, which tends to be associated with self-devaluation and self-centrality, becomes a self-fulfilling prophecy. Through exclusion, the degenerative alienation syndrome may be precipitated, thereby justifying the initial exclusion to those who initially excluded the individual.

In Chapter 2 it was shown that persons with low social interest orient themselves toward negative reinforcement more than positive reinforcement. It is now suggested that orientation toward negative reinforcement tends to perpetuate the exclusion process. The person with low social interest expects punishment as a result of a history of punishment in group situations. He orients himself toward negative reinforcement and this selective orientation tends to support and perpetuate his personal theory of behavior. Since he perceives more self-directed punishment, he may be expected to behave in an antisocial manner. This antisocial behavior, in turn, leads to increased exclusion and necessarily the reduced probability of positive reinforcement. In this manner, the victim of exclusion as well as those who initiated the exclusion find their behavior justified and render the possibility of conflict resolution increasingly remote.

The procedure for reversing the alienation process now becomes evident. Those who initiated the exclusion must begin to positively reinforce the excluded person and encourage the former member to rejoin the group so that the probability of positive reinforcement may increase. In order to facilitate de-alienation, however, it may also be necessary to train the former members in ways which will mand reinforcement from the group members. For example, he may be trained to positively reinforce others, which tends to evoke positive reinforcements from the other by virtue of the norm of reciprocity (Gouldner, 1960), that is, an expectation between most persons that one positive act deserves another in return.

De-alienation or resocialization will not be effected satisfactorily, however, until self-esteem, social interest, and self-centrality of the target person has changed toward some base line level of acceptance. Even though the target person's attitudes and even his behavior may change, unless the appropriate self–other orientations of the individual change away from the level associated with alienation, the personal system of the individual may revert to its earlier state of equilibrium associated with alienation. To achieve this stage of resocialization, the individual may require intensive retraining or therapy (*see* Patterson & Reid, 1970). It is proposed that measures of self–other orientation be used to assess the effectiveness of these training programs.

SUMMARY

Within the self–other orientation framework, a more explicit approach to the sociological concept of alienation is proposed. In turn, the behavioral correlates of the components of the alienation syndrome (low self-esteem, low social interest, and high self-centrality) were indicated. This two-step translation of the alienation syndrome concept to cognitive constancy and behavioral outcomes renders alienation more amenable to experimental inquiry. Recently, Henderson, Long, and Gantcheff (1972) have extended the alienation framework to apply to French-Canadian children.

CHAPTER 5

A Political Personality Syndrome

A second study which employs a pattern approach to self–other orientation is described here. Again, we shall be concerned with the key component of self-esteem but now in conjunction with complexity of the self concept. Again, too, the analysis begins in relation to a phenomenon, the successful politician, and develops toward cognitive and behavioral explanations. Most significantly, however, the study described here supports Lewin's social psychological theory of personality pertaining to differentiation-integration.

Greenstein (1967) has recently noted the lack of systematic research relating personality and politics, although observers proliferate examples of political events that were critically mediated by the personal characteristics of the key actors. In response to the "Tatterdemalion nature of existing work in the field" (Greenstein, 1968), a theoretical and methodological analysis of the area of research was rendered by James D. Barber, Rufus P. Browning, Alexander L. George, Harold D. Lasswell, Neil J. Smelzer, David J. Singer, and M. Brewster Smith (*see* Greenstein, 1968). In contrast to earlier work, the study presented here involves a social psychological theory of personality, self–other orientation, and measures of the basic personality constructs. The measures involve topological representations of the self in relation to significant others. The verbal demands of the measures are minimal, thereby minimizing cause for dissembling. The central construct is the social responsiveness of the political candidate. The dependent variable is election or appointment to political office.

The pattern of behavior viewed as crucial in American politics is the process of negotiation, accommodation, and bargaining among diverse groups under conditions of conflict. In attempting to control, mediate, or resolve conflict, the political actor may be responsive to few or many parties to the conflict.

The relative power of the diverse groups is assumed to be a variable relevant to the responsiveness of the political actor. In an environment in which a single group or a coalition is clearly dominant, consistent political behavior congruent with the opinions of the power component of the constituency may be the basis for recruiting candidates and for political survival. Persons who practice this approach to politics may be described as ideologues. The ideologue is responsive to a single dominant subgroup. On the other hand, where the balance of power among diverse subgroups is tenuous, a pragmatic approach to politics may be indicated. In this latter approach the politician seeks an *ad hoc* policy decision rather than a decision in terms of his own guiding principles or those emerging from the opinions of a given segment of the constituency. In this way, the pragmatic politician avoids opposition based on his expected voting behavior since his responsive behavior is difficult to predict.

The crucial concept which evolves from this analysis of political behavior is latitude of responsiveness. Responsiveness by A is defined as a change in opinion of person A in the direction of greater agreement with those of person B. The ideologue responds consistently to a relatively narrow range of opinions, those supported by the dominant group in the constituency. The pragmatic politician is responsive to a pluralistic constituency. It is now proposed that latitude of responsiveness is associated with two components of self–other orientation: self-esteem and complexity of the self concept.

SELF-ESTEEM AND RESPONSIVENESS

It will be recalled that self-esteem is used here as that component of the self system which is involved in the regulation of the extent to which the self system is maintained under conditions of stress. The person with high self-esteem has recourse to self-reinforcement. Social stimuli are mediated by the self system in such a way as to maintain consistency in behavior. In this way, the individual is somewhat insulated from the environment and is not completely subject to environmental contingencies. Thus, high self-esteem is associated with integration of the self system and consistency of social behavior. The individual is not a captive of events or does not feel compelled to accommodate the self to the situation.

S.S.—D

Persons with low self-esteem, on the other hand, do not possess a well-developed conceptual buffer for evaluative stimuli. In Witkins' terms (Witkins, Dyk, Foterson, Goodenough, & Karp, 1962), the person with low self-esteem is field dependent, that is, he tends to conform passively to the influence of the prevailing field or context. Since the individual's behavior is directly linked to immediate environmental circumstances and is not mediated and integrated through the self concept, he is inclined toward inconsistency (Mossman & Ziller, 1968).

The relationship between self-esteem and political candidacy has been discussed at length by both Lasswell (1930) and Barber (1965). Lasswell describes political figures as suffering from marked feelings of personal inadequacy or inferiority, who seek out political opportunities for compensating for these feelings.

COMPLEXITY OF THE SELF CONCEPT AND RESPONSIVENESS

The complexity of the self concept is defined by the number of facets of the self perceived by the individual. The earliest stage of self-awareness involves the separation of the self from the non-self. As the developmental process continues, the self concept becomes increasingly differentiated.

Following the first gross categorization of self and non-self, the infant begins to determine among other objects both social and material, and among his feelings and emotions. The relationship of the self to others, and particularly the parents, provides information about the self. As the child strives for independence from the parents, he learns to distinguish new aspects of the self. Group affiliations add further information about the self through comparisons and contrasts with the members and with other groups. By identifying with a group, the individual establishes that he is distinguished from those who are not in the group. The self is discovered by successive approximations in an external-internal direction. The non-self is more readily discovered than the self.

Inherent in the development process is the tendency to evaluate the self in comparison with others (*see* Festinger, 1954). Festinger's theory of social comparison is based on the assumption that a correct appraisal of one's own opinions and abilities in relation to those of others is presumed to derive from a more basic need for a clearly defined self concept (Ziller, 1964). Through the process of social comparison the individual establishes a frame of social reference with the self as a point of reference. In the process, the self is distinguished from other in terms of similarities and contrasts of opinions and abilities.

Expanding upon the theory of social comparison, it is now proposed that more meaningful encounters with a wide variety of others is associated with increased self-dimensionality or complexity of the self concept. In order to establish similarities and contrasts with a wide variety of others and in the process of making these comparisons, a more highly differentiated self-social concept evolves. Each person with whom the self is compared presents one or more facets different from those of other persons. The perceiver tends to code these facets as being included in or excluded from the self-definition. The inclusion of more facets within the self-definition increases self-complexity. Continuous confrontation with diverse others is assumed to encourage closer scrutiny of the self in terms of similarities and contrasts followed by the emergence of a more highly differentiated self concept. The result is a multifaceted self concept.

Thus, it is proposed that the self concept may also be described in terms of complexity, the degree of differentiation of the self concept, or in Lewin's terms (1935) the number of parts composing the whole. As one aspect of cognitive style, complexity of the self concept reflects the number of dimensions along which stimuli relevant to the self are ordered (*see* Harvey, Hunt, & Schroder, 1961). Assuming that facilitation of ordering and organizing stimuli is associated with attending to a wider range of stimuli, it is anticipated that individuals with complex self concepts may be aware of or consider a greater number of stimuli as being potentially associated with the self. In terms of interpersonal perception, the complex person has a higher probability of matching some facet of the self with a facet of the other person, since there are a larger number of possible matches. Thus, it is hypothesized that the complex individual is more inclined toward assimilation of self and others or perceiving similarities between self and others, whereas the simplex individual is inclined toward contrasting self and others. In general then, it is proposed that persons with more complex self concepts attend to a broader range of social stimuli, perceive more similarities between self and other, and are more responsive to others.

Allport (1961, p. 508) makes a similar assertion:

> As a rule people cannot comprehend others who are more complex and subtle than they. The single track mind has little feeling for the conflicts of the versatile mind . . .. Would it not follow, therefore, that the psychiatrist, since he deals with intricate mental tangles, should benefit by the possession of a complex personality?

Experimental support for the framework derives from a series of unpublished experiments by Alex Bavelas of Stanford University concerning the etiology of superstition. Bavelas found that persons with more complex theories tended to assimilate new information into the system with greater facility. In our present terms, this suggests that persons with more complex theories of the self will tend to assimilate new information into the cognitive system with greater ease, that is, they are more responsive to their environment.

In these studies, the same series of bits of information was presented on a screen to each of two subjects. The subjects, A and B, were separated and could not communicate with each other. After each presentation of information, the subject was required to make a response. Correct feedback was provided to subject A. The feedback presented to subject B was the same as that presented to A, that is, the feedback was non-contingent on B's responses. Subsequently, A and B were asked to describe what had occurred, that is to develop a theory which would fit the observations.

It was found that B developed a more complex theory than A. Complexity was measured by counting the number of words used to describe their theory.

Subsequently, A and B discussed what they had seen. It was found that B, the subject with a more complex theory, was able to persuade A that he was wrong. In the discussion, B reported observations which A had ignored. These observations were easily assimilated by A's complex theory, but B's simplex theory had to be abandoned in the face of the "new data."

Barber (1965, p. 224) describes two types of political candidates: those who have such high self-esteem that they can manage relatively easily the threats and strains and anxieties involved in the role of candidate, and those who have such low self-esteem that they are ready to become involved in the extraordinary procedures of political candidacy in order to raise their self-esteem. Serious doubts must be raised, however, about Barber's methodology which involved the assessment of interview responses as indicators of self-esteem.

Direct support of the hypotheses associating complexity of the self concept and responsiveness to diverse others is provided by a study by Thompson (1966). Persons with complex as opposed to simplex self concepts (complexity of the self concept was measured by enumerating the number of adjectives checked as descriptive of the self), were found to perceive strangers twenty years their senior as being more similar to themselves. Also children with complex as opposed to simplex self concepts were found to be more sociometrically popular (Ziller, Alexander, & Long, 1964).

THE SELF-ESTEEM–COMPLEXITY MATRIX (INTEGRATION-DIFFERENTIATION)

The four cells generated by high-low self-esteem and high-low complexity of the self concept provide gross categories of the relative responsiveness of persons with these patterns of self–other orientation. Thus, the high self-esteem, high complexity cell includes individuals with differentiated and integrated theory of social behavior. The high-high person is capable of assimilating new information concerning the self without jeopardizing the self system. These persons may be assumed to be responsive within moderate limits.

The low self-esteem, high complexity cell is assumed to describe the person with a very tentative theory of social behavior, a person who is responsive to a wide range of social stimuli, in terms of political behavior, a person who is responsive to a wide range of social stimuli.

The high self-esteem, low complexity quadrant is assumed to include persons with a closed theory of behavior. They are generally non-responsive. Rokeach's (1960) Dogmatism Scale may also be describing these individuals who render absolute rather than tentative judgments. With regard to political behavior, the ideologue is included within this cell.

It is somewhat more difficult to characterize succinctly persons in the low self-esteem, low complexity cell. It is tentatively proposed that they are highly responsive within a narrow range of social stimuli.

A framework similar to the coordinate analysis of responsiveness presented here is Lewin's (1935) theory of differentiation-integration. Development was described by Lewin as including an increase in the number of relatively independent subparts of the person (differentiation) and increasing the unity of the person (integration or organization).

Integration is not simply a reversal of the differentiation process. Through integration, an interdependence among the different systems of the person emerges and a restructuring of the entire system occurs. In the subsequent course of differentiation, however, new centers of the personality are developed out of the new personality structure. The process is cyclical and results, usually, in ever increasing levels of development.

Nevertheless, the integration of the person during development is not a simple restructuring of the inner personal system. Instead, it is a process by which a certain system (or subsystem) becomes dominant by imposing patterns of action related to certain needs. Here, as in the concept of self-esteem as used in the self–other orientation framework, integration is described by Lewin as including a control function. Differentiation (and self-complexity) is followed by integration (self-esteem) which functions as a reorganizing process which helps to reintroduce a degree of control by the individual over increasingly complex interrelationships among subparts and subsystems of the personality.

More recently, Witkins, Dyk, Foterson, Goodenough, and Karp (1962) and Schroder, Driver, and Streufert (1967) introduced differentiation and integration as central concepts in their theories of personality, although the constructs are confounded with each other in both theory and measure. The similarity between the present framework and Piaget's (1947) concepts of assimilation and accommodation should also be noted. Other related concepts include cognitive complexity (Bieri & Blacker, 1956) and cognitive tuning (Zajonc, 1960). Although there is a common theme in each of these approaches, the concept of complexity is protean and illusive. It is unreasonable to expect the discovery of a single approach which can account for much of the meaning of all of these seemingly related concepts. Focusing on the complexity of the self, however, and considering this as but one component of the self system, may prove to be a more productive strategy.

The present study explores the patterns of self–other orientation which occur most frequently among persons holding political positions. The findings are then cross validated with regard to winning an election for political office. Political districts in the region studied (Oregon), were assumed to be pluralistic. Thus, it was hypothesized that winning political candidates tend to be pragmatic or responsive politicians (low self-esteem, high complexity of the self concept). In addition, changes in self-esteem were analyzed in association with winning or losing an election for political office.

Subjects

The subjects included 91 politicians who had already won the primary election and were candidates in the general election for the legislature of the State of Oregon, 104 male elementary and high school teachers, 150 male school principals, and 44 school superintendents. The teachers were always from the same school building as one of the principals who, in turn, were usually under the supervision of one of the superintendents in the sample. The teachers' sample included one teacher from the same school as one of the principals who was closest in age to the principal.

The samples of school personnel were selected from the states of Oregon, Nevada, Washington, and Idaho. The school communities included in the sample were determined in part by geographic proximity. The total population of superintendents on a convenient automobile route were contacted within each state. One to ten principals within the same school district were chosen on the basis of minimizing travel demands. In small school districts all the principals were contacted; in very large districts, all those who could be contacted in a day were included. Eighty-two percent of the public school personnel approached agreed to complete the instruments and returned them to the research organization. The sample of politicians represents 90% of the candidates in the general election for state legislature approached by the data collectors. The politicians represent 60% of all candidates for the Oregon State legislature for that election year. Those excluded were in remote districts or could not be located on the days the data collectors visited the community.

It was assumed that the public school superintendency is a political position not unlike that of the state legislator (Wriston, 1959) in terms of the presses on the position with regard to responsiveness and conflict resolution in a pluralistic community. Indeed, it may be said that a superintendent of schools is a politician without benefit of political party. The teachers and principals were selected as a convenient control group of adult males. It was assumed, however, that the role of teacher was least associated with the role of politician.

Instruments

The data collector traveled to the community of the subjects and usually approached the subject personally concerning his participation in the study. The data collector was preceded by a letter explaining the nature of the project in general terms. The directions on the cover of the Self–Other Orientation Tasks for school personnel were: "The questions which follow are designed to provide an indication of the way you look at yourself in relation to significant other people. In this description of yourself and others, words are avoided. This is a social psychological instrument designed for research purposes only. Hopefully, it will tell us something about differences in the perceptions of self and others among educators in the states of Idaho, Nevada, Oregon, and Washington. This instrument has been approved by the Department of Health, Education, and Welfare, Office of Education. Please work as quickly as possible. It should require about fifteen minutes or less."

The political candidates usually completed the form while the data collector waited. School personnel returned the forms to the university office of the project director.

The measure of self-esteem was administered twice to a sample of 44 of the original sample of 91 political candidates — once about six weeks before the general election and a second time two to four weeks after the general election. The latter sample was determined simply on the basis of proximity to the data collector and availability.

The measures of self-esteem and complexity of the self concept were derived from two instruments in the Self–Other Orientation Tasks. The measure of self-esteem is a shortened adult form of the instrument described earlier. The instrument contains four items scattered throughout a test booklet which the subject is presented with, a horizontal array of circles, and a list of significant others such as doctor, father, a friend, a nurse, yourself, someone you know who is unsuccesful. (The remaining sets were (a) someone you know who is a good athlete, someone you know who is popular, someone you know who is funny, someone who knows a great deal, yourself, someone you know who is unhappy; (b) an actor, your brother or someone who is most like a brother, your best friend, yourself, a salesman, a politically active person; (c) someone you know who is cruel, a judge, a housewife, a policeman, yourself, your sister or someone who is most like a sister.) The tasks require the subject to assign each person to a circle in the horizontal array. The score is the weighted position of the self from left to right.

The measure of complexity of the self concept presents an adjective check list form of 110 high frequency adjectives selected from the Thorndike–Lorge Wordbook (1944). The subject is asked to check each adjective which he thinks describes himself. (*See* Appendix A, Item 5.) The measure of complexity of the self concept is the total number of words checked. The concept and measure derive from a study of accuracy of perceptual recall (Glanzer & Clark, 1963) in which it was suggested that the length of subject's verbalizations may serve as an index of perceived complexity of the stimulus. A similar assumption was made by Zajonc (1960). It has been found that persons with high complexity of the self concept tend to be more popular (Ziller, Alexander, & Long, 1964), have had a wider range of social experiences (Golding & Ziller, 1968), use wider category widths, and identify with a wider range of others (Thompson, 1966), and require more time to reach a decision in an information search-group decision making situation (Smith, 1967). It has also been found (Ridgeway, 1965) that persons who check a greater number of adjectives as descriptive of the self also rate themselves higher on a self-report measure of complexity of the self concept, and draw more lines connecting a circle which represents the self to circles which represent other people. Finally, a Pearson correlation of 0.50 ($p < 0.05$) was found between complexity of the self concept and perception of the self as located within as opposed to outside a field of significant other people. (Golding & Ziller, 1968).

Corrected split-half reliability coefficients in the present sample of subjects for self-esteem and the complexity of the self concept were 0.90 and 0.92 respectively, indicating that the measures are adequately stable. Self-esteem was also found to be negatively correlated with complexity of the self concept ($r = -0.22, p < 0.01$).

Results

Changes in the self-esteem of political candidates were analyzed with regard to the experience of winning or losing the general election. Candidates who were elected to office tended to gain in self-esteem (15 increased, 4 decreased, and 4 remained unchanged), whereas candidates who were not elected increased in self-esteem a lower percentage of the time and decreased in self-esteem a higher percentage of the time (8 increased, 11 decreased, and 2 remained the same). It is noteworthy that the eight candidates who failed to be elected, yet increased in self-esteem, were all non-incumbents. The publicity associated with candidacy may be reinforcing.

In analyzing the frequency of occurrence of patterns of self-esteem and complexity among teachers, principals, superintendents, and legislators (candidates who had been elected), the distribution of scores of the total sample (including candidates who lost the election) was divided with reference to the mean, and the frequencies with which the patterns occurred were tabulated (*see* Table 5.1). Only the political candidates who were elected to office were included in this analysis, however. It was readily noted that the high complexity, high self-esteem pattern occurred with lower frequency among superintendents and legislators. In order to test the significance of this observation, the four categories of subjects were analyzed with regard to high self-esteem and high complexity and with regard to high and low self-esteem and low complexity (*see* Table 5.1).

The results with regard to high complexity are statistically significant and indicate that superintendents and legislators in contrast with principals and teachers were described by the high complexity, high self-esteem

Table 5.1   Frequency of Personality Patterns Involving Self-esteem and Complexity of the Self Concept Among Teachers, Principals, Superintendents, and Legislators.

| | | | Self-esteem | |
			High	Low
Teachers	Complexity	High	28	21
		Low	33	22
Principals	Complexity	High	41	28
		Low	48	33
Superintendents	Complexity	High	4	11
		Low	17	12
Legislators	Complexity	High	9	1·1
		Low	19	19

X^2 (Teachers and Principals vs. Superintendents and Legislators, high complexity only) = 4.12, d.f. = 1, $p < 0.04$.

pattern proportionately less frequently. The results with regard to low self-complexity were not statistically significant.

In an effort to cross validate the previous results, the total sample of political candidates (not merely legislators) was divided according to the outcome of general election (*see* Table 5.2). Again, only the results with regard to high complexity were statistically significant.

Those elected to office showed the high complexity, high self-esteem pattern less frequently, but showed the high complexity, low self-esteem pattern more frequently. It must be noted that of 18 high-high candidates, only 5 (28%) were elected, whereas of 16 high complexity, low self-esteem candidates, 14 (88%) were elected.

By assigning scores of 1 and 0 to winning or losing the election, a 2×2

Table 5.2 Frequency of Personality Patterns Involving Self-esteem and Complexity of the Self Concept Among Elected and Non-elected Political Candidates.

			Self-esteem High	Low
Elected	Complexity	High	5	14
		Low	22	14
Non-elected	Complexity	High	13	2
		Low	10	11

X^2 (High Complexity Elected vs. High Complexity Non-elected) $= 9.95$, d.f. $= 1$, $p < 0.002$.

X^2 (Low Complexity Elected vs. Low Complexity Non-elected) $= 0.51$, d.f. $= 1$, N.S.

analysis of variance was conducted with regard to the data in Table 5.2. The main effects for self-esteem were statistically significant ($F = 5.51$, d.f. $= 1$ and 87, $p < 0.05$) as were the interaction effects ($F = 13.12$, d.f. $= 1$ and 87, $p < 0.001$). Candidates with low self-esteem as opposed to high self-esteem tended to be elected to office. Again, however, the results are largely attributable to the poor showing of candidates with high self-esteem and high complexity.

Finally, it was noted that of the 31 incumbents who were candidates for re-election, only one of them lost. The personality pattern of the non-elected incumbent was high self-esteem, high complexity.

Discussion

Quite unexpectedly, it was observed consistently that the high self-esteem, high complexity of the self concept pattern of personality was associated with non-election to a political office or non-appointment as public school superintendent. The high-high pattern appears to indicate the apolitical personality. On the other hand, as initially proposed, the high complexity, low self-esteem pattern (the pragmatic politician) appears to indicate the political personality, or at least the personality pattern associated with the highest probability of election or appointment to office.

The results are somewhat opposed to those of earlier studies which used a single variable approach and suggested that low self-esteem is associated with political candidacy because of the need for reassurance (Barber, 1965, pp. 224, 243). Table 5.2, for example, shows that self-esteem does not differentiate between those elected or not elected with regard to candidates with low complexity of the self concept, although the main effects with regard to self-esteem are significant. Previous results were not qualified adequately.

Of course, previous investigators have used observations or self reports as measures of self-esteem as opposed to the more indirect, limited verbal approach described here. Under conditions of self report, some persons proclaiming high self-esteem are simply describing what they half-believe themselves to be and would like to be, but they need continual confirmation (including self reports) in order to buttress their unsure self-image (Maslow, Hirsh, Stein, & Honegmann, 1945).

The results are also somewhat incongruent with the theoretical frameworks of Lewin (1935) and Schroder, Driver, and Streufert (1967). The latter theorists suggest that the highest level of adaptation is achieved by persons whose life space is highly differentiated (high complexity of the self concept in terms of self–other orientation) yet highly integrated (high self-esteem here), the apolitical personality in the present framework. It is now maintained that the focus of the earlier frameworks was individual adaptation within a social environment where the individual may select social encounters to a greater degree than a politician. The results of the present study suggest that the low self-esteem, high complexity personality pattern may be more viable in the sociopolitical environment in which social responsiveness is a critical social demand. The politician is required to be other directed, aware of a multiplicity of social presses since he is usually a member of a pluralistic political district.

In a follow-up laboratory study (Terbovic, 1970), subjects classified in terms of high and low self-esteem were placed in a teaching situation where the "student" (a confederate) was only permitted to turn on a red light indicating displeasure or a green light indicating pleasure with the instruction. The instruction concerned directions for drawing a figure composed of six equal-size rectangles.

The results showed that persons with low as opposed to high self-esteem valued more highly the feedback from the "student." Again, the results appear to support the main theme of this section that persons with low self-esteem are more responsive to others.

Of course, legislators may take different roles within the legislature which may be associated with different self–other orientation patterns. For example, legislators who are responsible for initiating, formulating, and seeking approval of new public policies (the lawmaker in Barber's terms, 1965), may be described by the high self-esteem, high complexity grouping. These legislators "are freed by virtue of exceptionally strong personal resources — particularly a deep sense of personal identity and self-acceptance — to deviate from the common path precisely because they are in possession of powerful techniques for dealing directly with accompanying strain" (Barber, 1965, p. 224). Of course too, other samples of politicians at different levels on the political structure and in different political units must be studied to examine the generalizability of the results.

In Riesman's (1954) terms the high self-esteem, high complexity personality is inner directed. He is also less responsive to diverse others, thereby reducing markedly the probability of election or appointment to political office in a pluralistic social unit.

The two components of self–other orientation, self-esteem and complexity of the self concept, have been interpreted throughout as being associated with Lewin's concepts of integration and differentiation. The four cells generated by the intersection of these bifurcated measures permit a more systematic analysis of the differentiation-integration nexus than was heretofore possible. The results of this study suggest that high differentiation, high integration of the self concept is associated with the inner-directed personality. The initial theoretical analysis suggested that high integration, low differentiation was associated with dogmatism, and high differentiation, low integration with social responsiveness. The fourth cell was not readily interpretable. It remains, however, to extend the meaning of these cells experimentally. Most significantly, however, the long held theoretical framework involving differentiation-integration assumes new promise in conjunction with the associated measures of complexity of the self concept and self-esteem which emanated from a self–other orientation framework.

CONCLUSION

In this and the preceding chapter, two patterns of self–other orientations were explored. It was emphasized at the outset that one of the advantages of the component approach to the self system is the opportunity to examine crucial patterns of self–other orientation. The method of searching for these patterns is crucial since a large number of patterns are possible. In the two instances described here, the search was assisted by earlier theoretical positions, the alienation literature, and Lewin's concepts of differentiation-integration.

Part III   Development of Self–Other Concepts

Throughout, it has been necessary to consider the evolution of the self concept. In describing the concept of social interest, for example, the continuous conflict between the need for independence and need for dependence was described throughout the life cycle. In the next two chapters, development of the self concept becomes the central concern.

In Chapter 6, studies dealing largely with age are discussed. The inexorable process of aging combined with the need for stability presents a continuous conflict for the individual. It is proposed here that the resolution of this conflict is reflected, in part, in the self concept.

Chapter 7 is concerned with environmental factors associated with the development of the self concept. These include geographic mobility, culture, family setting, and physical disability. Social reinforcement of individual behavior will vary according to the social setting and will be reflected in the person's social interest and self-esteem.

Together, these two sections describe the cognitive and the behavioral approaches to the study of the concept of the self. The cognitive approach tends to emphasize the primacy of the self concept as it is related to behavior. The latter approach emphasizes the influence of behavior on the self concept. The confluence of these two approaches is one of the most exquisite theoretical problems in psychology.

CHAPTER 6

Consistency and Change of the Social Self

A persistent dilemma for the student of social behavior as well as the person being studied is that of maintaining some semblance of stability under conditions of continual change (Lecky, 1945). A degree of stability or consistency with regard to perceptions of the self and others is required in order to reduce the complexity of the environment to manageable proportions. To borrow from another adage, it might be proposed that even if consistency did not exist, it would be invented. Even the "invented" consistency, consistency which exists only in the eye of the perceiver, is still a phenomenon with behavioral correlates. Persons act on the basis of their perceptions. Indeed, study of the self concept is based upon similar arguments.

On the other hand, consistency suggests non-responsivity to situational demands. Consistency under changing conditions is, in fact, a simple definition of non-adaptability or even dogmatism. In terms of the self concept, then, it must be asked, what is the utility of the concept of the self in a relatively kaleidoscopic environment? It is proffered here that the self concept is a perceived working theory of behavior. The self concept is subject to change, but in the intervals between change, the individual provides himself with a modicum of perceived stability. As previously stated, a degree of stability provides a point of reference and a point for projection of the self into the future. Like any theory, it also provides a basis for asking more meaningful questions and limits the regions of information search concerning behavioral decisions.

Essentially, the concept of the self as used here is provisional, thereby providing for a degree of adaptability. The strategy of using a concept of this kind is similar to that used by Lewin and embodied within his concept of "dynamic equilibrium." It is assumed that equilibrium is not the final goal of the organism. It is assumed that the organism tends toward a state of tension reduction and goal achievement, but this state is only a point in a continuum which includes a complexity of goals and new levels of organization of the individual and his environment. Similarly, the self is assumed to achieve a state of "dynamic definition," if you will, where the self is defined tentatively and remains relatively stable for a given time period prior to a new level of development.

The problem of developing a dynamic self concept which is useful within a given age category, and yet, can be responsive to new situations associated with increasing age, will be used to illustrate the dilemma of stability and change with regard to the self concept.

Sarbin (1962) has assumed too that the self, like other cognitive structures, is subject to progressive change. The change is usually in the direction from lower order perception to higher order and more complex perceptions. It should be underscored, however, that the complexity evolves from earlier more simplex concepts which are not discarded but are differentiated. Early conceptions of the self, then, are presumed to be primary and propaedeutic. If, then, the self system is to be adaptive to later situations, a modifier of some kind must be included within the system which facilitates change. Complexity of the self concept is one such modifier. Responsiveness to social norms (social interest) is assumed to be another. Through these mediators, the self system remains open to change.

Before examining data concerning the self concept at different age levels, an examination of some theoretical explanations of the development of the self system are examined, namely, those of Sullivan (1953), Sarbin (1962), and Brim (1966). Appropriately, these conceptions of the development of the self system emphasize, respectively, a social-psychoanalytic framework, a cognitive framework, and a social learning framework.

SULLIVAN'S INTERPERSONAL APPROACH

Harry Stack Sullivan (1953) describes the development of the person before birth and onward. In the early phases, the infant's experience lead to gross distinctions between the self and the non-self. The cues for differentiation are largely physiological and kinesthetic. The act of thumb sucking, for example, aids in the description of self boundaries.

The self as a system, however, begins (according to Sullivan) when the infant is subjected more and more to the social responsibilities of the parent. At this level of development, the infant learns that the environment is cooperative only under certain conditions. In more recent terminology, the socialization process begins when the parents begin to use contingent reinforcements. The inherent conflict between self and other becomes clarified, and in the process, the infant learns to distinguish the self from others while still being very much included with others. It is maintained here that this conflict between self and others is everlastingly in a state of flux requiring constant reintegration followed by differentiation. It is in this sense that we speak of self–other orientations as being in a state of dynamic equilibrium.

SARBIN'S COGNITIVE APPROACH

Sarbin (1962) presented a more systematic analysis than Sullivan, but again the process begins with an emphasis on the "somatic self" which is organized around responses to stimuli to the somesthetic, kinesthetic, proprioceptive, and cutaneous senses. The somatic self is the dominant facet of the self system throughout the first two years. As cognition becomes more complex with the addition of non-verbal and verbal language structures, however, the concept of the self takes on an autonomous organizing function. Stimuli are selected and organized in terms of the developing self system. In a sense, the person begins to respond to himself as a point of reference and as a person.

Finally, according to Sarbin, the social self emerges. With the development of the concept of "I," the child can more readily differentiate others. Thus, the differential roles of mother and father are readily perceived and integrated within the cognitive structure. Again, the cognitive structure itself begins to mediate behavior by the selection of stimuli attended.

There is a tendency in this cognitive system to emphasize the effects of early experience on later behavior, and an inherent tendency to argue for the stability of the self concept. Sarbin builds the possibility of change into the self system through the process of differentiation of the self concept and complexity of the substructures of the self system. Still, the problem remains within this cognitive orientation as to how the significance of the somatic self fades and the social self becomes dominant. Sarbin suggests that this is accomplished by reinforcement of selected responses, but he does not elaborate and it remains for those more concerned with socialization to indicate how this shift in emphasis is accomplished.

BRIM'S RESOCIALIZATION ORIENTATION

Brim (1966) has outlined the development of the self through the life cycle with an emphasis on socialization. Socialization as used here indicates the processes whereby the individual becomes an integral part of a larger social unit, such as the family, work group, and community. Usually, the demands of society upon adults are tailored for the capacities of the average man. Usually, then, the strain is not excessive. Under certain circumstances, however, rapid change in self–other orientations may be necessary, such as under conditions of upward mobility or disaster or even accelerated social change of a society. These environmental changes coupled with the normal demands for resocialization accompanying changes in expectations associated with age and position may endanger the adaptive processes.

It is conceded that there are limits to later-life socialization. Early learning is durable due to learning under conditions of partial reinforcement, frequency of learning situations, primacy, and intensity of rewards and punishments. Brim proposes that late-life adjustment is possible, nevertheless, if there is a continuity between the old and the new and if discontinuity is anticipated by introducing elements into childhood learning which facilitate change. One such series of elements suggested is an approach to conflict resolution. These may include withdrawal or the use of "metaprescriptions." The latter are simply specific indications of priorities in a choice situation, for example: "Side with your wife when she disciplines the children, even if you think she is wrong." Thus, Brim adds another modifier to the self system which facilitates change but permits a degree of stability. In this later case, the use of conflict resolution procedures, stability of sorts is attained through the utilization of an armamentarium of change processes. In this sense, capability of change becomes a facet of the self concept.

Unfortunately, none of the aforementioned frameworks concerning the development of the self concept included any supporting data. An analysis of the series of studies which follows indicates changes in self–other orientations with age, the relation of early self concept and later self concept, and differences in self concept associated with retardation in maturation.

KUHN'S "Who Am I?" TECHNIQUE

One of the most simplex and direct approaches to the exploration of the self concept as associated with age was conducted by Kuhn (1960) using the Twenty Statements Test of Self Attitudes. The TST consists of asking the respondent to make 20 different statements in answer to the single question, "Who am I?" addressed to himself. A content analysis is made of the responses. Of major interest, however, is the groups with which the individual feels identified as revealed by his responses.

An analysis was made of the protocols of 1185 individuals, ranging in school category from second grade through college and professional graduate school and age 7 through 24. As the subject increased in age, it was found that he identified himself increasingly by his association with various groups. The youngest used 5.79 group references, whereas the oldest used an average of 11.03 group references. It was also reported that as people retire, their group reference scores diminish.

DEVELOPMENT OF SELF–OTHER ORIENTATION

Group identification may be assumed to be related to social interest as it is defined with the framework used here. In fact, Kuhn's findings were supported in a series of studies by the author and his colleagues using the Self–Other Orientation Tasks (Ziller & Grossman, 1967; Long, Henderson, & Ziller, 1967; Long, Ziller, & Henderson, 1968).

The first study (Long, Henderson, & Ziller, 1967) involved all students (373) in an elementary school in a semi-rural community. They ranged in age from 6 to 13 years, were white and largely from middle-class homes. The children's form of the Self–Other Orientation Tasks was used. The form includes items measuring self-esteem, social interest, and identification with mother, father, teacher, and friend, and individuation (as opposed to majority identification). The individuation and identification items have not been described previously.

Individuation was defined as the degree to which a person differentiates himself from his peers. The extremes of this dimension were considered to be "like" and "different from" others. The measure of individuation included a large circular area containing a dispersion of ten small circles representing "other children." (*See* Appendix A, Item 6.) The subject was asked to select one of two circles at the bottom of the page to represent himself. The choice of a circle different from those representing peers (a circle with five parallel lines passing vertically through the area) was interpreted as a higher degree of individuation. Evidence supporting the validity includes a Pearson correlation $(0.50, p < 0.01)$ between the above measure of individuation and a self report of individuation.

Identification of the self with particular other persons was defined as the acceptance of the other person as a model for the self. Heider (1958) has suggested that when a person indicates that two objects "belong together" it may be assumed that a concept relates them. Thus, placing the self in close proximity to another person was assumed to indicate a high degree of identification with him.

In the Self–Other Orientation Tasks, the subject was presented with a row of ten circles with another person (mother, father, or teacher) located on the circle to the extreme left. He was asked to select one of the remaining circles to represent the self. The distance between self and other was measured in number of intervening circles. (*See* Appendix A, Item 7.)

In the task involving identification with friend, the subject was presented with two gummed circles (a red circle for the self and a green circle for friend). He was asked to paste them on a blank sheet of paper in any way he liked. The distance between the circles was measured in centimeters. Less distance was assumed to reflect greater identification.

Evidence supporting the validity of the former tasks include the finding that children living in a fatherless home identified less with the father than did children of the same age and socioeconomic class whose fathers were present in the home. A second finding of this same study (Long & Henderson, 1967) was that children rated by their teachers as being "shy with teacher" identified with the teacher less than those rated "friendly with teacher."

It was found that self-esteem was highest in the first grade, decreased markedly in the second grade, but tended to rise from the second through the sixth grade. Social interest increased steadily from the first through the sixth grade. Individuation also increased with grade. The results with regard to identification with teacher, however, indicated clearly that children who were in school longer identified with the teacher less. With regard to friend, however, there was a sharp increase in identification with increasing age. (*See* Table 6.1.)

The results with regard to social interest clearly support Kuhn's results. Increasing age is accompanied by increasing identification with groups of significant others. Before commenting on the other results, however, a second study will be reported concerning the self–other orientation of children in the sixth through the twelfth grades in school.

The second developmental study of self–other orientations involved 420 students (30 boys and 30 girls of the appropriate age for grade in each grade, grades 6–12) in four schools in Queen Anne's County, Maryland (Long, Ziller, & Henderson, 1968). The subjects were white, varied widely in socioeconomic class and academic ability and achievement, and

Table 6.1   Self–Other Orientation Scores for Grades 1–6 ($N = 26$ boys and 26 girls in each grade).

Measure	Mean (or %) Score for Each Grade						
	1	2	3	4	5	6	
Individuation (%)							
Boys	21	32	47	36	65	82	$X^2 = 31.85$
Girls	24	19	30	37	18	45	$p < 0.001$
Self-esteem							
Boys	4.7	2.9	30	4.3	3.6	3.8	$F = 3.16$
Girls	4.6	3.4	4.3	4.2	3.5	4.2	$p < 0.01$
Social Interest (%)							
Boys	36	59	47	55	45	71	$X^2 = 13.50$
Girls	47	53	53	67	64	72	$p < 0.02$
Identification (Mother)*							
Boys	8.3	7.3	7.5	9.2	7.9	9.2	$F = 5.24$
Girls	9.1	8.1	9.0	9.5	9.7	9.6	$p < 0.001$
Identification (Teacher)*							
Boys	6.8	6.5	5.9	5.6	4.0	4.4	$F = 4.64$
Girls	7.3	8.3	7.5	8.1	7.1	6.6	$p < 0.005$
Identification (Father)*							
Boys	8.2	8.2	9.0	8.9	8.2	9.2	$F = 2.14$
Girls	9.4	7.7	8.3	8.9	9.5	9.1	$p < 0.06$
Identification (Friend)*							
Boys	4.3	1.9	2.4	6.4	5.0	7.0	$F = 9.18$
Girls	2.1	0.3	3.6	4.2	8.5	9.4	$p < 0.001$

*In the measures of identification, scores were substracted from 10 in order that higher scores should represent greater identification. (From Long, Ziller, & Henderson. Developmental Changes in the Self-Concept During Adolescence. *School Review*, Vol. 76, 1968, pp. 210–230. With permission from The University of Chicago Press.)

lived in a rural area on the eastern shore of Maryland. Their ages ranged from 11 to 18. The measures were similar to those used in the earlier study with the exceptions that more items were used for each scale, and the measure of individuation was not included. The form included six self-esteem items, six items for social interest, and four items for identification similar to that in the study of students in grades 1–6 in which the focused persons were again "mother," "father," "teacher," and "friend."

Self-esteem increased with age level continuing a trend found in the earlier grades. Social interest, again continuing a trend, increased until the ninth grade and tended to level off. In an earlier section concerning alienation, it was found that the self-esteem of adults tended to diminish among the 22–39, 40–45, and 46–64 age groups as did social interest (Ziller & Grossman, 1967).

There is evidence then that self-esteem increases with age up to age 40 and then begins to decrease. Social interest also tends to increase with increasing age from age 6 to age 39, but beyond this latter age group social interest decreases. Since there is a tendency for all members of an age group to increase in self-esteem, it may be assumed that another and lower age group of persons are used as a lower point of reference. Those students in the fifth grade may use third grade students or second grade students as their points of reference, and it is possible to evaluate the self somewhat higher in some global way. The alternatives of looking backward is supporting in contrast only up to the 25–39 age category however, since the 40–45 age group tended to decrease in self-esteem.

A similar increase in social interest was noted following a similar parallel with age. This suggests that perceived membership within a social nexus of significant others is the basis for self-esteem. Significant others with whom we identify provide the social reinforcements which contribute to the development of a high evaluation of the self.

It will be recalled, that the alienated were presumed to have been excluded from a significant group of others, leading to a gradual reduction in self-esteem. The reverse tends to be the case for most other persons. Increasing age is associated with increasing identification with significant others and increasing self-esteem, at least up to age 40. It is possible, that this age is accompanied by a decreasing growth in the number of supporting groups of other persons, and in fact, the slow erosion of existing groups such as the family, through various forms of attrition such as the movement away from home of children and loss of parents and friends without replacement.

SUMMARY

Self–other orientations appear to change with age. Self-esteem and social interest both increase up to age 40, when a downward trend is observed. Nevertheless, the self–other orientation theory provides a working model for the individual for a personal theory of social behavior. The theory is modified in accordance with demands of the changing environment and its immediate presses, but a lag in the response of the self concept provides a degree of stability required for predictability and adaptability.

It has been suggested, however, that the environmental changes which accompany age may be the major determinants of changes in the self concept. Reinforcements in the social field are shown to have a profound effect in relation to the social self. The next chapter focuses on this emergent area of inquiry.

CHAPTER 7

The Ecology of the Social Self

As with the variable of age, the environment is a variable which resists the individual's attempts to change it. The environmental is, of course, more immutable than age since one need only wait a minute and age will change, in one direction, at least.

Thus, environment becomes an independent variable in our analysis of the development of the self concept. Unlike Barker (1968), however, the behavior setting will be explained in terms of the psychological field of the individual. For example, it is not enough to describe the self–other orientations of the child who moves frequently. More than this, is an inquiry into the locus of social reinforcements for the child who moves frequently. Again, a field approach is taken which includes a social learning orientation. In terms of social learning, the ecological concerns include the criterion for social reinforcement, sources of social reinforcement, and the effect of social reinforcement. Other psychological aspects of the environment include variations in range of choices, expectations of others, range of stimuli, and clarity of alternatives.

The criterion for social reinforcement may be expected to be determined, in part at least, by the characteristics of the family and the culture. Both constitute the pervasive social environment. One of the most extensive studies of the family environment as it relates to the self system was conducted by Coopersmith (1967).

FAMILIAL CORRELATES OF THE SELF SYSTEM

Coopersmith's studies were concerned entirely with self-esteem. Self-esteem was defined as a self-evaluation reflecting his attitude toward his capabilities and worthiness. The measure of self-esteem was a self report using such items as "I'm pretty sure of myself." The subjects were 1748 children attending the public schools.

Contrary to the findings by Ziller, Hagey, Smith, and Long (1969) and Rosenberg (1965), no relation between socioeconomic class and self-esteem was found. Also no relation between religion and self-esteem was found. Coopersmith suggests that these social categories are too remote and that the investigation should focus on the more immediate social environment.

For example, rather than socioeconomic class determined from father's income and occupation, the regularity of the father's employment was analyzed in relation to self-esteem. It was found that higher self-esteem was associated with regularity of father's employment. It was also observed that the extent of the father's job-related absence from home and the mother's rating of the stability of the father's employment was related to discrepancy between the child's self reports of self-esteem and the teacher's rating of his self-esteem. Discrepancy between self report and teacher's rating of self-esteem was interpreted as a defensive reaction. Children whose fathers are in unstable work situations are uncertain about their value. This uncertainty, however, is not to be equated with low self-esteem.

The parents of the children were also interviewed. On the basis of the interview data and ratings of the parents by the interviewers, it was found that mothers of children with high self-esteem are rated as higher in self-esteem and emotional stability than are the mothers of children with medium and low self-esteem.

Indirect evidence on the fathers of the children indicate that fathers of children with high self-esteem are more likely to be attentive and concerned with their sons, and the sons in turn are more likely to confide in their fathers. Also, the interaction between husband and wife in families of children with high self-esteem is described as more compatible and marked by greater ease of exchange.

It was also found that there were more previous marriages in the families of low self-esteem children than in the medium or high families. Finally, from reports of the decision making processes within the family, the investigators report their impression that the high self-esteem families establish clearer patterns of authority and areas of responsibility.

With regard to early history and experiences, it was found that self-esteem is higher among first and only children than in later born children. Mothers who were uncertain about methods of feeding and who shifted from breast to bottle early were more likely to have children with low self-esteem. Coopersmith concluded that children with high self-esteem tend to have more positive social experiences during the early years.

Other results of the study were based on questionnaire responses of the parents. It was found that the parents of children with high self-esteem were "more loving" and had closer relationships with their children than did mothers of children with lower self-esteem. They also reported more interest, concern about companions, and availability. Also, parents of children with low self-esteem report that they give less guidance but more harsh treatment. They are inclined to use punishment rather than reward. Coopersmith suggests that parents of children with low self-esteem are inconsistent in their regulatory behavior. Finally, it was observed that parents of children with low self-esteem were less demanding and more permissive in their attempts to control the behavior of the children.

The latter findings are interpreted by Coopersmith as indications of a lack of interest in their children and he proposes that the children also interpret the parents' behavior as indicating a lack of interest. Perhaps, however, this finding and many of the others may be interpreted within a context of criterion for reinforcement and frequency of social reinforcement.

It is now proposed that children with high self-esteem, as measured by Coopersmith, were socialized in such a way that they developed a clear understanding of the norms of the majority in the large community and were reinforced by parents for behavior consistent with these norms. High self-esteem, in this sense, is a concomitant of this pattern of behavior on a probability basis. Adherence to the norms of the majority has a higher probability of positive reinforcement by others leading to higher evaluations of the self. The higher probability of positive reinforcement also may be expected to be associated with a more stable perception of the social environment and more stable behavior. And as indicated at the outset, stability of behavior is associated with high self-esteem.

The father's presence may be interpreted as presenting a more available model for the norms of the majority. The father's attention and concern as well as more stable marriage patterns may be interpreted similarly. High self-esteem parents may be assumed to present a more stable view and model of the majority norms. Likewise, first born children may be expected to have had a more thorough indoctrination in the norms of the majority since there is no older child model to depend upon and since the parents are more available.

Coopersmith's studies, then, seem to indicate that low self-esteem develops from a poorly delineated basis for social reinforcement and subsequently, a lack of social reinforcement. The child with low self-esteem develops in an environment with poorly delineated models for behavior or conflicting models, whereas the child with high self-esteem has before him a clearly depicted model and is consistently reinforced for behavior which is congruent with the model's behavior.

Unfortunately, Coopersmith's data is derived largely from self reports. Under these conditions it is not always convincing that the interpretations evolved from the data rather than from the predilections of the investigator.

It is also regrettable that the investigation concerns itself only with self-esteem. The self–other orientations of the children were scarcely touched upon.

Perhaps, too, the investigation was narrow in the sense that it did not consider in any detail the potential effects of exclusion from the majority. If the norms of a monolithic majority are imposed upon everyone, the members of the minority will tend to receive fewer positive reinforcements. But it is an error to suggest that it is in some way the fault of the parents of the members of the minority group.

LOCUS OF REINFORCEMENT

Coopersmith's work was interpreted here in terms of the criterion of reinforcement. It was proposed that knowledge of and adherence to the norms of the majority was associated with greater probability of social reinforcement and resulting high self-evaluation on a self-report device. In this argument, the majority may be viewed as the source or locus of reinforcement. The concept of majority, however, is almost too inclusive. Other non-specific loci of reinforcement include society, the family, peers, neighborhood, and perhaps the self. The first two studies reported here pertain to society and the family as sources of social reinforcement.

Paralleling Hallowell (1955), it was assumed here that an individual's self–other orientations and his interpretations of his experiences with the self–other orientation framework are inseparable from the self–other orientations of his society. The society reinforces certain patterns of self–other orientations because these have functional importance in the maintenance of a human social order.

In this socialization process, the family is the instrument of society. The family may be looked upon as a micro-society mediating group which has the responsibility of inculcating the norms of a larger group. The family is uniquely suited for this role because of the assumed primacy effects of social experiences in the family and because of the child's dependency relationship. The dependency of the child provides the motivational basis for socialization. To obtain the required reinforcements (food, care, and affection) the child is oriented toward meeting the expectations of the key family members.

SELF–OTHER ORIENTATIONS OF ASIAN INDIAN CHILDREN

In the first study (Ziller, Long, Ramana, & Reddy, 1968) differences in family relationships between Asian Indian and American children were presumed to be related to different self–other orientations. Four components of the perception of self in relation to significant others were measured by means of the Self–Other Orientation Tasks. These tasks are uniquely applicable to cross-cultural research because in these measures the communication of the subject's self–other perceptions depends largely upon topological rather than verbal representations and arrangements of self and other. Here it is assumed that the meaning of psychological space across cultures is somewhat less difficult to determine than the meaning of a series of interrelated words.

The joint family experiences of the Asian child are presumed to have far-reaching implications for the child's self–other orientations. The joint family has been described by Murphy (1953, p. 29) as "the household of persons comprising the sons of a given pair of parents, together with their wives, children, and unmarried sisters, and all those (e.g., aged parents) who are dependent upon them." In India, the child's social environment is largely the joint family (Mandelbaum, 1959; Narain, 1964). According to Cormack (1961) "self . . . had no meaning save in relationship to family and serving that family" (p. 10).

In this social setting, the child may have many parent surrogates. The child may be nearly as close to his aunts as to his mother and, indeed, all females of the joint family may be thought of by the child as having essentially similar or even identical functions. In this way, the child is not disciplined by or responsible to a single individual. Within the extended family constellation, the Indian child is "prized, magnified, pushed forward, warmed, threatened, rebuked, idealized, fancied in grandiose terms of future achievement." "Children are the stuff of one's being. It is the warmth and closeness to them that makes life important, meaningful, continuous." Lois B. Murphy (in G. Murphy, 1953) goes on to say that the Indian children accompany parents or parent surrogates everywhere.

In support of these observations, Naedoo and Fiedler (1962) noted that Indian college students in America esteemed significant others more highly than did American subjects. Lois Murphy observed, too (in G. Murphy, 1953) that Indian children, in comparison with American children, were not exposed to as much conflict with authority. Fewer restraining forces emanated from Indian than American parental figures.

On the basis of these descriptions, one of the critical concepts emerging is the closed nature of the Indian family. A closed group (Ziller, 1965) is defined as a group in which the membership remains constant. An open group, on the other hand, is defined as an interacting set of persons in a constant state of membership flux. It has previously been proposed that open groups, in contrast with closed groups, have an expanded frame of reference. Thus, in closed groups where it is possible to insulate and isolate oneself, self-estimates may remain unchallenged or unchecked for long periods of time.

The aforementioned description of the familial nexus of Indian in comparison with American children indicates that the Indian child is more highly valued by the extended family, is more enmeshed in the family matrix which largely determines the child's social universe, is inseparable from parents and parent surrogates, is less separated from parents in terms of status barriers, and tends to be the focal point of the family, the family's reason for being.

The locus of social reinforcement for the Indian children is assumed to be the family. In addition, a high frequency of social reinforcement is expected from parents in the Indian society. Thus it was proposed that in contrast to the American child, the Indian child's self–other orientations reflect higher self-esteem, higher social interest, higher identification with parents but a lower range of identification with others, and higher self-centrality.

The Indian sample consisted of 50 boys and 50 girls from Form I of the M.V.D.M. High School in Vesakapatnam, Andhra, South India. The students ranged in age from 10 to 14 with a median age of 12. Information of their caste and number of siblings was obtained from their teachers and from the students themselves.

The American sample consisted of 50 boys and 50 girls from the public schools of Queen Anne's County, Maryland. These subjects selected from the sixth to eighth grades were white and were matched with the Indian children on the basis of age and sex. Information concerning father's occupation was obtained from the school records. Both samples varied widely in socioeconomic background. The Americans had significantly fewer siblings (Americans 3.09, Indian 4.09, $t = 3.79$, $p < 0.05$) and resided in a more rural area than the Indians.

The six items which constituted the self-esteem measure included the following sets of significant others: (1) doctor, father, friend, mother, yourself, teacher; (2) someone you know who is a good athlete, someone you know who is a good dancer, someone in your class who is funny, someone in your class who gets good grades, yourself, someone you know who is unhappy; (3) an actor, your brother or someone who is most like a brother, your best friend, the principal of your school, yourself, a salesman; (4) someone you know who is cruel, your grandmother, a housewife, a policeman, yourself, your sister or someone who is most like a sister; (5) someone who is flunking, the happiest person you know, someone you know who is kind, yourself, someone you know who is successful, the strongest person you know; and (6) doctor, father, a friend, a nurse, yourself, someone you know who is unsuccessful. The six items, designed to measure social interest were the same as those described in Chapter 2.

Two kinds of tasks were designed to measure identification. In both of these, physical distance is assumed to represent psychological distance, with greater identification associated with less distance. In the first of these, ten circles are displayed in a horizontal line. A significant other such as "mother" is located in the first circle to the left and in a second item as the last circle to the right. The task requires the subject to mark any of the other circles in the row which best represents himself. Distance in circle units from the significant other is the measure of identification intensity. Identification with "mother," "father," "teacher," and "friend" are examined. (*See* Appendix A, Item 7.)

In a study of disadvantaged school beginners, it was found that children separated from their natural fathers placed the self significantly farther from father than did those living with their fathers (no-father, 34% next to father; fathers, 60% next to father; $X^2 = 5.6, p < 0.02$; Long & Henderson, 1967). Girls in grades 9 through 12 located themselves next to mother more frequently than did boys (66% vs. 52%, $X^2 = 4.9, p < 0.05$; Long, Henderson, & Ziller, 1967). Finally, Head Start children rated as "shy with teacher" by their teacher located themselves farther from the teacher (3.5 vs. 4.7, $N = 24$ boys and 24 girls, $F = 4.43, p < 0.05$; Long & Henderson, 1966).

The second measure, identification (grouping), is assumed to reflect the social inclusiveness of the individual. In the four items that comprise the scale, the subject arranges arrays of 10 people including the self into groups. The four sets of others included: (a) doctor, father, friend, someone you know who is happy, mother, neighbor, yourself, someone you know who is successful, someone with whom you are uncomfortable; (b) doctor, father, friend, the funniest person in your class, mother, yourself, the strongest person you know, someone you know who is hard-working, someone you know who is unsuccessful; (c) someone you know who is a good athlete, your brother or someone most like a brother, a friend, a neighbor, yourself, a salesman, your sister or someone most like a sister, your teacher, someone you know who is unhappy; and (d) someone you know who is a good dancer, your father, a friend, someone you know who gets good grades, someone you know who is kind, a neighbor, yourself, teacher, someone with whom you feel uncomfortable. The number of others included within the self group is the measure of span of identification or social inclusion. The measure has been found to differentiate adult neuropsychiatric patients and normal controls (Ziller, Megas, & De-Cencio, 1964; Ziller & Grossman, 1967), and emotionally disturbed children from their normal controls (Long, Ziller, & Bankes, 1970). The normals were more inclusive.

The six items designed to measure centrality were distributed throughout the test booklet. The six items were the same as those described in relation to the alienation syndrome.

The American subjects completed the test in groups. Written instructions rendered the instrument self-administering. For the Indian subjects, the instructions for each item were read aloud in Telugu, the native language of the children, by an Indian experimenter.

Two by two analyses of variance were calculated for Indian and American boys and girls. Only the results with regard to the main effects of culture will be reported and discussed. In doing so, few significant results were lost and these appeared to contribute nothing to the meaning of the theory or clarity of the results.

The Indian students were found to represent themselves as having higher self-esteem, greater social interest, more self-centrality, and closer identification with mother, father, teacher, and friend. Indian children also included fewer others in the self grouping (*see* Table 7.1).

On the basis of an analysis of the Asian Indian joint family, it was hypothesized that Indian in comparison with American children would indicate higher self-esteem, higher social interest, higher self-centrality, higher identification with parents, and lower inclusion of other with self. The results were supporting in every case.

Taken as a whole, the results are consistent with the expectations associated with the characteristics of the Indian joint family. In comparison with the American adolescent, the life space of the Indian adolescent appears to be bounded by the family constellation. Self-identity and family

Table 7.1   Means and Analyses of Variance of the Self-social Constructs of Indian and American Children.*

Construct	Indian (N = 100)	American (N = 100)	F (Culture) (d.f. = 1/196)	p
Self-centrality	2.26	1.41	11.7	0.001
Social Interest	5.31	3.74	42.4	0.001
Self-esteem	28.10	20.55	65.6	0.001
Identification (mother)	2.83	4.43	16.6	0.001
Identification (father)	2.76	4.14	17.1	0.001
Identification (teacher)	3.69	7.56	62.2	0.001
Identification (friend)	3.42	4.72	10.3	0.005
Identification (grouping)	13.81	15.49	26.8	0.001

*The means represent the scores for boys as well as girls. None of the results with regard to the sex of the subjects were statistically significant. Two sex × culture interaction effects (identification with teacher and friend) were statistically significant but contribute little to the understanding of transcultural family effects. In order to conserve space these results are not reported. (From Ziller, R. C., Long, Barbara H., Romana, K. V., and Reddy, V. E. Self–Other Orientation of Indian and American Adolescents. *Journal of Personality*, 1968, **36**, 315–330. With permission.)

identity are thoroughly intertwined within a relatively closed social sub-system. The Indian student includes fewer others within the self grouping but identifies more closely with parents.

Indeed, the Indian child tends to identify more closely with others in general and shows greater social interest in addition. Again, these results may suggest a too thorough amalgamation of self and other (particularly with regard to "others" such as the family), suggesting again a degree of ego diffusion in Erikson's terms (1959). That is, self-identity and group identity overlap to such an extent that it is difficult to view self or other from an objective coign of vantage. As a result, prediction of the behavior of the self outside the group (here the family) may be difficult (Ziller, 1965). Nevertheless, within the joint family nexus, the results suggest that the Indian children have a higher need for affiliation or that the family is the locus of reinforcement for Indian children. Similarly, Ghei (1966) found that Indian college students in comparison with an American sample were higher on Edwards' (1959) measure of succorance.

The advantages and disadvantages of close ties within a closed group are further emphasized by the finding of higher self-centrality as described by Indian adolescents. Higher self-centrality has previously been associated with alienation (behavior problems, unpopular children, and children who move frequently). With regard to Indian children, self-centrality emerges from social environment in which the child is the focus of adult attention, within the family context. Outside of the favorable family context, however, self-centrality is presumed to be dysfunctional. Prediction of individual behavior by the self-centered child is inhibited by the failure to give adequate consideration to the responses of the other, the other who is also, in this case, somewhat self-oriented.

Yet the Indian adolescent was found to describe higher self-esteem than the American adolescent. In this regard, close identification within a highly supporting closed group appears to be advantageous. Nevertheless, this state of high self-esteem may be in jeopardy under open group conditions where the adolescent is outside the range of influence and support of the joint family. Indeed, the constellation of self–other orientations described here (high social interest, high identification, high self-centrality, and high self-esteem) may be functional in that the joint family system is perpetuated by the self systems that are generated within them. Thus, building on Ghei's (1966) hypothesis stated earlier, the self system which is functional in the joint family also serves to make for low transferability of the individual across social systems, thereby perpetuating the closed joint family system.

In an earlier study (Long, Henderson, & Ziller, 1967), it was noted that high identification with others, and particularly high identification with parents, is associated with high self-esteem. This observation is supported again by the present results. With regard to the Indian subjects, correlation coefficients between self-esteem and identification with mother was 0.44 ($p < 0.05$), identification with friend ($r = 0.37, p < 0.05$), identification with father ($r = 0.31$, $p < 0.05$), and with teacher ($r = 0.20$, $p < 0.05$). For the American subjects, only the correlation between self-esteem and identification with mother was statistically significant ($r = 0.30$, $p < 0.05$). These results indicate, at the very least, a close association between self-esteem and acceptance of and by others.

In the theory of self-social constructs, self-esteem must be viewed within a social context of significant others. Others provide a frame of reference within which the self is located and evaluated. Self-meaning is not an absolute, but a social relative. It is also proposed that there exists for each individual, but also for individuals in general, a relative ordering of significant others, and that the self-meaning is a function of the personal weighting of others and the others' evaluation of the person.

In addition, a serial ordering of the effects of significant others must be considered. Psychoanalysts have long noted the potential primacy effects of parent-child relationships. The present results support these observations and even hint at the relative weighting of the relative influences of others. Assuming that the order of correlations between identification and self-esteem indicates the relative influence of the subject of identification, it is noted that within the Indian sample, the order from most to least influence was mother, friend, father, teacher. Within the American sample, the only significant relationship between identification and self-esteem involved identification with mother.

Before wandering any further toward the boundaries of the data and the region of speculation, the inherent shortcomings of cross-cultural studies must be confronted. As Cattell (1963) has noted, making national comparisons such as these is both "invidious" and "notoriously tricky."

In the present study, the instruments used were equally unfamiliar to both samples, but the American group had probably had more experience with tests and testing. Moreover, since the instructions were translated, meanings might have shifted slightly. The data from the Indian subjects, however, show that the instructions were followed correctly.

More seriously, one may question whether the two samples, although matched for age and sex, were comparable. In the region of India in which the study was conducted, only 14% of the children in this age group were in school, according to the 1961 census. Thus, the Indian subjects in contrast with the Americans were among the educationally elite. The Indian sample also resided in a more urban area and had significantly more siblings.

The most crucial question, however, is whether or not the measures used in this study are valid for the Indian subjects. The internal consistency of the measures suggest that the measures possess consistent meaning for the Indian subjects. Cross-cultural validity for the esteem items was indicated by the finding that the position of the social object in the row was significantly related to the social status of the stimulus object. Thus, the "unsuccessful" person was placed most frequently in the extreme right position of the horizontal arrangement of significant others by both Indian and American students.

In this study, the utility of the Self-social Symbols Tasks in the study of personality and culture is indicated. In addition, the theory and results of the study have emphasized the critical nature of child-family relationships with regard to self–other concepts.

SELF–OTHER ORIENTATIONS OF KIBBUTZ CHILDREN

A second study* concerning locus of reinforcement was conducted in Israel, and compared children in a Kibbutz and children who attended a

---

*Dalia G. Leslie and the author conducted the original study.

religious school in Tel Aviv. The focus of the study was the orientation of the Kibbutz children with regard to the usual societal matrix of parents, teachers, and friends, but especially the parents.

The Kibbutz is an Israeli community whose main principles are economic collectivism and social equality (*see* Rabin, 1965). The organization is voluntary. Membership is motivated by the individual's efforts to realize economic and social justice through this democratic organization. All full-fledged adult members participate in the government.

The Kibbutz rather than the family has responsibility for economic and child rearing functions. Parents do have limited control and responsibility for their own children.

Kibbutz children are brought up in houses physically separated from their parents' houses and constitute an independent social unit. In each house is a small, homogeneous and stable peer group. It is a distinct cohesive unit and remains for the child the most important early social experience with the exception of family interactions. The communal values and education are transmitted by appointed educators and nurses.

The children keep regular daily contact with both parents for about three hours after the parents' work period. The parents return the child to his own peer group house in the late evening. Other contacts occur between parent and child when their schedules coincide for open periods of time.

The parents are the only stable object of emotional attachment which is exclusively the child's own. The child experiences a succession of nurses and teachers who are his caretakers, trainers, and socializing agents.

Such a unique organization has not been overlooked by social scientists. In general, the studies reveal no marked differences between children raised in a Kibbutz and other Israeli children or between Kibbutz and American children (Kaffman, 1965; Nagler, 1963; Barnett, 1965).

Some differences were observed by Rabin (1965), however, comparing Kibbutz children with children from rural families resembling those in the Western culture. Using standard tests including the Vineland Social Maturity Scale (Doll, 1946) and the draw-a-person technique, and sentence completion tasks, Rabin concluded that Kibbutz children in comparison with the children in the control groups tended to show less intense orientation toward parents but more orientation toward peers. Moreover, there tended to be a "dispersion of cathexis" among Kibbutz children. They tended to be oriented toward many others as opposed to a few significant others. This latter finding was attributed, in part, to a lag in the clear conceptualization of significant others in the environment stemming from the changing of the metapelet (mother surrogate) at the end of the first year of the child's life.

Bettelheim (1967) makes a similar observation. He notes (p. 260) that Kibbutz children have little opportunity to develop intimate relations with others. Here intimacy suggests "we select few" as opposed to "those impossible others." The Kibbutz society does not present a model, approve of, or provide opportunity for strong private feelings about a few others as distinguished from the group as a whole. Also, with the coming of adolescence, Bettelheim observed that the Kibbutz child begins to draw away from his parents and toward his youth group. Bettelheim's observations were made without the benefit of any objective devices, however, but were based solely upon personal observation.

These latter observations suggest that in terms of self–other orientations, Kibbutz children may be expected to show lower social interest and higher openness than a control group.

The subjects for the study were 25 boys and 25 girls from a Kibbutz who were in their seventh regular school year, were 12 or 13 years of age, and who had progressed to this school level at the customary rate. The comparison group consisted of 25 boys and 25 girls from a school affiliated with the Hebrew religion in Tel Aviv. The grade, age, and progress requirements for inclusion within the sample were the same as for the Kibbutz children.

The religious school was selected also because the intra-familial relations contrast with the Kibbutz conditions. Although there is no documentation of the difference, Israeli consultants in the project agreed that the children in the religious school were much more restricted in their social activities than most other Israeli children. These children spent much more of their time under the direct supervision of adults and in particular, with their parents, and that parents of children in religious schools tend to monitor their children's behavior more than most other children in Israel. Thus, the two groups tend to represent the extremes on a peer-parent orientation continuum which is hypothesized to be reflected in their social interest and openness orientations.

In order to facilitate the cooperation of the school personnel involved, the Self–Other Orientation Tasks used included only one item from the self-esteem scale (the set of significant others included someone who has failed, the happiest person you know, someone you know who is kind, yourself, someone you know who is successful, the strongest person you know), one centrality item, one social interest item, and one openness item.

Openness refers to the perceived number and breadth of associations with others whose location from the self is proximal or distal. In Horney's terms (1937), openness refers to "moving toward people" as opposed to remaining separated or moving away from others.

Openness pertains to the individual's perception of his initiative in seeking associations with others and his acceptance of others as associated. More than this, however, the extent of these associations is significant. Few associations may indicate guardedness with regard to others. The more open person is willing to endure the risk of social encounters (*see* Jourard, 1964).

The openness item used in the form sent to Israel is found in Appendix A, Item 8. A circle representing the self is located within a field of other circles which symbolize other people. The subject is asked to draw as many or as few lines as he wishes from the circle for the self to the other circles representing other people. The score for the item is simply the number of lines drawn between self and others. Split-half reliability uncorrected for length for 99 children was 0.64 when calculated in an earlier study using two similar items.

Evidence for the validity of the item was found in an earlier study in which members of a militant campus group (The Black Student Union) at the University of Oregon were found to use fewer connecting lines than any of the other campus groups.

The test forms were translated into Hebrew by one Israeli and translated back to English by another Israeli to check the validity of the translation. The language was changed where serious disagreement occurred. The data were collected in Israel under the supervision of the Minister of Education for Israel.

Kibbutz children in contrast to those attending religious schools showed lower social interest ($M_1 = 0.47$, $M_2 = 0.74$, d.f. $= 1$ and 94, $F = 7.89$, $p < 0.05$) and greater openness ($M_1 = 11.06$, $M_2 = 10.32$, d.f. $= 1$ and 94, $F = 2.29$, $p < 0.15$). With regard to openness, a closer examination indicated that the girls in the Kibbutz were the most open ($M = 11.50$). In addition, Israeli girls were found to be more self-centered than boys (0.67 vs. 0.38, $F = 5.64$, d.f. $= 1$ and 64, $p < 0.05$), but again, the girls in the Kibbutz were the most self-centered. This contrasts with the results of a study reported in the previous chapter in which no significant differences were found between American boys and girls with regard to self-centrality (Long, Ziller, & Henderson, 1968). These findings suggest that Kibbutz children do not perceive themselves as included within a matrix of others which is dominated by adults such as parents and teachers. Children attending religious schools, on the other hand, tend to perceive the self as included within the matrix of parents, teachers, and friends. This also suggests, in keeping with earlier observations, that Kibbutz children do not develop intimate relations with others, that is, that they avoid groups which tend to exclude others.

On the other hand, Kibbutz children tend to perceive the self as being associated with a wider range of others (openness). In keeping with earlier observations these results suggest that Kibbutz children related to a wide range of peers. These associations with others are diffuse. From these results, it may be deduced that the adult group is the locus of reinforcement for children in religious schools, whereas for Kibbutz children, the peer group is the source of reinforcement.

The difference found between Israeli girls and boys remains for others to explain. Like the Asian Indian children, however, the Israeli girl may be the cynosure of the culture.

At the very least, the results indicate the influence of environment on the schemata of self and others. How these schemata are associated with behavior remains to be established. The consistency of these schemata when the child leaves the Kibbutz also remains to be established.

CHANGING GROUP MEMBERSHIP

In the preceding section, a question was raised concerning changes in the locus of reinforcement which accompany changes in the environment, as for example, when the child leaves the Kibbutz. The next two studies describe the self–other orientations of black American children who were bussed into a new integrated school community and the self–other orientations of children who had changed communities frequently and expected to move frequently.

Myer (1968) examined the social interest and self-esteem of Negro children who were bussed from their own segregated neighborhood school areas to schools which had been attended almost entirely by white children. The one host school tended to accept the newcomers, whereas the other school tended to be rejecting.

The subjects were 240 fifth and sixth grade pupils who were recruited for the program by the staffs in the Negro schools. In discussing the bussing program with the Negro parents, the school officials emphasized the advantages of bussing their children to less crowded schools. The program was largely initiated by white members of the community.

Only the results with regard to two of the schools will be described here. In school W, over 50% of the people were in favor of the program, the district was one of the wealthiest in the community, and the principal expressed support of the school board's right to make the bussing decision.

In school V, the principal actively undermined the program, the section of the community in which this school was located was the only white area with public housing and a discernable welfare rate, and the parents were antagonistic to the bussing program.

In school W, the favorable environment, 100% of the Negro children wished to return at the end of the year as opposed to 4% of those attending school V. Eighty-five percent of the Negro mothers in school W wished their children to return to the school the following year as opposed to 0% in school V. Given these conditions in the adopted social environment, what were the self-esteem and social interest scores of the Negro children in the two schools?

The children's forms of the two instruments were administered to the Negro children at the end of the school year following the bussing experience. The self-esteem measure contained four items as did the social interest measure. It must be noted that the children had been assigned to school W and V on a random basis.

Myer reports that the children in school W located the self within the matrix of parents, teachers, and friends (social interest) 39% of the time, whereas the child in school V did so only 1% of the time. The children in school V, however, indicated higher self-esteem than the children in school W (3.05 vs. 0.98).

The results suggest that the children in school W in contrast to school V were more accepted and perceived themselves as included within the matrix of significant others within the new community, but that their self-esteem was much lower. The *lower* self-esteem revealed by the children in the *more* accepting communities may indicate that perceived acceptance by the new school community compels the child to use the new community rather than the old community as his frame of reference. He compares himself with children in the new community because they accept him and he perceives himself as included within this group. The new group, however, is in a more advantageous socioeconomic position, has a superior educational background, and is in the majority. It is hardly surprising, then, that the black child bussed into this community reveals low self-esteem.

His counterpart in the less accepting community need not alter his frame of reference. He does not perceive himself as included within the community, so he continues to evaluate himself in relation to other blacks who are more comparable in terms of socioeconomic background and education. In addition, he need not perceive himself as being in a minority position since he identifies with his own community.

In another sense, the locus of reinforcement for the blacks bussed into the accepting community is that new community, whereas the locus of reinforcement for the children bussed into the rejecting community is their old community. Those perceiving themselves as included within the new accepting community may receive fewer reinforcements, however, in terms of academic and socioeconomic status, which may indeed be the most central regions of reinforcement for children who do not associate with children in the new community under the usual neighborhood conditions where a wide variety of other status dimensions may be central, such as in a variety of game behaviors and social interaction in general. Faced with a limited range of criterion in which his status is not high, the black child reports lower self-esteem. Those who are rejected may also reject the new community as the crucial agent of reinforcement. In so doing, their self-evaluation is not challenged or changed,

The latter observation must be underscored. These interpretations suggest that segregation is self-perpetuating because the members of the segregated group must risk a reduced self-evaluation when they attempt to join a more heterogeneous group dominated by a white majority. Their self-esteem can be maintained with least effort within the segregated community.

This observation is similar to that suggested earlier with regard to Asian Indian children. The high reinforcement of the child within his own extended family tends to encourage him to remain within the extended family. Outside the extended family, the child must learn to adapt to a lower reinforcement rate. The lowering of reinforcement, then, produces a field of forces, if you will, which tends to control the mobility of the individual. Movement of the individual from one field of reinforcement to another now becomes a most significant social psychological problem. In examining this problem, it will be useful to trace the self-esteem, social interest, and perhaps the marginality of the individuals.

GEOGRAPHIC MOBILITY

The study of the transition between loci of reinforcement has not yet been conducted. A study has been conducted, however, which involved constant changes in loci of reinforcement (high geographic mobility) and self–other orientations (Ziller & Long, 1964).

Geographic mobility is an ubiquitous feature of modern American society, characteristic of certain segments of all social classes (Hollingshead & Redlich, 1953). Speculation about the psychological effects of spacial mobility has largely centered upon an assumed social isolation of the mobile person and the possible relationship of this isolation to mental disorders. The results of studies of such effects, however, have been equivocal and contradictory. Thus, Tietze, Lemkou, and Cooper (1942) examined the records of 1022 patients in Baltimore for rates of various psychoses in relation to mobility. The highest prevalence of mental disorders occurred among people living for the shortest time in the same house. Robins and O'Neal (1958), locating adults who had been problem children thirty years earlier in St. Louis, discovered a high incidence of both social problems and mobility. Hollingshead and Redlich (1953), on the other hand, found no significant relationship between psychotic disorders and geographic mobility, nor did Schmitt (1958) in his study of area mobility and mental health in Hawaii. Gabower (1959) likewise was unable to establish the negative effects of mobility in her study of children with behavior problems.

In the present study (Ziller & Long, 1964), the association was analyzed between spacial mobility and various components of the self concept without assuming a negative or positive relationship between spacial mobility and personality as a whole.

The child who moves frequently and who anticipates frequent geographic changes faces the prospect of a constantly changing social environment. If the self is defined primarily in terms of others, and others are constantly changing, the perception of self may be presumed to lack stability. A degree of consistency might be achieved, however, if self is taken as the point of reference regarding others, since the self is more constant than others from one geographic location to another. It is therefore proposed that the child who has moved frequently tends to perceive the self, rather than others, as central.

It was also hypothesized that high mobility children tend to identify with the majority to a lesser degree. The mobile child repeatedly finds himself dissociated, outside, or separated from groups of others. He does not belong. The group of others, by remaining separate, limits socialization opportunities for the newcomer. Of particular concern are the limited opportunities for consensual validation or the search for social reality. The mobile child's reference group is more remote and his views of the environment are not as readily referenced with regard to his peers.

The mobile child is not without recourse, however. In the search for social reality, a stable reference group is required. It is proposed that the

stable reference groups most available to the mobile child are the ubiquitous parents and teachers. Although in a sense these reference sources are
more remote, they provide the required foci for the establishment of
social reality and identity. Thus, it is proposed that high mobility children
tend to be oriented toward parents and teachers as loci of reinforcement.

The effect of spacial mobility upon self-esteem was unclear, and indeed,
there appears to be no ready rationale for predicting differences on this
dimension.

Subjects

Three groups of eighth grade students comprised the sample. Children
of this age were selected because there was sufficient opportunity to have
experienced multiple moves, and any possible effects of geographic mobility could have had adequate opportunity to accumulate and intensify.
In addition, it was assumed that self–other relationships were of critical
concern to children at this age.

Sample A, the group with the highest geographic mobility, was comprised of 83 students of both sexes from the Dover Air Base School,
Dover, Delaware. These students were all children of Air Force personnel, and had lived in an average of 6.9 communities. They all lived on the
air base, an extremely open community, where the usual tour of duty was
three years. In addition, the children of sample A not only had moved
frequently, but also expected to continue moving, at least until the retire-
ment of the father from the Air Force.

Sample B consisted of 76 students who had lived all of their lives in a
single community. These students were selected from the communities of
Milford and Harrington, Delaware, (populations according to the 1960
census were 5795 and 2495 respectively) located about 15 miles from the
Dover Air Base. In Harrington, approximately 50% of the eighth graders
met the low mobility criterion; in Milford, about 44%.

Because the high mobility sample was confounded by the military
nature of the community, a second control high mobility group was also
studied – a third group of children who had moved several times, but
whose fathers were civilians. Sample C was comprised of 60 children
from Dover Junior High School (Dover population in 1960 was 7250),
whose fathers were not in the Air Force, and who had lived in three or
more communities. Although the geographic mobility of this group was
not as high as might be desired for experimental purposes, this additional
sample made it possible to control for geographic area, and comparisons

with this second experimental group provided some information concerning the generality of the results involving the Air Force sample.

Instruments

Self–other orientations were again derived from the Self–Other Orientation Tasks. The tasks were self-administering and were completed by the subjects while assembled in large groups. The sequence of tasks was constant. Tasks designed to measure each of the components were scattered throughout the booklet.

The components were self-esteem (one item), social interest (one item), self-centrality (three items), and majority identification (three items). The measure of self-esteem presented a horizontal array of eight circles. The subjects were also presented with a list of persons including the self and asked to assign each person to a circle. The significant others included "doctor," "father," "friend," "the person with whom you are most happy," "mother," "the most successful person you know," and "the person with whom you are most uncomfortable." As previously noted, location of the self to the left was assumed to indicate high self-esteem.

The social interest and self-centrality items were the same as those included in Appendix A, Items 2 and 4, as described earlier.

The measure of majority identification was the same as that described earlier with regard to the study of Asian Indian children. (*See* Appendix A, Item 6.) In an array of ten small circles within an enveloping large circle, a given percentage (0%, 20%, or 30%) of the circles had four horizontal lines drawn through them. Choice of an unlined circle as to represent the self was coded as a unit of majority identification. A score of three was possible.

Self–Other Primacy

In addition to the Self-social Symbols Tasks, a task designed to provide a general measure of self versus other orientation was included. Each student was provided with two unlined sheets of paper ($8\frac{1}{2} \times 10$ inches) and was then allowed five minutes to write about themselves (on the first sheet) and about a friend (on the second), that is, only a total of five minutes writing time was permitted. The number of words used to describe the self and the number of words used to describe the friend comprised two separate scores from which it was possible to determine the relative amount of time directed toward description of the self as opposed to description of the friend.

The results in relation to geographic mobility are summarized in Table 7.2. Means for each of the three samples are shown, and statistical tests of the differences between Samples A and B, and between Samples C and B are reported. The results with regard to mobile (Air Force) and non-mobile comparisons (C vs. B) are mutually supporting, although fewer significant differences were found in the latter comparisons. (*See* Table 7.2.) Since the Air Force sample provides a more extreme mobile or open group, only these results will be discussed in detail.

The hypothesis relating centrality of self to geographic mobility was supported. Air Force children obtained a mean centrality score of 0.80 as compared with a score of 0.33 for the non-movers.

The results with regard to the hypothesis relating majority identification and high geographic mobility were also supporting. Air Force children selected the different circle to represent themselves more frequently than the low mobility children.

The hypothesis with regard to mobility and social interest was also supported by the results. A higher proportion of Air Force children than non-movers placed the self within the adult dominated triangular representation of society (59% vs. 33%, $p < 0.001$).

The self–other primacy measure also differentiated the Air Force sample from the non-movers. The highly mobile group wrote significantly

Table 7.2   Means and tests of significance of scores from Self-social Symbols Tasks among Mobile and Non-mobile Children.

Test	Means			Tests of Significance	
	Mobile Air Force ($N = 83$)	Mobile Civilian ($N = 60$)	Non-mobile ($N = 76$)	Non-mobile vs. Civilian *p*	Non-mobile vs. Air Force *p*
1. Majority identification	2.07	2.03	1.72	N.S.	$t = 2.02$ 0.05
2. Esteem (a) horizontal	4.7	4.8	5.2	N.S.	N.S.
3. Self-centrality	0.80	0.50	0.33	N.S.	$t = 4.61$ 0.001
4. Social Interest	0.59	0.50	0.33 $X^2 = 4.03$	0.05	$X^2 = 9.87$ 0.001
5. Self–Other primacy (a) self	42.60	50.00	48.80	N.S.	$t = 2.40$ 0.025
(b) other	33.20	34.00	27.60 $t = 2.00$	0.05	$t = 2.02$ 0.05

more words about their friend ($p < 0.05$), and significantly fewer words about themselves ($p < 0.025$) than did the children who had never moved.

Discussion

The hypothesis relating centrality of self with geographic mobility was supported by the data. It was initially proposed that under open group conditions where the social environment is constantly changing, the self, rather than others, evolves as a social point of reference. That self as a focal point may be associated with social isolation is implied by the finding in the previous study that sociometric isolates in the sixth grade placed self rather than friend, more centrally than sociometric stars (Ziller, Alexander, & Long, 1964) and the earlier finding that high self-centrality is one of the three facets of the alienation syndrome. Thus, while centrality of self may be a necessary dynamism under conditions of an ever-changing environment, this condition appears to foster a separation of self from others.

The highly mobile child in this study, as hypothesized, also represented himself as "different" significantly more often than did the children who had lived in only one community. In the initial theoretical framework, reduced majority identification by the mobile child was presumed to have evolved from repeated separation from peer group and the concomitant reduction of opportunities for consensual validation. In an earlier study (Henderson, Long, & Ziller, 1965), a lower degree of majority identification was found to be significantly related to the choice of an "alone," rather than a "group" condition. Thus, the mobile child appears to be indicating perceptions of social isolation. This conclusion is supported by the findings derived from an adjective check list in which mobile children described themselves not only as "different," but also as "unusual," "lonely," and "strange."

The findings related to the measures of social interest and self–other orientation may also be interpreted in terms of social isolation. A significantly higher proportion of the mobile as opposed to non-mobile children placed themselves within the triangular representation of societal structure (high social interest). Thus, although the mobile child reveals high centrality of self and minority identification, at once they perceive themselves as included within the nexus of parents, teachers, and friends. Previous research indicated that poor readers in contrast to good readers, sociometric isolates in contrast to sociometric stars (Ziller, Alexander, & Long, 1964), and Israeli children in religious schools as opposed to

Kibbutz children also place the self in the triangle of parents, teachers, and friends.

These cumulative results suggest orientation of the self within the adult dominated societal triangle of significant others provides a degree of structure in the social environment for those who find the general environment somewhat unstable or even threatening. Thus, the mobile child who lives within a constantly shifting social field has recourse to parents and teachers as points of references, and indeed, may find friends crucial in their social field because they have repeatedly experienced a loss of friends. In terms of Helson's (1959) adaptation level framework, the mobile child in contrast to the less mobile child does not take friends for granted. He is aware of the fact that friendships can be lost. This realization is less poignant for the non-mobile child.

A similar interpretation may be made with regard to the findings that more words are written by the mobile child about the friend and fewer about the self. For the child who moves frequently, establishing new relationships with others is an endless enterprise (*see* Gabower, 1959), since interpersonal relationships within open groups are necessarily short-lived and unreliable. The greater attention accorded to "friend" as opposed to "self" in this task may reflect this concern for friendship. The non-mobile child is less aware of the problem.

Altogether then, the self–other orientations of the mobile child include low identification with the majority, centrality of self rather than other, and high social interest. No significant difference between mobile and non-mobile children were found on the measures of self-esteem. It must be emphasized that the results do not warrant an interpretation which imputes maladjustment to the mobile child. In terms of locus of reinforcement, the results suggest that mobile children are more acutely aware of the significance of friends and other potential social reinforcers such as parents and teachers. Having experienced social deprivation, in a sense, the perpetual newcomer realizes the significance and value of friends.

The mobile child is also more self-centered, however. Thus, the mobile child reflects more social interest, yet is more self-centered. It is possible, however, that social interest and self-centeredness are both abutments of the self system under conditions of an ever-changing social environment. The mobile person is compelled to be more concerned about the self definition. Since the self is defined, in part, on the basis of significant others, and significant others are subject to repeated change with regard to the mobile child, the child again has recourse to stable significant others such as parents, as well as the ubiquitous self as points of reference. Thus, the mobile child may be said to be oriented toward stable significant others in an effort to maintain the self definition, but the others are seen in relation to the self, whereas for the less mobile child, the self is perceived in relation to significant others. For the mobile child, the self is the point of reference. For the less mobile child, others constitute the point of reference.

OVERVIEW

This section describes possible environmental correlates of self–other orientations. Included in the environmental considerations were the family, developmental stages, culture, and changing social environments. In the studies described here, the environment was examined as a source of social reinforcement. For example, evidence indicated that when the family is the locus of social reinforcement, the child indicates high self-esteem. In general, it was found that different social environments were associated with different patterns of self–other orientations. For example, the Kibbutz children tended to less orientation toward the nexus of parents, teachers, and friends than children attending religious schools in Israel. The results suggest that self–other orientations represent schemata developed in response to the stresses of the environment. Self–other orientations become, in this sense, adaptations to the social environment and represent relatively stable guides or cognitive controls for social behavior. In this sense, no personal map of the self and other is necessarily superior or inferior in general. Each cognitive map represents a personal representation of the self and other which is functional and even optimal for a given span of time under certain environmental conditions. Through these cognitive gymnastics, the individual achieves a satisfactory sense of social order and social control. Self–other orientations, in this sense, mediate adaptation to the social environment, and represent relatively stable guides or controls for social behavior. In the following section, these and previous emerging meanings of cognitive maps provide the basis for a more general approach to the theory of self–other orientation.

Part IV   Theories of Personal Change and Stability

The preceding chapters describe not only the content of the research area, but also the evolution of a theory of the social self. Location of the theoretical framework at this point is most fitting because it indicates that the theory of self–other orientation is, in fact, an evolving system of thought. A two-part framework of personal stability and change is presented. In the first section, the individual's control over interpersonal relations is emphasized. In the second section, a personal system is proposed for resolving the dilemma of control within a changing social environment.

CHAPTER 8

Toward a Theory of Self–Other Orientation

Three problems are central to the development of a theory of self–other orientation. First, why and how can a private thing like the self be understood only in relation to significant others? Second, how is the inherent conflict resolved between satisfaction of the needs of the self and the needs of the other? Third, given the changing personal and social field, how is the self concept maintained? The historical background to these problems are presented here along with an inchoate theory of self–other orientation which addresses the three problems in terms of a cognitive framework.

THE SOCIAL SELF

Following Descartes' concern with the self concept and his dictum, "I think, therefore I am," self-consciousness was introduced as a crucial concern of self theorists. John Stuart Mill provided one of the early definitions of the self when he wrote that "*the inexplicable tie . . .* which connects the present consciousness with the past one of which it reminds me, is as near as I think we can get to a positive conception of self. That there is something real in this tie, real as the sensations themselves, and not a mere produce of the laws of thought without any fact corresponding to it, I hold to be indubitable . . . this original element . . . to which we cannot give any name but its own particular one, without employing some false or ungrounded theory, is the Ego, or Self."

Pierce (1868) was perhaps the first to indicate that the self concept was more than intuitive but was inferred from commerce with objects and the testimony of other people. William James (1890) expanded Pierce's basic idea and described the material self, the social self, and the spiritual self. By the material self, James meant our connection with property, body, clothes, our immediate family, and our home. Social self referred to the recognition we get from others. He added that "*a man has as many social selves as there are individuals who recognize him* and carry an image of him in their mind." Often, however, in discussing the social self, he seemed to suggest that social support or, more anachronistically, social reinforcement, was important to an individual. The spiritual self was "the entire collection of my states of consciousness, my psychic faculties, and dispositions taken concretely."

It was the work of the sociologists Baldwin (1897), Cooley (1918), and Mead (1925), however, that initially developed the relationship between self and other. Baldwin describes a bipolar self which involves the self and the other. The individual has more control over the sense of self as opposed to the other. The other frequently behaves in a way which the individual does not anticipate, but these variations in the behavior of the other lead to the development of a new self concept. Baldwin suggests a spiraling interaction between the self and other leading to a more complex self concept.

No discussion of the self concept is complete without including the contribution of Cooley (1918). Cooley, too, emphasizes the interaction of self and other in the development of the self concept. His ideas emerge from the line of thought which began at least with Pierce (1868) and with James' (1890) "social self."

To Cooley, the "self and society are twin-born . . ." (1918, p. 5). This observation follows the earlier descriptions of the evaluation of the self concept from distinctions between the agent and object particularly as the object is social. The self and other mutually define each other. The definition of each concept emerges in juxtaposition to its companion concept. In so doing, however, the definition of self necessarily involves the other and its reverse. In addition, however, Mead accords the other or the social factor an equal weighting with the self. Earlier conceptions implied that the self is dominant, while the other sample formed the background.

Finally, Mead (1934) advanced the thesis of the social nature of the self concept when he introduced language as a connecting link. He noted that, whereas a facial expression can be observed only by the other, vocal behavior may be attended by both the speaker and the other person. The person may be both a speaker and a listener with regard to his vocalizations. In this way, the vocalizations are a stimulus to which both the self and the other may respond, and it is a rather simple step for the speaker to put himself in the place of the other and take "the attitude of others toward himself" (Mead, 1934, p. 90). Moreover, when the speaker repeats this role taking behavior across situations, a concept of the "generalized other" emerges, whenever the attitudes of others toward himself become organized and the individual becomes an object unto himself. It now becomes possible for him to conduct exchanges between the "I" and the "me."

Anticipating the theory of self–other orientation, the aforementioned ideas are distilled into the framework by simply assuming the salience of social stimuli, and social behavior are mediated by self–other concepts rather than self concepts.

SELF–OTHER CONFLICT

Inevitably, considerations of the relationship between the self and the other as they are perceived by the individual must include the way in which the inherent conflicts between the self and the other are controlled or resolved. It is assumed that individuals attempt to maximize satisfaction of personal needs. Two or more individuals, then, in a social situation are compelled to modify personal need satisfaction in the context of the needs of the other. An interpersonal approach to the theory and measurement of personality with its attendant considerations of conflict control underlies, in part at least, the work of Freud and the ego psychologists, Adler, Horney, Sullivan, and Schutz. Finally, an incunabular theory of self–other orientation will be presented.

The inherent conflict between self and other was at least tangentially stated by Baldwin (1897) and Mead (1934). In his discussion of the relationship between self and others, Baldwin noted behavior on some occasions which might be described as "slavishness," but counterbalancing bold aggressive behavior. For example, he describes how a child learns when and in what circumstances his mother will allow him to assert himself, and when she will require him to be docile and teachable. There are situational determinants, then, associated with the emphasis of either self or other in interpersonal relationships.

Much about the early theory of self–other orientation smacks of introspectionism, however. Little attempt was made by the aforementioned self theorists to seek behavioral outcomes of the proposed constructs. It remained for social psychological personality theorists to develop the significance of the social self with regard to individual and social behavior. In so doing, it becomes necessary to develop measures of the self concept, a problem which was easily ignored by earlier philosophically oriented scholars.

Mead (1934) analyzed the characteristic of vocalizations whereby the self and the other are at once the audience, thereby facilitating the ability of the speaker to put himself in the place of the other. In the present context, this is simply one of the first suggestions made by a social scientist for facilitating conflict resolution, between self and other, and to create conditions which will lead the self to view the self from the point of view of the others.

Dualism: Freud as an Example

Perhaps, the first systematic effort to describe the organism's efforts to control the conflict between self and other was proposed by Freud. As Jones put it, Freud was a stubborn dualist "seized with the conception of a profound conflict within the mind," and throughout his life he struggled to discover and define the nature and characteristics of the opposing forces (1953, Vol. III, p. 266). In his early discussions, he wrote of conflict between "the conscious" and "the unconscious" with "the censor" intervening between the two. Later, he wrote of conflict between "the id," "ego," and "the superego."

The instinctual responses of primordial man were assumed to emanate from "the id." The id is the source of psychic energy. It is closely associated with bodily processes from which its energy is derived. It tends to represent the individual's inner world and subjective experience. (In terms of self–other orientation, the id represents self-orientation.)

The id operates by the *pleasure principle*. Increases in energy level in the id are accompounded by immediate efforts to re-establish a state of equilibrium in the organism. Behavior guided by the id moves toward immediate gratification. The id is extremely responsive to changes in energy level.

The superego represents the expectations of traditional society as communicated to the child by the parents. In contrast to the id, the superego is associated with external and social concerns as opposed to internal, body, and self concerns. The superego represents the ideal rather than the real, and it is directed toward perfection rather than pleasure. The superego is incorporated with the expectations of the parents, but in time, self-control is substituted for parental control. (In terms of self–

other orientation, the superego represents other-orientation. The other rather than the self is the point of reference.)

The ego responds to the reality principle. It is capable of differentiating things in the mind and things as they exist in the external world. Nevertheless, Freud described the id and ego as overlapping. The ego is the organized part of the id. In the normal individual, the id and ego are "ego-syntonic." The ego smoothly integrates the forces associated with instinctual stimuli (the id), with societal expectations (the superego). At times, however, the ego is subject to severe strain under the conflicting pressures emanating from id and superego requirements. (In terms of self–other orientation, the ego may be best described as representing the processes by which the demands of the id and superego are reconciled.)

The Ego Psychologists' Control Mechanisms

Whereas Freud, at least in the early years, emphasized the impulsive behaviors associated with the id, a group of later psychoanalysts (Anna Freud, 1946; Hartmann, 1958; Kris, 1951; Rapaport, 1960) emphasized instrumental and controlled behavior of the normal individual. This functional behavior was mediated by sensory and perceptual responses, thought and language. Hartmann described individual striving for organization and compatability among behaviors. In his later years, Rapaport emphasized the ability of the individual to control and direct his own responses through attention and thinking. In contrast to Freud's description of man's instinctual urges, the ego psychologists describe the progression of normal persons toward independence from instinctual drives (ego — autonomy) and increasing independence from external stimulation (internalization, Rapaport, 1960). The ego functions which promote this independence include *patterns* or *sequence of behavior* such as inhibition, delay or postponement of behavior. Essentially, the ego psychologists were concerned with processes and mechanisms for behavior control.

As stated at the outset, social psychological theories of personality are concerned with the inherent conflict between self and others. In these terms, Freud and the neo-Freudian or ego psychologists may be freely described as being concerned with the reconciliation of the dual demands for personal satisfactions and the satisfaction of others. These dual, conflicting demands are now presumed to be mediated through cognitive control mechanisms (the ego) representing styles or sets for rendering competing demands compatible within a personality framework. Thus, the ego becomes a mediating or control mechanism between the competing demands represented by the id and the superego. The origins of this framework obviously are found within the works of Freud and the ego psychologists.

The Social Approach of Adler

Among Freud's followers, Adler (1927) broke with the instinctual assumption concerning the motivation of man as an individual and introduced social urges. The cornerstones of Adler's framework may be interpreted as the self (the "creative self") and the other ("social interest"). The self was viewed as the screening, organizing, and guiding mechanism mediating man and his environment.

In contrast to Freud, Adler emphasized consciousness and control. Man is ordinarily aware of the reasons for his behavior. He is conscious of his shortcomings as well as the goals toward which he is striving. Moreover, he is capable of planning and guiding his actions with full awareness of the implications for his self-realization. The person responds to his environment, but he is also partially responsible for selecting and interpreting the stimuli to which he responded. His responses are not instinctual or mechanistic but controlled.

Adler's framework and that of the ego psychologists are remarkably similar. In both systems, control mechanisms are emphasized which mediate man and his environment. For Adler, however, the environment was presumed to be largely social in nature.

In his early writings, Adler stressed the individual's strivings for personal superiority. Power and domination of others were emphasized and were presumed to emerge as compensatory behavior for deep seated feelings of inferiority.

In later writings, Adler shifted his emphasis toward social attachments. The term used by Adler was "social interest" and it was related to Freud's concept of ego-ideal or the superego. Social interest includes such behaviors as cooperation, other directedness, group identification, empathy, and in general, a concern for others in order to compensate for personal weaknesses but also to contribute to public welfare. The individual's thoughts and judgments take into account the characteristics and aspirations of others as well as of oneself. The common view is differentiated from the private view. Thus, Adler's initial concern with the individual, followed in later years by his concern for the group, depicts the inherent conflict between self and other which social psychological theories of personality must confront. For Adler, however, self and other were treated as a dichotomy rather than a duality, although the result of the conflict was often described. In summarizing the writings of Adler, Ansbacher and Ansbacher (1956) note that from 1918 on "the nondevelopment of social interest is considered together with increased inferiority feelings as the explanation for the egocentric striving" (p. 244).

In terms of self–other orientation, Adler seems to suggest a conflict between the self and the other in which the individual finds it difficult to reconcile the demands of each and resolves the conflict of interests by withdrawing. The result is egocentric striving.

For example, the problem of maladjustment is essentially a problem of lack of social interest. In every case, the pressure of social interest is acknowledged but it is qualified by a "but." The "but" is what is referred to now as a self interest. In the case of suicide and psychosis, the social interest disappears. The self–other conflict is resolved in favor of the self exclusively.

A variety of "safeguarding devices" such as egocentrism as described above are developed by the neurotic personality. Adler accepted Freud's concept of repression as one of these safeguarding devices but added others such as excuses for the self, depreciation of the other, accusations of self and other, and separation from others. Freud's defense mechanisms served as "protection of the ego against instinctual demands." Adler's safeguards, on the other hand, served to protect self-esteem from threats of external demands and life problems. Through these safeguarding tendencies, the neurotic individual manages to maintain some control over others' perceptions of himself. In terms of self–other orientation, Freud's defense mechanisms and Adler's safeguards may be interpreted as means of resolving the conflict between self needs and group needs. It remained, however, for Horney and Sullivan to develop the implications of the inherent self–other conflicts.

The Approach-Avoidance Framework of Horney

Karen Horney's work (1937) may also be interpreted in terms of the self–other conflict and resolution processes. Again, we will be particularly concerned with the conflict control mechanisms which are suggested. Horney's writings focused upon the relationship between the behavior of one person and that of another, for example, child-parent and member-culture. Again, the self–other orientation pattern is readily noted.

In her early writings, she pointed to two primary sets of response sequences, those concerned with *satisfaction* and those concerned with *security*. Response patterns of a positive affective sort, such as those associated with eating or sexual intercourse are concerned with "satisfaction." In terms of the rubrics used in this section, these satisfactions are associated with the self in contradistinction to the other. Other behaviors, however, are associated with "security" or the reduction of basic anxiety. In terms of self–other orientation, the latter behaviors are somewhat more concerned with the relationships between the self and the other.

In later writings, Horney extended her thinking and postulated a "search for unity" between these conflicting behaviors directed toward satisfaction versus security. As a consequence, there was a constant personal anxiety of being "split apart." Descriptions of the manner in which the neurotic individual resolved the conflict became her major contribution. She did not characterize normal behavior in this regard, however. Nevertheless, the direction is suggested.

Anxiety emerges from predominantly negative behavior toward the child by others. The child, in turn, develops habitual patterns of behavior for dealing with these interpersonal difficulties. These include "moving away from people," "moving against people," and "moving toward people."

Moving away from people is conflict resolution through withdrawal. The child separates himself from others rather than becoming a member or an opponent of others. He attributes his behavior to a lack of commonality with others and a lack of understanding by others.

Moving against people is an aggressive approach to conflict resolution. The child assumes that others are hostile toward him and he resolves to fight. He basically distrusts others. The attack on others is both defensive and vengeful. The child wants to be stronger than others so that he may be safe. He also punishes the hostile others.

By moving toward people, the child resolves interpersonal difficulties by trying to win the affection of others and by becoming dependent on others. The child acknowledges his own helplessness and seeks safety in complete conformity. Still, his estrangement and fear remain, and indeed, may be heightened by the decrease in interpersonal control. His temporary safety is achieved at the cost of long term adaptation.

The neurotic individual is particularly anxiety ridden because of the possibility that his established pattern of behavior will be disrupted and that he will be exposed. Essentially the neurotic individual maintains control over interpersonal situations through deception of the self or the other and lives in constant fear of exposure. One of the goals of therapy is to re-establish pressing personal control over what happens to himself without the necessity of deception. In attempting to establish these controls, cognitive processes are emphasized. These include the processes of attention to events and their consequences and perception of relationships between events.

Horney emphasized more than anyone before her, the inherent conflict between self and other and the neurotic personality's cognitive approach to resolving this conflict. It remained for later scholars to become concerned about the normal personality's methods of resolving these interpersonal cônflicts, and indeed, to make the conflict more explicit.

Dynamisms: Harry Stack Sullivan's Conflict Control Mechanisms

Perhaps, the major contribution of Harry Stack Sullivan to the area of self–other orientation was his descriptions of control mechanisms which would help to minimize the inherent conflict between self and other. In his framework, personality is defined as the behavior of a person in relation to one or more other persons. The unit of study is not the person but the person in relation to another person. The person tends to develop habitual ways of reacting to another person or persons. Sullivan (1953) refers to these patterns of behavior as "dynamisms," and they include feelings, attitudes, or overt behaviors. The key dynamism in terms of self–other orientation is the self system.

The self system is a dynamism which develops in an effort to control anxiety. For Sullivan, anxiety evolves from interpersonal relations. Originally the anxiety arose from the relations between child and mother and was transmitted to other social relations. In order to control this potential anxiety, the individual develops various protective measures and supervisory controls over his behavior. In cognitive terms, the self system is a mediating mechanism which transforms inputs in such a way as to be minimally disrupting. The child learns, for example, that he can avoid certain difficulties by conforming to his parental wishes.

A less adaptive dynamism for resolving interpersonal conflicts is apathy. Under conditions of apathy, all tensions and needs are markedly attenuated. The mechanisms appear to be clearly related to withdrawal. It is used because it is effective in reducing anxiety.

Other control mechanisms suggested by Sullivan include "focal awareness" and "consensual validation." In his efforts to avoid anxiety and establish equilibrium or consistency, the range of stimuli to which the person (through the self system) responds becomes increasingly restricted.

The self system effectively controls the stimuli to which the person attends. Personal integration is maintained through exclusion. Excluded are those things which will go all right in any event and those things which the person has found that he has not been able to do anything about.

Thus, while these controls maintain security or reduce anxiety, there is a tendency for the self system to interfere with one's ability to live constructively with others. The person is not adequately responsive or flexible. In more modern terminology, it is suggested that control mechanisms must be considered along with arousal mechanisms. Indeed, it is the balance or resolution among these alternate mechanisms which is the central concern of self–other orientation.

One corrective mechanism suggested by Sullivan for an overemphasis on control, but yet in a sense, is also a control mechanism, is "consensual validation." Consensual validation is a tendency to subject one's observations and analyses with regard to the self in comparison through exchanges with others concerning comparable experiences. The exchange leads to agreement, improved ability to communicate with others, and the ability to draw generally useful inferences about the actions and thoughts of others. Thus, the pervasive condition of conflict between self and other is assumed, and approaches to interpersonal conflict resolution are outlined by Sullivan.

In abstracting from Sullivan's writings, I have placed in bold relief his concern with the control functions of the self system. He was not as explicit as I have suggested. Still, like the ego psychologists, Sullivan moves in the direction of control mechanisms. His thinking was truncated, however, by a level of development in cognitive psychology which was far below the theoretical developments in self-social frameworks.

The theoretical systems developed by Adler, Horney, and Sullivan established the basis of social psychological theories of personality. All suffer from the same shortcoming, however. The development of these theories was truncated by the failure to develop a suitable methodology. Each, in a sense, built a closed system; new objective data was not introduced into the system and the theory became increasingly involuted or "parataxic," to use Sullivan's own language. Each observer tends to use a private communication system.

Schutz's Social Psychological Approach

In 1958, an interpersonal theory of personality was published by Schutz which promised to combine theory, measurement, and research. As soon as measurement is introduced in the systematic analysis of personality, it tends to become the point of focus, perhaps because it is the major problem faced by the investigator. In discussing Schutz's work, the emphasis shifts toward the analysis of personality measurement.

Any approach to the study of personality sooner or later must confront the problem of the number of variables, factors, or coordinates that are to be considered. Schutz considers a three-factor system. Probably one of the implicit assumptions of most personality theorists is that there exists only a limited number of variables which account for the majority of variance in human behavior. In addition, problems of information organization and communication contribute to the press toward simplification of the system. Schutz's search for relevant variables was guided by a theory of interpersonal behavior and an admitted press toward reduction.

The three interpersonal variables of the resulting system stem from needs for inclusion, control, and affection. Inclusion is defined as "the need to establish and maintain a satisfactory relation with people with respect to interaction and association" (p. 18). "Satisfactory relation" includes a psychologically comfortable relation with people, which is defined by each person as being somewhere on a dimension ranging from initiating social behavior with all other people to initiating social behavior with no one, and always eliciting behavior of others toward the self to never initiating interaction. If examined closely, the control of interaction is seen to be with the self or the other or some combination of these. The direct conflict between self and other is implicit.

In general, the essential component of inclusion is identity. The individual wishes to feel significant and worthwhile. In order to achieve this goal, however, others must first know who he is and be able to distinguish him from others. Failure to feel included arouses anxiety. Unsuccessful resolution of inclusion needs leads to a feeling of alienation, of being different and unaccepted.

Schutz's second variable is control, which is defined as the "need to establish and maintain a satisfactory relation with people with respect to control and power" (p. 18). Here "satisfactory relation" includes (1) a psychologically comfortable relation with people somewhere on a dimension ranging from controlling all the behavior of other people to not controlling any behavior of others, and (2) a psychologically comfortable relation with people with respect to eliciting behavior from them to never being controlled by them.

Again, is seen the press for control and the opposing press to be controlled. Schutz offers no information concerning the resolution of these processes, or as compartmentalized behavior. He sees no necessary relation between the individual's controliing behavior and his behavior toward being controlled.

Schutz is describing a power component in interpersonal relations. Here he borrows from Horney. He seems to be suggesting that power relations between self and a variety of others are inconsistent. It is possible to be high in relation to the power of one person yet perceive oneself as low in power in relation to another.

The third variable is affection which is described as "initiation of close personal relations with others." Again, however, the component of self-esteem is introduced when Schutz describes the need for affection as being associated with the need to feel that the self is lovable.

The concepts used by Schutz evolve largely from the social psychological theories of Adler and Horney who were concerned with the concepts of self-esteem, social interest, and power. The measures used in measuring and testing the concepts are entirely self report. Examples of the items include: (a) I try to be with other people, (b) I let other people decide what to do, and (c) I try to be friendly to people.

OVERVIEW

From this brief review, a trend may be deduced with regard to social psychological theories of personality. A number of components or self–other relations recur. They include self-esteem, power, and social interest or inclusion. There also emerges a greater concern with the process by which the variables to be included in the system are selected.

In addition, more modest expectations are suggested concerning the behavior for which a given personality theory purports to possess utility. Freud hoped to encompass human behavior in its infinite complexity within the confines of the system generated by his assumptions and constructs. More recent theories are concerned with social behavior, albeit broadly conceived social behavior. Moreover, Schutz hints that at this stage of the art, it may be more strategic to seek variables critically relevant to certain behavior rather than to seek behavior encompassing variables.

Finally, all approaches to the study of personality reviewed here begin with the subject's description of his relationships with others. In each case, however, the reports are mediated somewhat by the observer. Freud, Adler, Horney, and Sullivan translated interviews with patients into a meta-language or a personality theory. In the process of translation, the framework of the theorist has been imposed on the patients' attempts to describe the self-social matrix from the point of view of the self. Thus, Horney and Sullivan are concerned with the motivations of the subject, his basic needs and his attempts to reduce anxiety. When a meta-language is developed, the therapeutic process is complicated by the necessity of again translating that language to the subject. In this sense, the therapist, rather than the subject becomes the point of focus. The subject is given the task of attempting to understand the therapist, and through this process, understand the self.

The communication system developed by Schutz is subject to a similar criticism. The basis of the communication is the self report of the subject, but the fundamental language is selected by the therapist (self reports which the subject may or may not review). In all social psychological theories of personality reviewed here, the constructs that emerge from the language of the subject remains unvalidated. When a given word is used, the meaning of that word is subject to wide variations among persons and between persons with different backgrounds, experiences, roles, and orientations. In the process, the meaning of the constructs from the point of view of the patient may be difficult to determine.

It is a maxim in psychological research that progress is at least tripartite and involves theory, measurement, and research. Progress in the area of social psychology as it relates to personality has perhaps not been slow as much as it has not been balanced with regard to the three-part assumption of progress in science. The theory and experimental approaches await the development of a new approach to the measurement of personality, or a new approach to communication by the subject to the scientist but concerning primarily the subjects perceptions and meanings. A phenomenological approach is proposed.

Self theories of personality have been reviewed in terms of a conscious-unconscious dichotomy, a unitary concept of the self as opposed to a multi-component concept, and finally with regard to emphasis on social factors. In reviewing social-psychological theories of personality in the latter category, control mechanisms associated with the inherent self–other conflict were underscored. Finally, the problem of measurement was introduced in describing Schutz's framework. Against this background, a theory of self–other orientation will be described. The theory of self–other orientation is social psychological, phenomenological, multifaceted, and focuses upon self–other schemata which are assumed to operate as control mechanisms or what Sullivan refers to as dynamisms.

S.S.—F

SELF–OTHER ORIENTATION

The self concept is learned in much the same way as any other concept. Its ubiquity and its significance, however, introduce some special factors in self concept learning. For example, since new information about the self is continually available, the self concept is subject to continuous differentiation followed by reintegration. Additional information about the self may be assimilated initially by a simple collection process. Continuous additions, however, threaten to render the boundaries of the self concept unclear, and a periodic reintegration is usually proposed. It is proposed here that social schemata are the bases of self-integration, and that these social schemata are relatively enduring.

A fundamental assumption of self–other orientation theory is that self–other relations and self-delineation are a universal and constant concern. Self-delineation is imposed by social environmental demands. It is necessary under the press of a continuous series of social decision making situations to develop schemata which will aid the processing of self-social stimuli and facilitate decisions for social behavior under conditions of rapid presentation of social events.

As it was stated briefly in Chapter 1, representational concepts facilitate the organization of behavior along given abstract dimensions. Through these concepts, various acts of the individual are categorized according to the same dimension even though some of the characteristics of the acts may differ greatly. It is, however, by virtue of these categorizations that a certain amount of consistency in behavior is achieved. As social experiences accumulate and are organized according to self–other concepts, a degree of independence from external control is acquired. The self–other concepts function as "internal monitors" or organizing agents for social behavior. Social stimuli are selected, categorized, and responded to in terms of these mediating internal controls. It is through these controls that a modicum of behavioral consistency is possible, or at least that the subject perceives his behavior as being somewhat consistent.

The perception of behavioral consistency is assumed to be reinforcing in and of itself. Consistency of behavior may suggest to the actor that he has control of his behavior, at some minimum level at the very least. Thus, behavioral control has an acquired value and the use of mediating concepts, such as self–other concepts are self-reinforcing.

In the cognitive theory of personality proposed here, social adaptation is presumed to be mediated by self-social constructs. It is proposed that social stimuli are screened and translated into personal meaning through crude topological mappings of the self in relation to significant others, including the self as perceived in the past (Social Stimuli → Self Concept → Social Response.)

The fundamental framework of the theory of self–other orientation is Brunswik's (1956) theory of perception. In this framework, the interaction of the organism and the environment is stressed. Cues of the environment are processed by the individual in relation to his needs or sets. Certain cognitive processes intervene between the stimulus and the response. Stimuli must be selected and organized according to the needs of the organizer and in terms of some system which reduces the information to be stored and facilitates information retrieval and general utility (*see* Neisser, 1967).

In terms of interpersonal perception, social stimuli are presumed to be mediated by constructs which map the relationship of self and others. Here social stimuli are assumed to be the most significant, and in keeping with this social emphasis, self–other concepts rather than simply self concepts are assumed to be the crucial mediators of social stimuli and social behavior. These social schemata include self above other, with other, more than other, separated from other, included with other, similar or dissimilar to other, more central than other, different than others, close to others, and connected with others. With the aid of these gross mappings of the relationships between self and other, information concerning the relationships involving self and other in new circumstances is readily coded and decoded, thereby facilitating decision making significant for interpersonal behavior.

As with Sullivan's dynamism, self-social constructs make for stability under kaleidoscopic social conditions. In this sense, the social constructs act, to some degree, as defense or control mechanisms as they might be labeled by ego psychologists.

Similarly, Klein (1951) has proposed that all theories of adaptation are concerned with the resolution of tension and an effort to establish equilibrium between the inner and outer systems. In his efforts to establish equilibrium, the individual puts to use his perceptual, cognitive, and motor processes. These processes are the tools or potentials for adaptation. These equilibrating mechanisms or ego controls include "leveling" and "sharpening" among others. Leveling involves overlooking differences between objects in an array, whereas sharpening involves a heightened sensitivity to details (differentiation). It has been found that people develop definitive modes and patterns of perceiving which are adaptive for them. It is now proposed that self–other orientations are similar perceptual patterns or ego controls for interpersonal adaptation.

Perhaps, the cognitive orientation of the self-definition described here is most closely associated with the thinking of Hilgard (1949) and Hebb (1960). In an article which reviews the history of writing about the "defense mechanisms," Hilgard proposed a broader view of what he called the "inferred self," a concept facilitating the comprehension of continuity, permanence, or persistence of patterns or motives and attitudes throughout a person's life history — the important human motives being "interpersonal both in origin and expression."

Hebb (1960) described the self concept as a set of mediating processes arising out of experience, in part connecting the body image and in part a pure fantasy of an immaterial self. It is a real fantasy in that it affects behavior.

The framework for interpersonal behavior proposed here attempts to link social experience to perceptions of others, to social behavior, and reactions of others to the individual. In this framework, the crucial link is between social experience and social behavior which is mediated by self–other orientations. (*See* Fig. 8.1.)

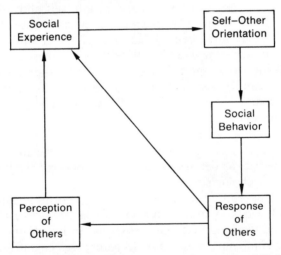

Fig. 8.1   A framework for linking social experience and social behavior.

It is proposed that social experience is coded by the individual in terms of self–other orientations using preverbal mappings of self and significant others (self above other, with other, different than others, etc.). Consistent with the principles of Brunswik, Hilgard, and Hebb described above, these self–other orientations mediate social behavior.

The association of self–other orientations with social behavior is mediated in turn, however, by social perception. Thus, for example, the individual who maps himself apart from parents, friends, and teachers may be expected to perceive himself as independent of or excluded from others and behaviorally tend to move toward activities which do not require companionship.

Social behavior, in turn, is linked to social reaction in much the same way as Leary (1957) has discussed the echoing stimulus-response chain between persons. Submissive behavior, for example, tends to be associated with dominant reactions from others. Social behavior and responses of others constitute social experience and complete the self-social cycle.

Again, in the approach described here, the focus is on self–other orientations as they reflect various social experiences (for example, what are the self–other orientations that characterize the geographically mobile children?), and as they are associated with perceptions of others, social behavior, and responses of others to the subject.

Ten components of self–other orientation have been proposed: (a) self-esteem, (b) social interest, (c) self-centrality, (d) identification, (e) majority identification, (f) complexity, (g) power, (h) openness, (i) inclusion, and (j) marginality. In the scanning, information search, and decision making processes which are presumably involved in self–other orientations, these components may well be arranged in a hierarchy of use. Some are more important and are applied more frequently than others. For example, self-esteem may be assumed to be high in the response hierarchy for most subjects. Majority identification, however, may be higher in the response hierarchy for black Americans.

The framework presented here is open ended. It emerges against the background of a long history of ideas which have attempted to increase our understanding of a most exquisite theoretical problem which attends the confluence of individual and social psychology. I have suggested that measurement has been one of the missing links.

Most important, however, is that the measures derive from a method of communication which fits the information. The medium must be congruent with the message in order to maximize communication. The English language was not invented to communicate mathematical principles, so a language of mathematics was generated. Moreover, as the problem area of mathematics changes, so does the mathematical language. New mathematics or systems of logic emerge with new problems.

It is now proposed that the topological arrangements of self and others provide an optimal method for communicating information about the individual's cognitive representations of self-social perceptions. This proposal is based on the asumption that non-verbal communication is the learned method for expressing personal feelings regarding the relationship between the self and the other. Non-verbal communication requires close attention by the other to receive the message in order to learn the idiosyncratic language of the sender. Non-verbal communication is intimately shared communication in that the message is not imposed on the receiver. The message is subtle, can be ignored often with impugnity, and requires careful monitoring and personal knowledge of the other. It is also assumed that the record of the expression of self–other orientation must also be non-verbal in order to be more congruent with the face to face non-verbal behavior.

Still, the methodology of self–other orientations described here is probably limited to certain problem areas. New methods of communication between the subject and the scientist must be forthcoming as new social psychological problems are investigated.

CHAPTER 9*

A Helical Theory of Personal Change

In the previous chapter the evolution of the concept of the social self was deduced particularly as the concept relates to the process of maintaining a degree of stability in an ever-changing environment. In the present chapter, the change process is central. How are the guidance systems of the individual altered?

A HELICAL THEORY

A synthesis of four subsystems of personal change is proposed here from which there evolves a helical theory of personal change. The subsystems include attitude-value change theories, behavior modification, role theory, and self theories. The components of the personal change framework are assumed to form a hierarchical system beginning with attitudes (the least resistant to change) to self concept (the most resistant to change). A change in any one of the components of the system creates a state of disequilibrium and a press toward congruence for the components lower in the system. In a sense, Festinger's Theory of Cognitive Dissonance is differentiated, extended, and reintegrated here.

Individual and social change is inherent, yet stability or at least predictability is often the preferred state (Lecky, 1945). Under these circumstances, the human compromise must involve the monitoring of social change and the adaptation of group and individual processes in an effort to maintain control over the changing system. Social scientists' investigations of the control of individual and social change have been fractionated. Social psychologists in departments of psychology have

*This chapter is a revision of an earlier paper by Ziller (1971).

147

focused on attitude change (*see* McGuire, 1968). Social psychologists in departments of sociology have examined the problem of personal change in relation to role and self concept under the rubric of role strains within role theory (*see* Secord & Backman, 1964). Clinical psychologists and sociologists have both studied in depth changes in the self concept (Rogers, 1951; Brim & Wheeler, 1966). Finally, a burgeoning area in clinical psychology is behavior modification (Bandura, 1969).

Unfortunately, each of these subtheories is compartmentalized. Paraphrasing Cassirer (1944, p. 21), each subtheory is autonomous and becomes a Procrustean bed on which the empirical facts are stretched to fit a preconceived pattern. The result is a complete "anarchy of thought."

A confluence of the four aforementioned frameworks is proposed here leading to a general theory of personal change. A brief outline of the basic components of the framework is described along with the fundamental assumptions of the system of thought. A more elaborate description of each subsystem is developed later along with the connections between the subsystems within the general theory of personal change. Although each subtheory points toward a general theory of personal change, each has a limited purview and the framework of each does not provide an adequate basis for integrating the extensive research findings. Moreover, taken as a collective, the subtheories fail to provide a working basis for a thorough understanding of personal change because they are unwieldy, are not generalizable in their entirety, and do not consider the joint effects of the different frameworks. A synthesis is required which points out some of the shortcomings of the separate frameworks and leads to a restructuring of the frameworks at a higher level of abstraction for greater generalization.

The core of the personal change theory is a Guttman type hierarchy of potentially changeable personal characteristics including attitudes, values, behaviors, roles, and self concepts. It is assumed here that the characteristics are ordered on an underlying dimension of ease of change. Attitudes are the least difficult to change, and the self concept is the most difficult to change. Values, behavior, and role are ordered on a continuum somewhere between these two extremes.

Self Concepts
Roles
Behaviors
Values
Attitudes

In defining the components of this hierarchical system of personal change, a close association will be sought between the definition of the component and the method of measurement of the component usually used in the experimental literature. This approach is particularly important with regard to the definition of attitudes. Much of theory and research in the area of attitude change are closely related, only if the reader is willing to overlook the fact that attitudes are usually measured through self reports with their inherent shortcomings. Under these conditions, the resulting theory can be deluding. Most important, however, directions for a new framework may be obscured. With regard to attitude change theory, it is proposed here that diffuse definitions of attitudes along with aggrandizing theories have served to truncate the development of a vital theory of attitude change within a system of personal change. Nevertheless, the contribution of the research may be reclaimed by limiting the range of meaning of the studies and by organizing the findings within a more complete system of thought.

Attitudes

A frequent definition of attitude is a person's predisposition to behave in a certain way (Jones & Gerard, 1967). Newcomb (1950, pp. 118–119) defines attitude as a state of readiness for motive arousal. "An individual's attitude toward something is his predisposition to perform, perceive, think and feel in relation to it." In discussing the function of attitudes, Katz, Sarnoff, and McClintock (1956) have included an ego defensive function. In one way or another, these definitions indicate a link between attitudes and the remaining four components in the system of personal change. The nature of the association is not indicated, however.

In the present context, attitude is defined as a self report and a public statement of the person's disposition at that point in time to behave in a certain way. The self report nature of attitudes is stressed because most measures of attitudes used in experiments ask for a verbal self report or an opinion (Bem, 1967). The inherent shortcomings of the self report must be underscored here (Kelly, 1955, p. 268; Polanyi, 1966, p. 4).

In addition, however, the definition of attitude emphasizes its social component. The opinion is usually made public. The report is presented to someone. Thus, expectations between the self and the other become involved.

Values

Values are most often defined as a cluster of attitudes. In this sense, a higher level of abstraction is indicated. Values, too, usually are measured by public self reports. Nevertheless, it is often assumed that attitudes are more susceptible to change than values (Hollander, 1967, p. 117), again suggesting the proposed hierarchical ordering assumed here.

Behaviors

A behavior is a response in relation to a situation as a stimulus. Behavior occurs in the context of a situation as opposed to an attitude or value which occurs in response to a question. When a verbal statement is made in response to a question raised in a non-voluntary situation, the verbal response is distinctly not a behavior in the present sense. If, on the other hand, the statement is volunteered by the individual, the verbal response approaches a behavior as described here. In the latter case, the individual assumes a greater responsibility for the act. Watson (1930) included verbal responses within the behavior category, but this assumption led to an unnecessary diffusion of the behavior definition.

Roles

A person occupying a place in a social relation, such as a mother, expects herself and is expected by others to relate and behave toward other persons in the social system according to certain norms. Certain behaviors are relevant to the role. If these behaviors are not forthcoming, the social system is less predictable leading to some interference in the group interaction, social processes, and perhaps reduced performance. In some roles, the latitude of expectations is more narrow than other roles.

In some sense, a role assumes a degree of commitment to a social relationship. The person occupying a position expects and is expected to behave in certain ways because the members of the social system have made an implicit agreement to do so. It is also probably assumed by the members of the social system that they will signal the other members of the group before they change their behavior in any appreciable degree. An element of trust is involved making for stability and predictability within the social unit.

Self Concepts

In the personal change system described here, the self concept is restored to a significant position. The self concept is more difficult than attitudes to measure, but we can scarcely afford to have theory construction dictated by the relative convenience of constructing measures.

It may be assumed that prediction is facilitated by the organization of relevant elements into a conceptual system. In the search for relevant elements, perhaps the most ubiquitous elements in the field should receive highest priority. Self concept, then, emerges as a high priority and crucial construct in the search for elements in social psychological theories of behavior and behavior change.

Most significant, in terms of the theory of personal change, the self concept is relatively stable. It is subject to change and is responsive to long term situational changes, but a lag in the change process is inherent. This lag assures a degree of stability within the personal system which serves as a point of reference in an otherwise kaleidoscopic social environment. Self–other orientations serve as control mechanisms for social adaptation by serving as screening and guiding representations.

ASSUMPTIONS OF THE PERSONAL CHANGE SYSTEM

The Hierarchical System

It has already been indicated that the five components of the change system are assumed to constitute a hierarchy of difficulty of change. Attitudes are the least difficult and self–other orientations are the most difficult. The other components fall somewhere between. No simple scale is suggested, however.

Commitment

The relative difficulty of change of the components is attributable, in part, to the relative commitment associated with each of the components. Commitment refers to a reduction in further alternatives associated with a particular choice (Roby, 1960). Having committed oneself at a particular level in the change hierarchy is associated with greater predictability for the individual. For example, having reported certain attitudes is less restricting than having accepted a certain role such as group leader. Violation of the expectations associated with the expression of an attitude is more acceptable to the self and others than violation of role expectancies. The greatest commitment is associated with the self–other orientations. The latter constructs are designed particularly to function rapidly under conditions of limited time demands and stress. The self–other orientations are associated with the stability, regularity, and consistency of personal behavior. The individual ceases to monitor rigorously the thinking processes associated with these constructs. They serve as a sub-system of reference which facilitates adaptation. To change these on a daily basis would require a prohibitive amount of effort, or there would be much less opportunity to attend to matters external to the self.

Expression of an attitude on a questionnaire is associated with con-siderably less commitment. The self concept is associated with a reduction in alternatives and is subject to more controls. It is implied throughout, that a more rapid change is possible as one moves down the hierarchy. Attitudes are subject to the most rapid change. Changes in self–other orientations are slow, but it is proposed here that this relative stability is functional. The instability of attitudes may also be functional in that a degree of flexibility is possible within a relatively stable personal sys-tem. Before exploring this possibility, however, it will be necessary to examine the assumption of the press toward consonance among the components in the personal system.

Equilibrium of the Personal System

The personal system is such that if one of the components is changed, a state of disequilibrium is effected within the system. It is assumed that in this imbalanced state there is a tendency for the components lower in the hierarchy to change in a way which will render the components con-gruent. For example, if an individual changes roles, the next most prob-able change would involve attitudes, then values, followed by behaviors.

Even though there is a tendency for the press to move downward in the hierarchy, it is assumed that a change in one component will also establish a press toward change in components higher in the system. A change in attitudes, for example, is assumed to exert some press toward changes on behavior, role, and self concept but with diminishing force with regard to the higher level components.

A differential time factor for change is assumed to operate as one moves up the hierarchy as opposed to down the hierarchy. Thus, the press on behavior change under conditions of attitude change is less than the press on attitude change under conditions of behavior change. Never-theless, if the press functions over time, it will increase. Still, it will take longer to change behavior through a change in attitudes than it will to change attitudes through a behavior change. For example, a change in attitudes toward premarital sex will not influence sexual practices to the same extent that a change in sexual practices will influence attitudes.

If more than one of the components are changed, the state of disequilibrium will vary in relation to the pattern of changed components. Under conditions where all components have been changed with the exception of the role, there will be a strong press toward changing roles. For example, if an individual's attitudes, values, behaviors, and self concept have changed regarding marriage, there will be a tendency to marry or obtain a divorce depending upon the original state. On the other hand, if only one's attitudes have changed toward marriage, the press toward change in the other components of the personal system with regard to marriage will be relatively weak, and the probability is higher that the attitudes will change in order to re-establish congruence in the system rather than a change in the entire system.

It is proposed that the individual is required to monitor the self-social system constantly in order to maintain the congruence of the self concept and social field. In the event of incongruence, the individual is most likely to alter his attitudes. It is assumed here that a change in attitudes requires the least effort and also is the least threatening to the self system as a control and predictive system. The change will have left intact the major components of the self system.

An attitude change also serves to reduce social pressures for change. In a sense, attitude change is a social defense mechanism. For example, overt agreement with the majority opinion is a low cost exchange which still permits covert disagreement. Indeed, in a sense, each of the components below the self concept may be interpreted as a defense mechanism in that the individual may maintain the self system intact yet adapt to social presses through changes in attitudes, values, behaviors, or even roles.

As already stated, it is assumed that in the event of a change at one level in the hierarchy, the entire system is in jeopardy to some extent. A press is generated to change other aspects of the system toward congruence, especially those components lower in the hierarchy. Under conditions where more than one component has changed, the system is subject to greater strain. For example, if behavior is changed in addition to an attitude change, the probability of changing values increases toward 1.00. The probability of changing roles also probably increases. It is quite likely, for example, that behavior modification techniques are effective, in part, by a change in attitudes *prior* to behavior change attempts. Indeed, when examined, most approaches to personal change will reveal a multiple entry strategy.

Since the greatest disequilibrium is created by changing components higher in the system, the optimal strategy of personal change would seem to be dictated: change the self concept. Self theorists base their approach on this premise. Yet, the foregoing sections have stressed some formidable obstacles to this approach. A more complete consideration of this problem is postponed for a later section.

The preceding discussion of the press toward balance in the personal system suggests that balance is the optimal state of the system. This would be true if the social and physiological fields of the person were constants. Given the continuous change of the environment, however, it is now proposed that a state of disequilibrium may suggest movement toward adaptation of the organism and the environment. In this sense, a tentative change in attitudes permits experimentation with the personal system with a minimum of cost — a pilot study of the personal system, if you will. Little commitment is involved, and the system may return to a state of equilibrium very rapidly and with relatively little difficulty if the self monitoring processes so indicate.

Increasing commitment is made as changes in the other components proceed. The hierarchy suggests an orderly progression up the scale. Attitude changes are tried first, then values, behaviors, roles, and finally the self concept changes, in turn, under favorable circumstances. But more dramatic changes in the personal system are possible. The probability of a high rate of change may itself be a characteristic of the personal system associated with risk. Indeed, Mossman and Ziller (1970), have recently found that persons with high acceptable rates of change for themselves tend to use coercion more frequently in a persuasion situation.

Self–Other Orientation Hierarchy

The self concept is, therefore, the most crucial component of the system. It is the most resistant to change and more time is required for change. Moreover, if the self concept is changed, there is a higher probability that other components in the system will change.

As indicated in the definition of the hierarchical components, however, there are assumed to be multiple components of self–other orientations. It is now proposed that these components themselves may be arranged in a hierarchy associated with personal change. Three components of the self–other orientation framework are relevant: complexity of the self concept, social interest, and self-esteem. It is assumed that complexity of the self concept is most amenable to change, social interest next, and self-esteem least.

Self-esteem has already been described in terms of consistency of the self system. The person with high self-esteem is presumed to have developed an integrated self system through which the individual readily assimilates new information or screens out irrelevant social stimuli. High self-esteem is assumed to underly personal stability.

Social interest (*see* Chapter 2) is an Adlerian concept referring to the range of a person's affectionate interest and concern. In terms of self–other orientation, social interest is assumed to involve inclusion of the perception of the self with others as opposed to the perception of separation from others. Inclusion involves a willingness to be subject to the field of forces generated among others and the self. Social trust is suggested. Indeed, it was demonstrated earlier (Chapter 2) that persons with high as opposed to low social interest are more inclined to monitor a positive as opposed to a negative source of reinforcement. It is assumed here that the stability of persons with high social interest is maintained through group norms.

Complexity of the self (*see* Chapter 5) concerns the degree of differentiation of the self concept, or in Lewin's (1935) terms, the number of parts composing the whole. A person with high complexity of the self concept requires more words to describe himself.

It is now proposed that the individual with the more complex theory concerning self–other relations is less likely to be seriously disturbed by new experiences which momentarily appear to be incongruent with the system. This proposition derives by extrapolation from a series of unpublished studies by Alex Bavelas of Stanford University concerning the etiology of superstition. It was observed that persons with more complex hypotheses or theoretical systems concerning a given phenomenon were able to assimilate new information into the system with greater facility.

Complexity of the self concept may be similar to "self-actualization" as described by Maslow (1954). Maslow suggests that in self-actualized persons "many dichotomies, polarities, and conflicts are fused and resolved." Emerging from this, self-actualized persons are simultaneously selfish and unselfish, individual and social, rational and irrational, and so on. Essentially, Maslow seems to be proposing that self-actualized persons are not simply described or categorized, that is, they are complex. In the present context complexity of the self concept is also associated with stability of the self system through cognitive processes such as tolerance for dissonance.

The assumed hierarchy among these three components of self–other orientation again suggests that strategies of personal change directed toward the self concept may be accomplished with greater facility if they begin with a concern for complexity of the self concept, in order to render the self system more adaptive. Changes in social interest are also a concern for personal change in that the individual with high social interest is more responsive to positive reinforcements from others (*see* Chapter 2). Finally, a change in self-esteem may follow in relation to a series of positive experiences associated with responsiveness to others. Indeed, an effective program to change self-esteem may not be possible to achieve directly but rather must emanate from social interest and the attendant positive social reinforcements. Again, a multiple intervention strategy is suggested directed simultaneously at complexity of the self concept and social interest, but ultimately self-esteem.

COGNITIVE, CONATIVE, AND AFFECTIVE COMPONENTS

The five components of the personal system derive in part from the classic classification of human process: knowing, acting, feeling. The cognitive component of the personal system concerns the organization of the information field into units which facilitate communication. These units are what has been referred to as attitudes and values. The latter is the more abstract unit.

The behavioral component has already been so named within the original system. To the behavioral component must be added the role component which incorporates the expectations of the others as well as certain behaviors.

Finally, the affective facet includes self–other orientations as they are described here. Here feelings are assumed to be expressed not by verbal reports such as attitudes, but rather in terms of the perceptions of the self in relation to significant others. The feelings have been incorporated within the self system. Indeed the feelings referred to here may be ineffable. Thus, self–other orientations cannot be measured using standard methods of communication. A meta-language is required. One such approach is the use of spatial paralogic. The system of personal change described here includes some of the most central characteristics of the human state, and it is in this sense, that the proposed theory is general.

A SYNTHESIS OF FOUR MICRO-THEORIES OF PERSONAL CHANGE

The theory of personal change is essentially an integration of the theories of attitude change, behavior modification, role theory, and the theory of self–other orientation. The theory of personal change has almost appeared piecemeal in the literature. Usually, however, one or another of the components is emphasized to the exclusion of some and the de-emphasis of others. Often many of the components are described but are not incorporated within the framework. More general frameworks seem to be avoided in preference for more readily testable micro-theories, but in so doing the modesty of empiricism may lead to theoretical myopia.

1. Attitude Change Theories

As stated earlier, the topic of attitude change has been the component of personal change most studied by social psychologists. Indeed, McGuire (1968, p. 136) states unequivocally that attitude research in the last decade has returned to the dominant status within social psychology that it had 30 years ago. This emphasis is somewhat difficult to defend, however, on the basis of the relationship between attitude change and behavior change (Fishbein, 1967). Fishbein concludes that traditional measures of attitude are not likely to be related to behavior in any consistent manner. He contends that earlier investigators have usually questioned the measures of attitudes. They have argued that traditional measures are oversimplified. Most measures only consider an individual's "affective feelings," and fail to take his cognitions and conations into consideration. Fishbein then suggests that most investigators attempt to resolve the attitude-behavior problem by expanding the definition of attitude to include affective, cognitive, and conative components. I would add that the social psychologists may also have been seduced by the rela-tive ease of conducting attitude research, and reduced the dissonance by exaggerating the importance of the research topic.

Support for Fishbein's claim that investigators of attitudes expand its definition of attitude to include affective, cognitive, and conative com-ponents to offset the inadequacy of the measures of attitudes may be found in the definition of attitude by Newcomb (1950), and Secord and Backman (1964). Newcomb writes that an individual's attitude toward something "is his predisposition to perform, perceive, think and feel in relation to it," (pp. 118–119). Similarly, Secord and Backman (p. 99) note that "In a broader sense, an individual's entire personality structure and hence his behavior may be thought of as organized around a central value system comprised of many related attitudes." Both statements at least indicate that attitudes are merely part of a personal system. Unfortunately, the emphasis is misplaced on the attitude component of the system. More significantly for the development of a general theory of personal change are the proposed relationships between attitudes and other components of the five-component helical personal system.

Attitudes and Values

In reviewing studies which have examined the relationship between attitudes and the other components in the change hierarchy, there is convincing evidence that a person's attitude toward an object is a function of his value orientation (Fishbein, 1963; Rosenberg, 1960). Rosenberg's study may be used as a model to investigate the relative position of the components in the change hierarchy. In this study, eleven deeply hypnotized subjects were given post-hypnotic suggestions part of which follows:

"When you awake you will be very much in favor of Negroes moving into white neighborhoods. The mere idea of Negroes moving into white neighborhoods will give you a happy, exhilarated feeling . . .. Also, when you awake you will be very opposed to the city-manager plan. The mere idea of the city-manager plan will give you a feeling of loathing and disgust" (p. 43).

The subjects, of course, were told that they would have no memory of the suggestion when they emerged from the hypnotic state. Value questionnaires were administered to the hypnotized subjects and to a control group of non-hypnotized subjects both before and after the trance session. The hypnotized subjects showed a greater change than the non-hypnotized control subjects in the structure underlying their attitude toward the issues. It was concluded that the experimental subjects had adjusted their beliefs concerning the perceived instrumentality of furthering or hindering their values to bring them into greater agreement with the hypnotically induced change in attitude.

Unfortunately, the reverse procedure was not conducted to examine the effect of a change in values on attitudes. It is only through this approach that the hierarchy can be established. Unfortunately, too, the definitions of attitudes and values are not clear. In terms of the hypnotic induction, the study may easily be interpreted as involving self–other orientations (as induced) and attitude or value changes, thereby supporting the proposed change hierarchy.

Nevertheless, Rosenberg's approach may well serve as a model experiment for testing the relationship among the various components. For example, a change in self–other orientation may be induced hypnotically followed by an examination of changes in behavior and attitudes. In a second phase of the study, behavior change may be induced hypnotically followed by an examination of changes in self–other orientation and attitudes. A final phase of the study would involve hypnotically induced attitude change followed by an examination of behavior change and change in self–other orientations.

Attitudes and Behaviors

The first major breakthrough in attitude research leading to the theory of personal change was made by Festinger (1957). Essentially, Festinger's theory concerning dissonance reduction indicates that a behavioral act is associated with an attitude change.

Festinger's ideas stem from a balance theory orientation (Heider, 1958). For example, when inconsistencies exist between two attitudes, the organism will strive for consistency by reducing or increasing the positive stance toward one of them. In point of fact, however, most of the experiments which examine the theory of dissonance-consonance are concerned with imbalances between behavior and attitudes. In most instances, the subject finds that he has committed himself to a certain course of action which is inconsistent with his attitudes. Since behavior involves more of a commitment, a change in attitude consistent with the behavior is usually found. Equilibrium is re-established with a minimum of cost, since it is easier to change one's attitude rather than try to redress a situation.

In one experiment (Smith, 1961), subjects ate chocolate fried grasshoppers as part of a survival training program in a military setting. The subjects were instructed to eat the grasshoppers under the supervision of either a controlling (very military) or permissive leader. Under the more severe leader, the subjects reported that the taste of the grasshoppers was less objectionable.

The experiment clearly indicates the prepotent effect of act in relation to attitude. In an effort to highlight the dissonance-consonance framework, however, other facets of the experiment are overlooked which may place the experiment within the broader context of a theory of personal change. Most significantly, the experiment was conducted under military classroom conditions. Under these conditions, the subjects may readily perceive themselves as models of military behavior under the conditions where the leader was himself an exaggeration of the model military leader, or even more so when the leader did *not* assume the expected leadership role. The role of the subject must be underscored. The effects, then, stem not only from the act of eating the grasshopper, but most significantly from expectations associated with the role of an exemplar. It is quite likely that most experiments concerning personal change involve several of the components of the proposed hierarchy.

In support of the latter proposition, an experiment by Zimbardo, (1960) is instructive. Pairs of friends were led to believe that they disagreed either a little or a great deal in their judgments of a case study of juvenile delinquency. The importance of the rating of the case was varied by telling some pairs that their judgments represented basic values, personality tracts, and outlooks on important life problems. Other pairs were told that their judgments did not mean much. It was found that change toward the friend's position is directly proportional to the significance of the judgment in relation to the self. Thus, the self concept is an important consideration in attitude research. The question that is never asked, however, is the relative strength of influence on attitudes among self–other orientations (self-esteem, social interest, complexity of the self), roles, behaviors, and values. The focus is solely on attitudes rather than the personal system. More important, for theory construction, it is necessary to separate the potential effects from the various components of the personal change system as they relate to attitudes. Focusing on behavior as it relates to attitudes is likely to lead to a narrow analysis of the process, to diffuse definition of concepts, and even to misplaced emphasis.

Confusion is also introduced into the theoretical framework concerning attitude change in that the direction of the effect is not indicated, although it is sometimes implied that attitude change leads to changes in values, behavior, and self concept.

Bem (1967) proposes a somewhat different interpretation of these studies and supports it with a series of pinpointing experiments. In Bem's studies, the individual is described as standing back and observing his own overt behavior in relation to a situation and making inferences (attitudes) from the association of behavior and the situation. For example, just as a communicator is more persuasive to others if he is known to be receiving no payment for his communication, so too, it is found that he is more likely to believe himself under such circumstances (Bem, 1965). Although self-observation is central to Bem's framework, the concept of the self is eschewed.

Bem's explanation is supported in a study (Davison & Valins, 1969) using drug inductions. It was found that if an individual believes that he is responsible (the subject is told that what he was told was a drug injection was, in fact, a placebo) for engaging in a behavior which is incon-

, his attitude will more readily change and
behavior than if he believes that external
ponsible for his behavior.
ger, Bem, and Davison and Valins, the
en behavior change and attitude change.
he more dominant variable.

Attitu

The after behaviors pertains to role changes.
Evidence o support the relationship between role
change a he more directly applicable studies involve role ge.
The rela level in the personal change hierarchy
(roles) and) has also been explored extensively.
The usual exp playing as it relates to attitude change
(Janis & King, 1956; Scott, 1957; Brehm & Cohen,
1962). Subjects, ther person's point of view, changed
their attitudes more were merely exposed to the other's
point of view. The e been seriously questioned, however, in terms of des 965). Nevertheless, if the subject
perceives himself as p *teacher or student*, through the act
of presenting an argum er persons, there is an increased
likelihood that the subje rate the attitudes in question in
accordance with the exp hers and himself relative to the
role of teacher or student. Proper adoption of the role may become the
issue of central concern, and attitudes consistent with this role are readily
adopted. Commitment to a role takes precedence over commitment to an
attitude.

Of course, commitment to a role is far greater in a natural situation
than under conditions of role playing, and attitude change would be
expected to accompany role changes. A unique opportunity to examine
the relationship between role change and attitude change occurred in an
industrial setting where some rank-and-file workers were promoted to
foremen and others to shop stewards. Later, some of these same recently
promoted foremen were returned to their former positions (Lieberman,
1956).

Individuals whose attitudes were the same before they changed positions showed consistent changes in attitude in the direction of their new
reference groups, shop stewards or foremen. Moreover, the foremen who

returned to their rank-and-file status reverted to
years earlier.

To this point, the possible effects of attitude char _ ⌐.. ιoιe change has
not been considered. Executive training programs often assume that a
change in attitudes relevant to the role leadership will create sufficient
imbalance in the personal system to effect a change in role behavior. It is
hoped that by changing crucial attitudes, role behavior may be effected.
Since the role is defined by the expectations of others as well as the self,
however, the probability of such a change is extremely small. In addition,
there is always the question as to whether or not attitudes crucial to the
role have been selected for change. It is entirely possible that only the
actor's perceptions can determine this. Thus, the self–other schemata of
the actor become a consideration.

Attitudes and Self Concepts

The association between self–other orientations and attitudes is being
stressed increasingly by investigations (Smith, 1968; Sherif & Sherif,
1967; Jones & Gerard, 1967). Smith, for example, refers to attitudes as
mediators of self–other relations. Somewhat earlier, Lifton (1961)
referred to a "death and rebirth" process associated with attitude change.
He suggests that a revulsion within the individual is required before
attitude change is effective. A similar process was described by Schein
(1951) with regard to the Chinese attempts to "unfreeze" the attitudes of
American prisoners of war prior to reindoctrination (brainwashing). The
process is not unlike that used by military recruiters in resocializing new
members of the military services in the United States (Smith, 1949;
Erikson, 1958).

The integration of personality, behavior, values, and attitudes is perhaps best illustrated in the following statement by Secord and Backman
(1964, p. 99): "In a broader sense, an individual's entire personality structure and hence his behavior may be thought of as organized around a
central value system composed of many attitudes."

Sherif and Sherif (1967), however, have made the link between the self
concept and attitudes central to their theory of attitude change. They
state (p. 2) that a "person's attitudes defines for him what *he is* and what
he is not, that is, what is included within and what is excluded from his
self-image." More than this, however, Sherif and Sherif (1967) suggest
that the self concept is the most cogent determinant of the personal system. It is assumed, first, that regardless of the nature of the environment,

the individual is the center of his social space. It is the individual's apprehension of the environment that is incorporated and translated into beliefs, values, and actions. Of course, extrapersonal stimuli are important causal antecedents, but these stimuli are first subjected to selective and modifying processes within the individual. "The self serves as the final screen channeling the course of development of social attitudes" (p. 19). In terms of the self–other orientation framework, the screening processes referred to by Sherif are assumed to utilize self–other schemata or images. Furthermore, these images are relatively enduring making for a degree of personal stability.

As the components of the personal system become more distal to each other, the probability diminishes that a change in the lower component in the hierarchy will influence the higher level component, particularly with increasing age. It has been noted repeatedly that the consistency of children's attitudes increases with age (Horowitz, 1936; Stevenson & Stewart, 1958; Vaughan, 1964; Wilson, 1963). This suggests that as the personal system stabilizes, attitude change is less likely to create a press toward change in other components of the personal system.

Earlier, self-esteem was defined in terms of consistency or stabilization of behavior. It may be expected, then, that persons with high self-esteem are more likely to move toward redressing disequilibrium. For example, it may be expected that persons with high self-esteem are less likely to change their attitudes to begin with. In response to a dissonant situation, the person with high self-esteem is also more likely to overcome the imbalance by cognitive work, that is, Festinger's (1957) dissonance-consonance hypothesis is more likely to be upheld by persons with high self-esteem. The latter proposition was upheld in studies by Gerard, Blevans, and Malcolm (1964) and Malewski (1962). A large number of studies have confirmed the positive relationship between self-esteem and susceptibility to persuasion (Janis & Field, 1959; Cohen, 1959; Leventhal & Perloe, 1962).

In examining the relationship between attitude change and the self concept, it becomes increasingly clear that the investigators of attitude change hope to extend their findings with regard to attitudes to the topic of the self or even more generally to personality by the simple expedient of expanding the definition of attitudes to embrace the concepts of the ego and behavior. In so doing, social psychologists may have paralleled the perils of psychotherapists who accepted the changed verbal self reports of clients in a clinical setting as equivalents of behavior changes and personality changes. A similar cognitive leap or self-deception is practiced by adolescents who hope that their self concept will somehow be enhanced simply by repeatedly reassuring themselves of their personal worth, behavior notwithstanding.

Kelman (1961) suggests that there are three distinct processes of social influence: compliance, identification, and internalization. "*Compliance* can be said to occur when an individual accepts influence from another person or from a group because he hopes to achieve a favorable reaction from the other" (p. 62). The expression of an opinion even though the person privately disagrees with the expression is instrumental. At the very least, it is a defense mechanism. In the personal change hierarchy, compliance is equivalent to attitude change.

"*Identification* can be said to occur when an individual adopts behavior derived from another person or a group because the behavior is associated with a satisfying self-defining relationship to this person or group" (p. 63). This definition approximates the social learning approach to behavior modification which is the third level of the personal change hierarchy.

"*Internalization* can be said to occur when an individual accepts influence because the induced behavior is congruent with his value system" (p. 65). Literally interpreted, internalization is similar to a change in the self concept.

To refer to all of these as attitude changes, aggrandizes the concept of attitudes and results in a misplaced emphasis on attitude research and the theories derived thereof. Indeed, it is proposed here that the emphasis of research should be distributed over the five levels, but that the major concern should be with the self concept rather than attitudes.

2. Behavior Change

Approaches to behavior change which derive from a learning framework are grouped under the rubric of behavior modification (Bandura, 1969; Frank, 1969). The approaches include modeling, positive reinforcement, negative reinforcement, and desensitization. Usually, the approach pertains to the clinical goal of treatment (Watson, 1962). The behavior modification approach usually is directed toward a narrowly defined behavioral objective. For example, the objective of the personal change training may be the elimination of smoking behavior. The approach avoids focusing upon inner agents and forces associated with smoking or even attitudes toward smoking. The objective is no more than the elimination of smoking behavior itself. Moreover, role considerations and the self concept are usually outside the field of concern. Change is effected through positive reinforcement of the desired behaviors or behaviors in the direction of the desired outcome or punishment of undesirable behaviors in the Skinnerian tradition (Skinner, 1953). Under some problem conditions, modeling of the desired behaviors is reinforced.

One of the other characteristics of the behavior modification approach to personal change is the flexibility, or indeed creativity, encouraged on the part of the trainer. The nature of the reinforcement is often selected for the particular subject and circumstance.

For example, Ayllon and his associates conducted an extensive program of research in the development of reinforcement procedures for the change of gross behavior disorders in adult psychotics. In the early studies (Ayllon & Michael, 1959), nurses and hospital attendants were trained to record "base line" data of the frequency with which patients exhibited certain behavior. Reinforcement contingencies — usually in the form of social attention and food reward — were arranged in the hospital setting to bring about the desired changes. Bizarre forms of behavior were ignored or were not reinforced with social attention. More rational response patterns were supported by the nurses. In so doing, psychotic verbalizations were markedly reduced or completely eliminated (Ayllon & Haughton, 1964).

Behaviors and Attitudes

The relation between attitudes and behavior from the point of view of behavior modification is quickly dismissed by Bandura (1969) as relatively inconsequential. He avers that persons who profess to be interested in attitude change are not interested in attitudes *per se* — their principle aim is behavior change. It is proposed that the attitude-change approach is selected as a means of behavior change under conditions where the behavior in question cannot be directly elicited and reinforced for practical or other reasons. However, the available data provide little or no support for the effectiveness of persuasive communications with regard to overt actions (Fleishmann, Harris, & Burtt, 1955; Levitt, 1965; Maccoby, Romney, Adams, & Maccoby, 1962).

Behaviors and Roles

The relationship between role change and behavior change is rarely discussed directly in reference to behavior modification. It is now proposed, however, that the topic of social learning and imitation (Bandura &

Walters, 1963) may meaningfully be discussed in relation to role changes and behavior changes.

Perhaps, the most common definition of role (Biddle & Thomas, 1966) is the set of prescriptions defining what the behavior of a member in a given position should be. In terms of social learning, this definition suggests that only certain behaviors consistent with the expectations of the group members are reinforced by the group members. For example, it has been found that lower-class patients expect a therapist to assume an active, medical role in the interview, and if he does not, they do not return (Overall & Aronson, 1963). Given the social forces directed toward the individual occupying a given social position to behave in prescribed ways, a change in roles congruent with a desired change in behavior would appear to be a most simple and direct method of personal change. The same forces that prescribe role behaviors, however, also tend to prevent or restrict role change. The actor becomes dependent upon given reinforcements associated with role behaviors. Role changes occur infrequently, however. But role playing is a suitable and readily available substitute.

In the usual role playing situation (Cameron, 1947; Moreno, 1934; Newcomb, 1950), there are no explicit instructions of how the actors should behave, although they may be aided by descriptions of positive models. In contrast, role playing in the experimental or therapeutic situation usually involves instructions to the subject or patient to imitate the behavior of a real-life or symbolic model (Bandura & Walters, 1963). As Bandura and Walters point out (p. 91), role playing is particularly effective (in experimental situations, at least) since the role player dependently accepts the assigned role and then is reinforced for reproducing the model's behavior.

Exposure to modeling stimuli may be viewed as a variation of role playing or vicarious role playing. A model, often on film, is positively reinforced or punished for a particular behavior or behavior sequence. The viewer's subsequent behavior in similar situations is observed to be related to the model's behavior. Bandura (1969, p. 120) attributes the effects of modeling to three factors: (1) the observer may acquire new response patterns, (2) observation of modeled behavior and their consequences to the performer may strengthen or weaken inhibitory responses in observers, (3) the behavior of others often serves only as discriminative stimuli for the observer. An example cited is the situation where a person gazes intently into a display window and others respond in a similar manner.

The relation between behavior change and role change is not thoroughly analyzed as a synthesis of role theory and behavior. In the description of social learning and imitation, behavior modification approaches attempt to subsume role theory. A more balanced view suggests that imitation and social learning processes depend to a large extent upon a change in the role of the subject. The subject assumes the role of student. The therapist often assumes the role of teacher along with the attendant expectations involving the subject as a student. Or, for example, when a behavior modifier intervenes in a family or group situation, the therapist disturbs the existing status pattern and generally makes possible a restructuring of the status hierarchy. In addition, the decision to participate in the experience with the change agent may itself represent an attitude change which may be propaedeutic to behavior change. All those who base their personal change processes on one of the components in the personal change hierarchy attempt to incorporate a wide number of psychological processes within the framework by broadening the definition of the process or by failing to recognize the contribution of other frameworks.

Behaviors and Self Concepts

By way of amelioration, behavior modification theorists have recently attempted to incorporate mediating constructs such as self-esteem within their framework (Bandura, 1969, p. 91; Wahler & Pollio, 1968). Wahler and Pollio demonstrated that behavioral changes produced in a boy through social reinforcement altered favorably his self-evaluation as well as his evaluation of others. In another instance, Bandura (1969, p. 37) invokes the concept of self-esteem to explain personal stability under conditions of minimal external social support or conflicting contingencies of reinforcement which are frequently encountered in the social environment. Eysenck (1959) anticipated a facet of the proposed theory of personal change when he suggested that the way to change the self concept is to change behavior.

More generally, behavior therapists are compelled to consider cognitive factors which influence human behavior and even autonomic functioning (Rackman & Teasdale, 1969). In aversion therapy as applied to alcoholism, for example, it may be necessary to invoke cognitive factors to explain why a patient avoids drinking outside the treatment room even though he knows that drinking will not be followed by an electric shock.

Cognitive factors have been shown to have a profound influence on conditioning and extinction (Spence, 1965; Grings, 1965). As early as 1937, Cook and Harris reported that the magnitude of a GSR was increased when the subject was told that he would receive an electric shock, and decreased when he was told he would not receive shock. It is proposed here, that cognitive factors associated with the social self influence social behavior in a way similar to that in which experimental sets influence learning behavior.

Furthermore, it is proposed here that role frameworks and the imaginal processes associated with self–other orientations may be necessary to explain the long term effects of behavior modification. One of the questions which haunts the behavior modifiers is the long term effect of a change in a given behavior. Few follow-up studies have been conducted. It is recognized, however, that return of the patient to his original environment frequently leads to the attenuation or extinction of the trained response. Similar observations have been made by T-group trainers (Campbell & Dunnette, 1968).

In an effort to make the individual less susceptible to the development of future maladaptive behavior without the assistance of a therapist, behavior therapists have begun to teach their patients self-control procedures. In these procedures, the subject is at once the patient and therapist (Ferster, Nurnberger, & Levitt, 1962; Goldiamond, 1965; Homme, 1965). For example, in an effort to control eating behavior, an individual can arrange to buy food on a daily basis, and he can buy food which requires a great deal of preparation (Ferster, Nurnberger, & Levitt, 1962). Self–other orientations are assumed to be cognitive control mechanisms or, in a sense, self-control mechanisms in that the self–other orientations presumably developed under conditions of behavior therapy are extended to similar situations, thereby extending the treatment.

The above observations are consistent with the personal change framework proposed here, which assumes that an imbalance in the system at any one level creates a state of disequilibrium in the system. This imbalanced state is rectified most easily by altering the elements lower in the hierarchy, in this case, the specific behavior rather than the role or self concept.

. For example, it is frequently noted that individual therapy with married adults not infrequently is associated with a subsequent divorce. The divorce, it is now assumed, may be a change in the personal system congruent with a behavior change or change in the self concept leading to stabilization of the personal system. It is also suggested that unless a change in role and self concept is observed, the behavior change will be relatively short lived. A synthesis of the levels of the personal system must be effected before change is assured at any one level.

Behavior change processes are seen to involve attitude changes, role changes, and changes in the self concept, that is, behavioral change must be viewed within the context of the personal change system. A compelling question is whether or not there is an optimal level to begin the process of personal change. Consideration of the behavior modification approach to fear responses is suggestive (Bandura, 1969, pp. 74–75).

Bandura proposes that the establishment of complex social behavior and the modification of existing response patterns can be achieved most effectively through a gradual process in which the subject participates in an orderly learning sequence that guides him stepwise toward more demanding performances. A sequence of intermediate goals should be outlined that lead gradually to more complex modes of behavior.

With regard to fear responses such as snake phobias, the therapist first devises a ranked set of situations to which the client responds with increasing degrees of anxiety. Initially, the subject is exposed to the least threatening event under favorable conditions (the therapist is present) until his emotional responses are extinguished. Subsequent steps in the treatment process involve a gradual increase in the fear arousing properties of the aversive situation until emotional responsiveness to the most threatening stimuli is extinguished.

The personal change hierarchy may be assumed to be a similar stepwise guide toward more demanding performance. Attitude change is the least demanding, followed by value change, behavior change, role change, and changes in the self concept. The individual is desensitized to change by gradual increases in the degree of commitment. A change in attitudes is tentative or even preparatory. It is still easy to turn back. It is less easy to return to an earlier role, but it is still possible. In this process, change is accomplished at a rate which the individual can accommodate.

3. Role Change

Definitions of role usually indicate the relationship of the concept with other components of the personal change system but particularly behaviors and the self. Newcomb, Turner, and Converse (1965, p. 323) write that role "refers to the behavioral consistencies on the part of a person as he contributes to a more or less stable relationship with one or more others." More generally, role is usually defined in terms of the behavioral expectations of the self and others for a person in a particular unit in a social unit (Sarbin, 1964). In terms of behavior modification, a role is a set of social behaviors which tend to be supported consistently by other members of the social unit, by the self, and by other individuals in the social field. In cognitive terms, role is an abstract pattern of ideas that is learned by the members of a social system (Jackson, 1966).

The ease with which an individual can conform to the expectations of others relative to a given role is assumed to vary from individual to individual as well as across roles. The difficulty in conforming to role expectations is usually referred to as "role strain" or "role conflict." Role conflict may arise from a variety of sources (Secord & Backman, 1964, p. 488). Conflict may arise when: (a) one expectation requires behavior that in some way is incompatible with another, (b) when an individual occupies two or more positions simultaneously, (c) when the individual's attitudes are incongruent with the role, and (d) when the individual's self concept is incongruent with the role expectations.

Thus, in describing role conflict, role theorists have had recourse to all levels of the personal change theory. Again, however, no integrated approach to the levels was attempted, although the hierarchy is sometimes implicit. For example, Reckless, Dinitz, and Murray (1956) suggest that the self concepts of "good" boys in a high-delinquency area serve as insulation against engaging in delinquent behavior. The boys defined themselves in such a way that engaging in delinquent behavior was incompatible with their self definitions.

A variety of processes have been described (*see* Secord & Backman, 1964, pp. 519–520) which contribute to the resolution of role conflict. These include the development of a hierarchy of priorities in role obligations and restrictions on multiple position occupancy. Also actors who are particularly subject to sanctions are protected in a variety of ways. Finally, two roles may be amalgamated.

Roles and Self Concepts

Rarely do role theorists indicate a relationship between role change and changes in the self concept. Jackson (1966) pinpointed the difficulty of exploring the relation between self and role as the need for a more precise and operational definition of self as a system. Vincent (1964), however, found an increase in self-acceptance (using the California Personality Inventory) after marriage. An increase in self-esteem following election to the state legislature has also been noted by Ziller and Golding (1969).

Perhaps, the most obdurate problem in role theory concerns the confluence of the concepts of self and role. The synthesis of these two concepts is critical in that a solution may lead to a more fruitful integration of individual psychology and sociology.

Newcomb (1950) confronted the problem and discussed it in terms of the relationship between self and others. He observed that since role behaviors involve a relationship between self and others, they are bound to be influenced by the ways in which oneself and others are perceived. The role behavior of a politician who perceives himself as superior to others is quite certain to be different than a politician with a lower self-estimate.

Studies of occupational socialization also support the hypothesized selective interaction of self concept and role. Secord and Backman (1964) note that individuals reduce role strain by tending to interact only with those who confirm their self concept. Hoe (1962) also interpreted data relating discrepancies between the self concept and perception of the teacher role as indicating that large discrepancies led to dissatisfaction and dropout from the profession. Finally, Stern and Scanlon (1958) found that selection of medical specialization was related to personality patterns, thereby minimizing the necessity of a change in the self concept. These studies again appear to support the assumption of the personal change theory that the self concept is more resistant to change than role.

Newcomb (1950) also suggests that the adoption of social norms associated with certain roles become "interiorized" in that they become part of the psychological make-up. The child, for example, not only *absorbs* but comes to use the frames of reference which he finds the people around him using. Thus, Newcomb assumes an interaction between self–other concepts and roles. Role behaviors may influence the self concept, and the self concept may influence role behaviors.

In a more recent statement of role theory, Sarbin (1968) elaborates on the concept of interiorization. He refers to the intensity of role enactment as "organismic involvement." At the low end of the assumed continuum, the actor participates with minimal effort and visceral activity. The example is cited of a ticket seller at a neighborhood theater during a slow period of business. At the other end of the continuum such as may occur during religious conversions, the self and role are as one. An extreme example of the role's usurption of the self is under voodoo conditions.

Sarbin (1968) also hypothesizes that the congruence of self and role leads to more convincing role enactment. Self-role congruence is assumed when the person seems to like the role, is involved in it, and is committed to it. This fit between the self and role is ordinarily described by saying that a person is not well suited to a particular role, or that the job does not fit his personality. This statement in itself assumes the dominance of the self concept over the role. Indeed, Sarbin assumes implicitly the self–other orientation and role behavior hierarchy described here in the personal change system (*see* Sarbin, 1968, p. 524). Sarbin also assumes implicitly the remaining elements of the personal change hierarchy, although he suggests that attitudes and behavior levels are equivalent and are expected to change simultaneously following a role change (pp. 555–556).

Roles and Behaviors

The most explicit statement of the relationship between role and behavior as well as role and attitudes was found in an earlier report by Sarbin (1964). Sarbin cites evidence that gastric hunger contractions are influenced by role enactment (Lewis & Sarbin, 1943).

Role enactment also influences performance. Moreno's (1934) pioneer work in psychodrama is based partially on this assumption.

Sarbin also indicates the bridge between role enactment and behavior modification (1964, p. 197). In the usual role playing situation the actor is in the presence of an audience which provides cues for expected behavior and also reinforces behavior which meets those expectations. For example, Zimmerman and Bauer (1956) showed that an imagined audience characterized as holding certain attitudes that were in opposition with the material to be learned and remembered influenced the retention of the material. Again, although the other components of the personal change system are sometimes related to role theory, the framework is constricted. The identity of the theory is preserved at the cost of narrowness.

The bridging concept between role theory and behavior modification is socialization. Socialization is usually defined (Secord & Backman, 1964) as an "interactional process whereby a person's behavior is modified to conform with expectations held by members of the groups to which he belongs" (pp. 525–526). Both attitudinal and behavioral changes occurring through learning are relevant. It has remained for behavior modifiers, however, to make the major contribution to the socialization framework (Bandura & Walters, 1963; Parke, 1969). The latter works, in turn, have not benefited from a consideration of role theory. Each group of investigators appear to be content within the more defensible but more limited micro-theories (Merton, 1957). A move toward the amalgamation of the two frameworks is suggested in Sarbin's (1968) updating of the role theory chapter in *Handbook of Social Psychology*. He devotes one page to behavior modification and social learning (p. 548). More concretely, Jackson (1966) has developed a measurement model for norms and roles which provides a tool for investigating whether more emphasis is placed upon reward or punishment in the social control process.

4. Self Theories

The personal change theory proposes that the self concept is the anchoring characteristic of the system. Assuming the hierarchical arrangement of the elements in the system, it is readily understandable why the history of the study of personal change is dominated by a concern with the self in relation to significant others. If a change in the self can be effected, a higher probability is created for changes in the remaining elements. Yet, those who have subscribed to self theories have not demonstrated convincingly the efficacy of their frameworks.

Self theories are phenomenological. The individual's subjective view of himself in relation to significant others is presumed to mediate social stimuli and social responses. The serial order effects involved among these variables are not ignored with impunity.

As has already been indicated, the self concept emerges as an overarching cognitive category out of the individual's interaction with his environment. The self concept, in turn, increasingly acts as a regulator of behavior, particularly in critical or novel situations (Jones & Gerard, 1967, p. 184). The self concept is a personal theory of behavior to which the individual has recourse under novel conditions or when inconsistency threatens. The phenomenal self assumes monitoring and steering functions under conditions of stress, but is itself shaped by outcomes of behavior.

It is assumed here, that through the self concept as a mediating construct, the individual maintains stability, yet permits adaptability of the personal system through social monitoring procedures. The monitoring processes focus upon personal records of changes in the social environment as well as changes in personal attitudes, values, behaviors, and roles. The monitoring processes vary in degree of systematization, but at the very least, gross deviations from some informal base line is assumed to be within the range of awareness of most persons.

For the most part, the monitoring processes function in the service of the stability of the self concept: the maintenance of a congruence between the phenomenal field of experience and the conceptual structure of the self. Such a condition of congruence Rogers notes (1951, p. 532) would represent freedom from internal strain and anxiety.

In support of the proposed hierarchy of personal change, Rogers (1951) observes that the individual will maintain a self picture completely at

S.S.—G

variance with reality. The individual hopes that events will change so that it will not be necessary to change the self concept.

Adaptability of the personal system derives from the characteristics of the system which permits incongruence among one or more elements of the hierarchy. As noted at the outset, it is assumed that attitudes may be changed without too much threat to the personal system. The disequilibrium created by a change in attitudes is not so great as to force a restructuring of the entire system. The conflict among levels of the personal system may remain "encapsulated" at that level.

Similarly, values, behaviors, and even roles may each be changed without threatening the overall stability of the self system, although with somewhat more threat than may be incurred by a change in attitude. Until new attitudes and behaviors become incorporated into the self system, however, a return is imminent to the original state consistent with the intact self concept. A stable change or learning is effected only when a change in the self concept is achieved (*see* Maslow, 1954, p. 111).

A change in the self concept which accompanies learning also represents a critical commitment to the learning objective. Under novel conditions or conditions of stress, the new stimulus-response connection is not buffered by mechanisms which examine the congruence of the connection and the self concept. The learning has been assimilated within the self system and the response is no longer under the control of the self concept. The learning has become "interiorized." For example, in a recent study by the author, married as opposed to dating dyads (who differ in degree of commitment to each other) were found to use different schemata concerning the relationship between a man and a woman.

Thus, it is proposed that the self concept is the ultimate level of the personal change hierarchy. Those who would effect change in attitudes, values, behavior, or roles are necessarily concerned with a change in the self concept, for it is assumed here that unless a change in the self concept is achieved which is congruent with changes at lower levels in the hierarchy, the lower level change is likely to be reversed and the organism returned to the initial state of equilibrium. Thus, for example, it is proposed that unless a positive change in self-esteem accompanies changes in behavior of the child following behavior modification procedures, the therapy should be continued until such time as the desired change in the self concept is observed.

Indeed, clients are assumed to function with different ranges of acceptable rates of change, and these rates, in turn, have been found to be related to social behavior (Mossman & Ziller, 1970). Acceptable rates of change of the self system is itself, then, another aspect of the self concept.

Several other facets of the self concept (here, self–other orientations) have been described earlier in this paper. These include self-esteem, social interest, and complexity of the self. Of these, self-esteem is assumed to be associated with the stability of the self system. Persons with high self-esteem are more consistent in their behavior across situations (Mossman & Ziller, 1968). This consistency is assumed to derive, in part, from the subject's willingness to impose personal structure on the system, thereby exerting some control over the situation. The person with high self-esteem in contrast to those with low self-esteem is less a victim of his environment and more a controller or even creator of his environment.

The second component of self–other orientations is social interest or the perception of the self as included within the force field of significant others. It has previously been found that persons with high social interest tend to monitor positive as opposed to negative social reinforcements. It is readily seen that unless the social interest of the individual is changed, very little may be accomplished by changing his attitudes toward other persons.

Although Roger's self theory is consistent with many of the propositions of the present framework, approaches to personal change which stem from his self theory also suffer from the failure to consider other elements of the personal change hierarchy. Also, Rogers was compelled to depend upon self reports for his measures of the self concept.

One of Roger's major assumptions was that the self concept can be changed directly. It was assumed that (a) the self develops out of the organism's interaction with the environment, (b) the self may introject the values of other people, (c) the self strives for consistency, (d) the organism behavior is consistent with the self, and (e) the self may change as a result of maturation and learning.

In order to change a dysfunctional self concept, a non-threatening therapeutic micro-social environment is arranged through a client-therapist dyad. Under these warm and accepting conditions, the person is encouraged to explore slowly the feelings which threaten his security. Slowly, too, these hitherto threatening feelings are assimilated into the self-structure. Rogers also posits the need for a continuous monitoring process to see whether a change in the client's value structure is required.

For an evaluation of the self concept, Rogers relied on Stephenson's (1953) Q-technique. In this approach, a number of items describing the self ("I am a submissive person") are sorted along a scale in terms of how the client sees himself. Next, the same cards are again sorted along the same scale in terms of how the person would most like to be.

Although in terms of the personal change hierarchy, the Rogerian method may be subsumed under the self–other orientation level, it is apparent again that a multi-level strategy is probably in operation. By the act of volunteering for counseling, the person becomes a client with the therapist. The client is subtly encouraged to play the role of therapist with regard to himself under the supervision of a master therapist. Certain behaviors under these role conditions are supported by the therapist. Finally, and unfortunately, the outcome of the therapy is not a change in the self concept, but rather a self report of change. In terms of the personal change framework, the focus of the therapy is not the self, but simply a series of attitudes about the self. An index of the extent to which these attitudes are interiorized is outside the scope of the measuring devices.

As suggested earlier, perhaps a direct approach to changing the self-esteem component of the self concept is impossible. A change in the self concept is the desired outcome of personal change procedures but the change processes must involve changes in attitudes, values, behaviors, and roles. Only when these changes are reflected in the self-social schemata of the person is there much assurance that the personal system has reorganized and has achieved a new state of equilibrium required for personal stability. If the desired changes in the self–other orientations have not been achieved, the client is likely to revert to earlier attitudes, behaviors, and roles.

The pivotal point of the theory of personal change concerns the proposed cognitive outcomes and the communication of the proposed social schemata. A number of social schemata have been identified including social interest, complexity of the self concept, self-centrality, openness, identification, inclusion, power, and marginality. These cognitive maps of self and others are assumed to screen and order social stimuli and in general mediate the social response. They are assumed to operate a cognitive control mechanism to which the organism has recourse, particularly under conditions of stress. It is also assumed that these schemata are enduring relative to roles, behaviors, values and attitudes, but like the other components of the personal change hierarchy, they too are subject to change albeit much more slowly.

Heretofore self theorists have been concerned almost exclusively with the social schemata of self-esteem (Wylie, 1961; Coopersmith, 1967). With the advent of a component approach to social schemata, self theories need no longer be restricted to the narrow confines associated with the concept of self-esteem. Programs of personal change may be designed to fit the patterns of self–other orientations which are most significantly involved for the individual. It is not necessary to assume that every personal problem stems from concerns with self-esteem, although it does appear to be a key concern. Moreover, more complex patterns of personal change may now be explored and the outcomes evaluated. The alienation syndrome is an example.

The major criticism of self theories comes from those concerned with behavior theories, but particularly those who adhere to the behavior modification framework (Bandura, 1969; Mischel, 1968). Usually, the utility of the internal constructs is denied. The criticisms are well founded and stem from the history of psychoanalysis with the proliferation of constructs which elude measurement and experimental verification.

The conflict between these two theoretical positions is one of the oldest in psychology. The initial conflict between S-R theories versus gestalt psychology has given way to the conflict between behavior modification and self theories. Increasingly, however, one finds that each school of thought moves in the direction of the opposing school. S-R theories have introduced intervening constructs leading to more extended connections between the stimulus and the response (*see* Berger & Lambert, 1968). Cognitive theorists have remained somewhat less compromising (*see* Zajonc, 1968). Bandura (1969) uses the concept of self-esteem repeatedly, and in another classic account of behavior modification frameworks (Frank, 1969), a critique of behavior modification suggests that this area too may have recourse to intervening constructs, such as the subject's perception of the situation.

In the present paper, self theories are combined with cognitive frameworks to develop a theory of self–other orientation and accompanying measures of the central constructs employing cognitive maps of self and others. Concepts of the self are discussed by most theorists in the area of personal change. These concepts are dismissed with alacrity by many, but with reluctance by some. Progress in science is tripartite and includes theory, measurement, and research. Perhaps, a theory of personal change has been truncated by the failure to develop adequate measures of the self concept.

OVERVIEW

An omnibus framework for personal change has been described here which incorporates theories of attitude and value change, behavior modification, role theory, and self theories. The pivotal construct concerns self–other schemata, cognitive maps of the self in relation to significant other persons. It is assumed that these social schemata include self-esteem, social interest, self-centrality, self-complexity, power, identification, majority identification, openness, inclusion, and marginality. These constructs are assumed to mediate social stimuli and social responses. Changes in social schemata are assumed to be the ultimate objective of all approaches to personal change.

Five approaches to personal change were discussed beginning with attitude change, value change, behavior change, role change, and changes in the self concept. The five change approaches are assumed to describe a hierarchy of personal change. The hierarchy derives from the relative resistance to change associated with the five components. For example, attitudes are less difficult to change than behaviors. Social schemata are the most resistant to change and make for the stability of the system. The individual is less committed to attitudes than self concepts. The ease of change at some levels in the hierarchy makes for flexibility within stability of the personal system. Given the flexibility within the system, the organism is required to constantly monitor changes in attitudes, values, behavior, roles, and the self in order to maintain congruence among these components of the personal system.

Under conditions where one of the elements of the hierarchical system is changed, a state of disequilibrium is effected and a press toward equilibrium is generated. The press is greater toward components lower in the hierarchy, however. A change at the higher levels is assumed to be associated with greater imbalance and a greater likelihood of a change in the self system. Thus, changes at several levels of the hierarchy simultaneously may be expected to lead to a change in the self system.

Finally, a change at various levels of the self system may indicate the relative meaning of an event for the individual. For example, a change in attitudes but not the self concept following an event such as marriage may indicate that the event is less meaningful for the person than for another person whose attitudes as well as his self concept had undergone a change following the event. Thus, the meaning of an event such as marriage, divorce, loss of a position, and promotion may be estimated by examining the profundity of the change in the personal system ranging from attitudes through behaviors to the self concept.

The theory of personal change contrasts with most micro-theories of personal change reviewed here which emanate from a few basic constructs such as attitudes or roles. Within a limited field, these uni-factor theories seem to summarize most elegantly the existing research, and undoubtedly form the basis for useful processes of personal change within a limited area of application. The shortcomings of these micro-theories appear when they are aggrandized and used in lieu of a more general theory of personal change. It is then that micro-theories serve as the Procrustean beds for many applied situations which do not fit neatly within the limited purview. More important, however, micro-theories tend to truncate the development of more universal frameworks by fostering chauvinism.

A more helical approach to theory development is required. Micro-theories may serve as points of reference within a more open theoretical system.

One of the crucial tests of the proposed helical theory of personal change should involve two groups of subjects under conditions of behavior modification in relation to a given behavior disorder. It is maintained that the duration of the treatment effects will be longer for those subjects whose behavior changes are accompanied by appropriate changes in self–other orientations.

Essentially, a chain of middle range theories of personal change has been proposed here. Links have been proposed between theories of attitude change, value change, behavior modification, role theory, and the self system. Perhaps, however, this chain of theories or helical approach is but an intermediate step toward the development of a more unified theory of personal change. Nevertheless, the helical approach to theory construction is an alternative to middle range theories (Merton, 1957) and general theories.

NEW DIRECTIONS

The self concept has been deduced from its early conception through the initial stages of a new approach and its evolution into a more complex system, and to the resulting reintegration of five micro-theories and their accompanying research. Now the search continues.

One of the indicated areas of development concerns monitoring the meaning of critical life events and environments. This approach involves repeated administration of the Self–Other Orientation Tasks across such events as the first job, marriage, first child, geographic relocation, divorce, illness and the like. It is assumed that the meaning of critical life events is reflected in changes in various facets of the self concept. Self–other orientations become a means of measuring the nature of meaning.

The approaches presented here may also be extended to the area of inter-group perception and inter-group stability and change in much the same way as self–other perception has been examined here. For example, the approach may be used to examine how members of groups such as branches of a business organization or nations perceive themselves in relation to other units in the system. In this process new concepts of own-other group may be identified, examined, and tested in laboratories and natural settings, and, again, new-group frameworks may be expected to emerge. The search continues.

Appendix A   Examples of Items from the Self–Other Orientation Tasks

Item 1 Self-esteem

The circles below stand for people. Mark each circle with the letter standing for one of the people in the list. Do this in any way you like, but use each person only once and do not omit anyone.

F — someone who is flunking
H — the happiest person you know
K — someone you know who is kind

S — yourself
Su — someone you know who is successful
St — the strongest person you know

Item 2 Social Interest

The circles below stand for your Parents, Teachers, and Friends. Draw a circle to stand for *Yourself* anywhere in the space below.

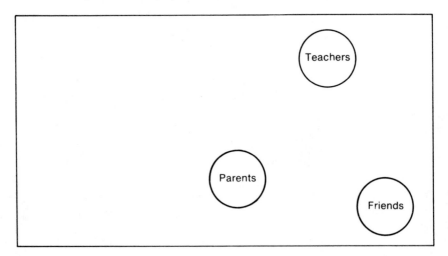

Item 3 Marginality

The two figures below stand for two groups of people you know. The small circles stand for other people. Draw a circle to stand for *Yourself* anywhere in the space below.

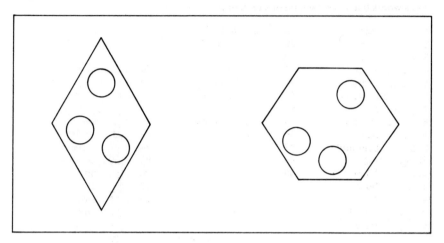

Item 4 Self-centrality

In the large circle below, draw two circles—one to stand for *Yourself* and a second to stand for a friend. Place an *S* in the circle for self and an *F* in the circle for your friend.

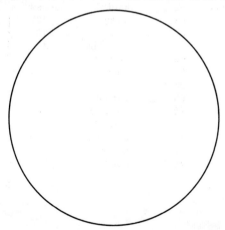

Item 5   Complexity of the Self Concept

Instructions: Here is a list of words. You are to read the words quickly and check each one that you think describes YOU. You may check as many or as few words as you like —but be HONEST. Don't check words that tell what kind of person you *should* be. Check words that tell what kind of a person you really are.

1. _____ able	38. _____ faithful	75. _____ popular
2. _____ active	39. _____ false	76. _____ proud
3. _____ afraid	40. _____ fine	77. _____ quiet
4. _____ alone	41. _____ fierce	78. _____ quick
5. _____ angry	42. _____ foolish	79. _____ responsible
6. _____ anxious	43. _____ friendly	80. _____ rough
7. _____ ashamed	44. _____ funny	81. _____ rude
8. _____ attractive	45. _____ generous	82. _____ sad
9. _____ bad	46. _____ gentle	83. _____ selfish
10. _____ beautiful	47. _____ glad	84. _____ sensible
11. _____ big	48. _____ good	85. _____ serious
12. _____ bitter	49. _____ great	86. _____ sharp
13. _____ bold	50. _____ happy	87. _____ silly
14. _____ brave	51. _____ humble	88. _____ slow
15. _____ bright	52. _____ idle	89. _____ small
16. _____ busy	53. _____ important	90. _____ smart
17. _____ calm	54. _____ independent	91. _____ soft
18. _____ capable	55. _____ jealous	92. _____ special
19. _____ careful	56. _____ kind	93. _____ strange
20. _____ careless	57. _____ large	94. _____ stupid
21. _____ charming	58. _____ lazy	95. _____ strong
22. _____ cheerful	59. _____ little	96. _____ sweet
23. _____ clean	60. _____ lively	97. _____ terrible
24. _____ clever	61. _____ lonely	98. _____ ugly
25. _____ comfortable	62. _____ loud	99. _____ unhappy
26. _____ content	63. _____ lucky	100. _____ unusual
27. _____ cruel	64. _____ mild	101. _____ useful
28. _____ curious	65. _____ miserable	102. _____ valuable
29. _____ delicate	66. _____ modest	103. _____ warm
30. _____ delightful	67. _____ neat	104. _____ weak
31. _____ different	68. _____ old	105. _____ wild
32. _____ difficult	69. _____ patient	106. _____ wise
33. _____ dirty	70. _____ peaceful	107. _____ wonderful
34. _____ dull	71. _____ perfect	108. _____ wrong
35. _____ dumb	72. _____ pleasant	109. _____ young
36. _____ eager	73. _____ polite	
37. _____ fair	74. _____ poor	

Item 6   Majority Identification

All of the circles within the square stand for other people. Choose any *one* of the two circles on the right to stand for *Yourself*, and draw one like it anywhere in the square.

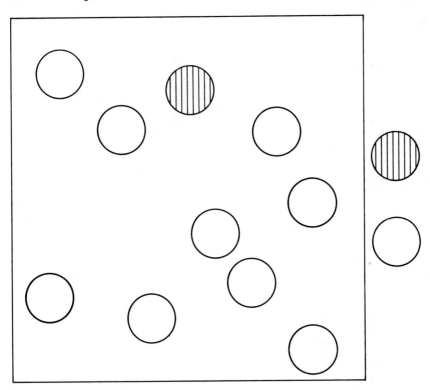

Item 7   Identification

The "M" below stands for your *Mother*. Choose one of the circles to stand for *Yourself*, and place a "Y" in it.

Item 8   Openness

The circle marked "Y" stands for *Yourself*. The other circles stand for other people. Draw as many or as few lines as you wish *from the circle for Yourself* to the circles which stand for other people.

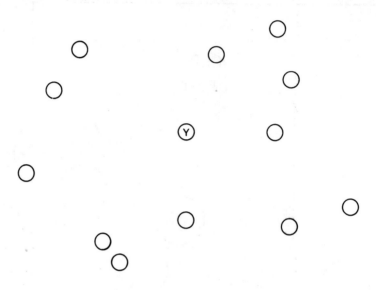

References

Adler, A. *The Practice and Theory of Individual Psychology.* New York: Harcourt, 1927.

Adorno, T. W., Frenkel-Brunswik, E., Levinson, D. J., & Sanford, R. N. *The Authoritarian Personality.* New York: Harper, 1950.

Allport, G. W. *Pattern and Growth in Personality.* New York: Holt, Rinehart and Winston, 1961.

Ansbacher, H. & Ansbacher, Rowena. *The Individual Psychology of Alfred Adler.* New York: Baur Books Inc., 1956.

Aronfreed, J. *Conduct and Conscience.* New York: Academic Press, 1968.

Asch, S. E. Studies of independence and conformity: A minority of one against a unanimous majority. *Psychological Monographs*, 1956, **70**, 1–70.

Ausubel, D. P. *Ego Development and the Personality Disorders.* New York: Grune & Stratton, 1952.

Ayllon, T. & Haughton, E. Modification of symptomatic verbal behavior of mental patients. *Behavior Research and Therapy*, 1964, **2**, 87–97.

Ayllon, T. & Michael, J. The psychiatric nurse as a behavioral engineer. *Journal of the Experimental Analysis of Behavior*, 1959, **2**, 323–334.

Baldwin, J. M. *Social and Ethical Interpretations in Mental Development.* New York: The Macmillan Company, 1897.

Bales, R. F. *Interaction Process Analysis, a Method for the Study of Small Groups.* Reading, Massachusetts: Addison-Wesley, 1950.

Bandura, A. *Principles of Behavior Modification.* New York: Holt, Rinehart and Winston, 1969.

Bandura, A. & Walters, R. H. *Social Learning and Personality Development.* New York: Holt, Rinehart and Winston, 1963.

Bandura, A. & Whalen, C. K. The influence of antecedent reinforcement and divergent modeling cues on patterns of self-reward. *Journal of Personality and Social Psychology*, 1966, **3**, 373–382.

Barber, J. D. *The Lawmakers.* New Haven: Yale University Press, 1965.

Barker, R. G. *Ecological Psychology.* Stanford, California: Stanford University Press, 1968.

Barnett, L. D. The Kibbutz as a child-rearing system. A review of the literature. *Journal of Marriage and the Family*, 1965, **27**, 348–349.

Bell, W. Anomie, social isolation, and the class structure. *Sociometry*, 1957, **20**, 105–116.

Bem, D. J. An experimental analysis of self-persuasion. *Journal of Experimental Social Psychology*, 1965, **1**, 199–218.

Bem, D. J. Self-perception: An alternative interpretation of cognitive dissonance phenomena. *Psychology Review*, 1967, **74**, 183–200.

Bendix, R. & Lipset, S. M. Karl Marx' Theory of social class. In R. Reinhard, & M. Lipset (Eds.), *Class, Status & Power*. Glencoe, Illinois: The Free Press, 1953.

Berger, S. M. & Lambert, W. W. Stimulus-response theory in contemporary social psychology. In G. Lindzey & E. Aronson (Eds.), *Handbook of Social Psychology*, I (Second Edition). Reading, Massachusetts: Addison-Wesley, 1968, pp. 81–178.

Berkowitz, L. *Aggression: A Social Psychological Analysis*. New York: McGraw-Hill, 1962.

Bettelheim, B. *The Children of the Dream*. New York: The Macmillan Company, 1967.

Biddle, B. J. & Thomas, E. J. *Role Theory*. New York: Wiley, 1966.

Bieri, J. & Blacker, E. The generality of cognitive complexity in the perception of people and inkblots. *Journal of Abnormal and Social Psychology*, 1956, **53**, 112–117.

Bills, R. E., Vance, E. L., & McLean, O. S. An index of adjustment and values. *Journal of Consulting Psychology*, 1951, **15**, 257–261.

Blau, P. & Scott, W. R. *Formal organizations*. San Francisco: Chandler Publishing Company, 1962.

Borgatta, E. F. A systematic study of interaction process scores, peer and self assessment, personality and other variables. *Genetic Psychological Monographs*, 1962, **65**, 219–291.

Brehm, J. W. & Cohen, A. R. *Explorations in Cognitive Dissonance*. New York: Wiley, 1962.

Brim, O. G. Socialization through the life cycle. In O. G. Brim & S. Wheeler, *Socialization After Childhood: Two Essays*. New York: Wiley, 1966.

Brim, O. G. & Wheeler, S. *Socialization After Childhood: Two Essays*. New York: Wiley, 1966.

Brunswik, E. *Perception and the Representative Design of Psychological Experiment*. Berekely, California: University of California Press, 1956.

Cameron, N. The paranoid pseudo-community. *American Journal of Sociology*, 1943, **49**, 32–38.

Cameron N. *The Psychology of Behavior Disorders, A Bio-social Interpretation*. Boston: Houghton Mifflin, 1947.

Campbell, J. P. & Dunnette, M. D. Effectiveness of T-group experience in material training and development. *Psychological Bulletin*, 1968, **70**, 73–104.

Caplow, T. *Principles of Organizations*. New York: Harcourt, Brace, & World, 1964.

Carrigan, Patricia M. Extraversion-intraversion as a dimension of personality: A reappraisal. *Psychological Bulletin*, 1960, **57**, 329–360.

Cassirer, E. *The Essay on Man*. New Haven: Yale University Press, 1944.

Cattell, R. B. The nature and measurement of anxiety. *Scientific American*, 1963, **208**, 96–104.

Christie, R. J. Jahoda, Marie. *Studies on the scope and method of "The authoritarian personality."* Glencoe, Illinois: The Free Press, 1954.

Cohen, A. R. Some implications of self-esteem for social influence. In C. I. Hovland &

I. L. Janis (Eds.), *Personality and Persuasibility*. New Haven: Yale University Press, 1959, pp. 102-120.

Cook, S. W. & Harris, R. E. The verbal conditioning of the *G.S.R. Journal of Experimental Psychology*, 1937, **21**, 202-210.

Cooley, C. H. Personal competition. *Economic Studies*, 1899, **4**, 73-183.

Cooley, C. H. *Social Process*. New York: Scribner's Press, 1918.

Coombs, C. H., Raiffa, H., & Thrall, R. M. Some views on mathematical models & measurement theory. *Psychological Review*, 1954, **61**, 132-144.

Coopersmith, S. A method for determining types of self-esteem. *Journal of Abnormal and Social Psychology*, 1959, **59**, 187-194.

Coopersmith, S. *The Antecedents of Self-esteem*. San Francisco: Freeman, 1967.

Cormack, M. L. *She Who Rides a Peacock: Indian Students and Social Change*. New York: Frederick A. Praeger, 1961.

Crowne, D. P. & Marlowe, D. *The Approval Motive*. New York: Wiley, 1964.

Crowne, D. P., Stephens, M. W., & Kelly, R. The validity and equivalence of tests of self acceptance. *Journal of Psychology*, 1961, **51**, 101-112.

Cumming, Elaine; Dean, Lois R.; Newell, D. & S., & McCaffrey, Isabell. Disengagement – a tentative theory of aging. *Sociometry*, 1960, **23**, 23-35.

Cumming, Elaine & E. Henry, W. E. *Growing Old: The Process of Disengagement*. New York: Basic Books, 1961.

Davis, K. *Human Relations at Work*. New York: McGraw-Hill, 1967.

Davison, G. C. & Valins, S. Maintenance of self-attributed and drug-attributed behavior change. *Journal of Personality and Social Psychology*, 1969, **11**, 25-33.

Dean, D. G. Alienation: its meaning and measurement. *American Sociological Review*, 1961, **26**, 753-759.

DeSoto, C. B. Learning a social structure. *Journal of Abnormal and Social Psychology*, 1960, **60**, 417-421.

DeSoto, C. B., London, M., & Handel, S. Social reasoning and spatial paralogic. *Journal of Personality and Social Psychology*, 1965, **2**, 513-521.

Deutsch, M. Trust and suspicion. *Journal of Conflict Resolution*, 1958, **4**, 265-279.

Deutsch, M. Trust, trustworthiness, and the F-Scale. *Journal of Abnormal and Social Psychology*, 1960, **61**, 138-140.

Diggory, J. S. *Self-evaluation*. New York: Wiley, 1966.

Diggory-Farnham, S. Self-evaluation and subjective life expectancy among suicidal and nonsuicidal psychotic males. *Journal of Abnormal and Social Psychology*, 1964, **69**, 628-634.

Ditz, G. W. The internal-external dichotomy in business organizations. *Industrial Management Review*, 1964, **6**, 51-58.

Doll, E. *Vineland Social Maturity Scale*. Minneapolis, Minnesota: Educational Test Bureau, 1946.

Drake, St. Clair & Cayton, H. R. *1962 Black Metropolis*. New York: Harper & Row, 1962.

Edwards, A. L. *Edwards Personal Preference Schedule*. New York: Psychological Corporation, 1959.

English, W. H. Minority group attitudes of Negroes and implications for guidance. *Journal of Negro Education*, 1957, **26**, 99-107.

Erikson, E. H. *Young Man Luther: A Study in Psychoanalysis and History*. New York: Norton, 1958.

Erikson, E. H. Identity and the life cycle. *Psychological Issues*, 1959, **1**, 1-171.

Etzioni, A. Human relations and the foreman. *Pacific Sociological Review*, 1958, **1**, 1–37.

Eysenck, H. J. *The Dynamics of Anxiety and Hysteria*. New York: Frederick A. Praeger, 1957.

Eysenck, H. J. Learning theory and behavior therapy. *Journal of Mental Science*, 1959, **105**, 61–75.

Fairweather, G. W. *Social Psychology in Treating Mental Illness*. New York: Wiley, 1964.

Faunce, A. *Problems of Industrial Society*. New York: McGraw-Hill, 1968.

Federn, P. *Ego Psychology and the Psychoses*. New York: International University Press, 1959.

Ferster, C. B., Nurnberger, J. I., & Levitt, E. B. The control of eating. *Journal of Mathetics*, 1962, **1**, 87–110.

Festinger, L. A theory of social comparison processes. *Human Relations*, 1954, **7**, 117–140.

Festinger, L. *A Theory of Cognitive Dissonance*. Evanston: Row, Peterson, 1957.

Feuer, S. Leadership and democracy in the collective settlements of Israel. In W. Gouldner (Ed.), *Studies in Leadership*. New York: Harper and Brothers, 1950, 375–395.

Feuer, S. What is alienation? the career of a concept. In M. Stein & A. Vidich (Eds.), *Sociology on Trial*. Englewood Cliffs, New Jersey: Prentice-Hall, 1963.

Fishbein, M. An investigation of the relationship between beliefs about an object and attitude toward that object. *Human Relations*, 1963, **16**, 233–239.

Fishbein, M. Attitude and the prediction of behavior. In M. Fishbein (Ed.), *Readings in Attitude Theory and Measurement*. New York: Wiley, 1967.

Fleishmann, E., Harris, E., & Burtt, H. Leadership and Supervision in Industry: An Evaluation of a Supervisory Training Program. Columbia-Ohio State University, Bureau of Educational Research, 1955.

Frank, C. M. *Behavior Therapy*. New York: McGraw-Hill, 1969.

Freud, Anna. *The Ego and the Mechanisms of Defense*. New York: International Universities Press, 1946.

Freud, S. *Psychopathology of Everyday Life*. New York: The Macmillan Company, 1914.

Fromm, E. *The Sane Society*. New York: Rinehart, 1955.

Gabower, Genevieve. *Behavior Problems of Children in Navy Officers Families: As Related to the Social Conditions of Navy Family Life*. Washington, D.C.: Catholic University American Press, 1959.

Gardner, B. B. & Whyte, W. F. The man in the middle: position and problems of the foreman. *Applied Anthropology*, 1945, **4**, 1–28.

Gerard, H. B., Blevans, S. A., & Malcolm, T. Self-evaluation and the evaluation of choice alternatives. *Journal of Personality*, 1964, **32**, 395–410.

Ghei, S. N. A cross-cultural study of need profiles. *Journal of Personality and Social Psychology*, 1966, **3**, 580–585.

Glanzer, M. & Clark, W. H. Accuracy of perceptual recall: an analysis of organization. *Journal of Verbal Learning and Verbal Behavior*, 1963, **1**, 289–299.

Goldiamond, I. Self-control procedures in personal behavior problems. *Psychological Reports*, 1965, **17**, 851–868.

Golding, Lynn H. & Ziller, R. C. Social-psychological implications of discreditable stigmata. Unpublished manuscript, University of Oregon, 1968.

Gordon, C. & Gergen, K. J. *The Self in Social Interaction*. New York: Wiley, 1968.

Gouldner, A. W. The norm of reciprocity: a preliminary statement. *American Sociological Review*, 1960, **25**, 161–178.

Greenstein, F. I. Personality and politics. *Journal of Social Issues*, 1968, **24**, 1–172.

Greenstein, F. I. The impact of personality on politics: An attempt to clear away underbrush. *American Political Science Review*, 1967, **67**, 629–641.

Grings, W. Verbal-perceptual factors in the conditioning of autonomic responses. In W. Prokasy (Ed.), *Classical Conditioning*. New York: Appleton-Century-Crofts, 1965, pp. 71–89.

Hallowell, A. I. *Culture and Experience*. Philadelphia: University of Pennsylvania Press, 1955.

Hammer, E. Negro and white children's personality adjustment as revealed by a comparison of their drawings (H.T.P.). *Journal of Clinical Psychology*, 1953, **9**, 7–10.

Hartmann, H. *Ego Psychology and the Problem of Adaptation*. New York: International Universities Press, 1958.

Harvey, O. J., Hunt, D. E., & Schroder, H. M. *Conceptual Systems and Personality Organization*. New York: Wiley, 1961.

Hebb, D. O. The American revolution. *The American Psychologist*, 1960, **15**, 735–745.

Heider, F. *The Psychology of Interpersonal Relations*. New York: Wiley, 1958.

Helson, H. Adaptation level theory. In S. Koch (Ed.), *Psychology: A Study of Science, Vol. I, Sensory, Perceptual, and Physiological Formulations*. New York: McGraw-Hill, 1959.

Henderson, E. H., Long, Barbara H., & Gantcheff, Helene. Self–other orientations of French and English Canadian adolescents. *Canadian Journal of Psychology*, 1972.

Henderson, E. H., Long, Barbara H., & Ziller, R. C. Self-social constructs of achieving and non-achieving readers. *The Reading Teacher*, 1965, **19**, 114–118.

Hilgard, E. R. Human motives and the concept of the self. *American Psychologist*, 1949, **4**, 374–382.

Hoe, Betty H. Occupational satisfaction as a function of self-role congruency. Unpublished master's thesis. University of Nevada, 1962.

Hollander, E. P. *Principles and Methods of Social Psychology*, London: Oxford University Press, 1967.

Hollingshead, A. B. & Redlich, F. C. Social Stratification and psychotic disorders. *American Sociological Review*, 1953, **18**, 163–169.

Homme, L. E. Perspectives in psychology—XXIV: Control of coverants, the operants of the mind. *Psychological Record*, 1965, **15**, 501–511.

Horney, Karen. *Neurotic Personality of Our Times*. New York: Norton, 1937.

Horowitz, E. L. The development of attitudes toward the Negro. *Archives of Psychology*, 1936, **28**, No. 194.

Horton, J. The dehumanization of anomie & alienation: a problem in the ideology of sociology. *British Journal of Sociology*, 1964, **15**, 283–300.

Hurlock, Elizabeth B. *Developmental Psychology*. New York: McGraw-Hill, 1968.

Inhelder, B. & Piaget, J. *The Growth of Logical Thinking*, New York: Basic Books, 1958.

Jackson, J. A conceptual and measurement model for norms and roles. *Pacific Sociological Review*, 1966, **9**, 35–47.

James, W. *Principles of Psychology*. New York: Holt, 1890.

Janis, I. L. & Field, P. B. Sex differences and personality factors related to persuasibility. In C. I. Hovland & I. L. Janis (Eds.), *Personality and Persuasibility*, New Haven: Yale University Press, 1959, pp. 55–68.

Janis, I. L. & King, B. T. The influence of role-playing on opinion change. *Journal of Abnormal and Social Psychology*, 1954, **49**, 211–218.

Jones, E. *The Life and Work of Sigmund Freud*. New York: Basic Books, 1953, 3 vols. (21).

Jones, E. E. & Gerard, H. B. *Foundations of Social Psychology*, New York: Wiley, 1967.

Josephson, Eric & Mary Josephson (Eds.) *Man Alone: Alienation in Modern Society*. New York: Dell, 1964.

Jourard, S. M. *The Transparent Self*. New York: Van Nostrand, 1964.

Jung, C. G. *Psychological Types*. New York: Harcourt, Brace, 1923.

Kaffman, M. A comparison of psychopathology: Israel children, Kibbutz and other urban surroundings. *American Journal of Orthopsychiatry*, 1965, **35**, 509–520.

Kanfer, F. H. & Marston, A. R. Determinants of self-reinforcement in human learning. *Journal of Experimental Psychology*, 1963, **66**, 245–254.

Katz, D. I., Sarnoff, I., & McClintock, C. G. Ego defense and attitude change. *Human Relations*, 1956, **9**, 27–46.

Kelly, G. A. *The Psychology of Personal Constructs*. New York: Norton, 1955.

Kelman, H. C. Processes of opinion change. *Public Opinion Quarterly*, 1961, **25**, 57–78.

Killian, M. & Grigg, C. M. Urbanism, race, and anomie. *American Journal of Sociology*, 1963, **67**, 661–665.

King, B. T. & Janis, I. L. Comparison of the effectiveness of improvised versus non-improved role-playing in producing opinion changes. *Human Relations*, 1956, **9**, 177–186.

Klein, G. S. The personal world through perception. In R. R. Blake & G. V. Ramsey (Eds.), *Perception: An Approach to Personality*, New York: Ronald Press, 1951.

Kris, E. On preconscious mental processes. In D. Rapaport, *Organization and Pathology of Thought*. New York: Columbia University Press, 1951, pp. 474–493.

Kuethe, J. L. Social schemas. *Journal of Abnormal and Social Psychology*, 1962, **64**, 31–36.

Kuhn, M. H. Self-attitudes by age, sex, and professional training. *Sociological Quarterly*, 1960, **1**, 39–55.

Lashley, K. S. The problem of serial order in behavior. In S. Saporta (Ed.), *Psycholinguistics*, New York: Holt, Rinehart, and Winston, 1961, pp. 180–198.

Lasswell, H. D. *Psychopathology and Politics*, Chicago: University of Chicago Press, 1930.

Leary, T. F. *Interpersonal Diagnosis of Personality: A Functional Theory and Methodology of Personality*, New York: Ronald Press, 1957.

Lecky, P. *Self-consistency: A Theory of Personality*. New York: Island Press, 1945.

Leventhal, H. & Perloe, S. I. A relationship between self-esteem and persuasibility. *Journal of Abnormal and Social Psychology*, 1962, **64**, 385–388.

Levitt, T. *Industrial Purchasing Behavior: A Study of Communication Effects*, Boston: Harvard University Press, 1965.

Levy, D. M. Oppositional syndromes and oppositional behavior. In P. H. Hock & J. Zubin (Eds.), *Psychopathology of Childhood*. New York: Grune & Stratton, 1955, pp. 204–226.

Lewin, K. *A Dynamic Theory of Personality*. New York: McGraw-Hill, 1935.

Lewin, K. *Field Theory in Social Science*. New York: Harper & Row, 1951.

Lewis, J. H. & Sarbin, T. K. Studies in psychosomatics: The influence of hypnotic stimulation on gastric hunger contractions. *Psychosomatic Medicine*, 1943, **5**, 125–131.

Lieberman, S. The effects of changes in roles on the attitudes of role occupants. *Human Relations*, 1956, **9**, 385–402.

Lifton, R. J. *Thought Reform and the Psychology of Totalism: A Study of Brainwashing in China*. New York: Norton, 1961.

Litzker, D. R. Internationalism as a prediction of cooperative behavior. *Journal of Conflict Resolution*, 1960, **6**, 426–430.

Long, Barbara H. & Henderson, E. H. Self-social concepts of disadvantaged school beginners. Unpublished manuscript, Goucher College, Towson, Maryland, 1966.

Long, Barbara H. & Henderson, E. H. Social schemata of school beginners: some demographic correlates. Proceedings. *75th Annual Convention, American Psychological Association*, 1967.

Long, Barbara H., Henderson, E. H., & Ziller, R. C. Development changes in the self-concept during middle childhood. *Merrill-Palmer Quarterly*, 1967, **13**, 201–216.

Long, Barbara H. & Kramer, R. The self concept of lower class female trainees. Unpublished manuscript, University of Delaware.

Long, Barbara H., Ziller, R. C., & Bankes, J. Self–other orientations of institutionalized behavior problem children. *Journal of Consulting Psychology*, 1970, **34**, 43–47.

Long, Barbara H., Ziller, R. C., & Henderson, E. H. Developmental changes in the self-concept during adolescence. *School Review*, 1968, **76**, 210–230.

Maccoby, N., Romney, A. K., Adams, J. S., & Maccoby, E. E. *"Critical periods" in seeking and accepting information*. Stanford: Stanford University Institute for Communication Research, 1962.

MacLeod, R. B. The phenomenological approach to social psychology. *Psychological Review*, 1947, **54**, 193–210.

Malewski, A. The influence of positive and negative self-evaluation on post-decisional dissonance. *Polish Sociological Bulletin*, 1962, **3–4**, 39–49.

Mancuso, J. C. (Ed.) *Readings for a cognitive theory of personality*. New York: Holt, Rinehart and Winston, 1970.

Mandelbaum, D. G. The family in India. In R. N. Asshen (Ed.), *The Family: Its Function and Destiny*. New York: Harper & Row, 1959.

Manis, J. G. & Meltzer, B. N. *Symbolic interaction*. Boston: Allyn & Bacon, 1967.

Mann, R. D. A review of the relationship between personality and performance in small groups. *Psychological Bulletin*, 1959, **56**, 241–270.

Maslow, A. H. *Motivation and personality*. New York: Harper and Brothers, 1954.

Maslow, A. H., Hirsch, Elissa, Stein, Marcella, & Honegmann, Irma. A clinically derived test for measuring psychological security-insecurity. *Journal of Genetic Psychology*, 1945, **33**, 24–41.

McClintock, C. C., Harrison, A. A., Strand, Susan, & Gallo, P. Internationalism—isolation, strategy of the other player, and two-person game behavior. *Journal of Abnormal and Social Psychology*, 1963, **67**, 631–636.

McDill, E. L. Anomie, authoritarianism, prejudice, and socio-economic status: an attempt at classification. *Social Forces*, 1961, **39**, 239–245.

McGuire, W. The nature of attitudes and attitude change. In L. G. Lindzey & E. Aronson (Eds.), *Handbook of Social Psychology* (Second Edition), Vol. III. *The individual in a social context*. Reading, Massachusetts: Addison-Wesley, 1968.

Mead, G. H. *Mind, self, and society*. Chicago: University of Chicago Press, 1934.

Mead, G. H. The genesis of the self and social control. *International Journal of Ethics*, 1925, **35**, 251–273.

Merton, K. *Social theory and social structure*. Glencoe, Illinois: The Free Press, 1957.

Meier, Dorothy & Bell, W. Anomie and differential access to the achievement of life goals. *American Sociological Review*, 1959, **24**, 189–201.

Mischel, W. *Personality and assessment*. New York: Wiley, 1968.

Mizruchi, Ephraim H. Social structure and anomie in a small city. *American Sociological Review*, 1960, **25**, 645–654.

Moreno, J. L. *Who shall survive?* Washington, D.C.: Nervous and Mental Disease Publication Co., 1934. New York: Beacon, 1953.

Morgan, J. J. B. Effects of non-rational factors in inductive reasoning. *Journal of Experimental Psychology*, 1944, **34**, 159–168.

Mossman, B. M. & Ziller, R. C. Self-esteem and consistency of social behavior. *Journal of Abnormal Psychology*, 1968, **73**, 363–367.

Mossman, B. M. & Ziller, R. C. Acceptable rates of change and the use of coercion in a persuasion situation. Paper read at the West Coast Small Group Meetings, Los Angeles, California, 1970.

Murphy, G. *Personality*. New York: Harper and Brothers, 1947.

Murphy, G. *In the Minds of Men*. New York: Basic Books, 1953.

Mussen, P. H. Differences between TAT responses of Negro and white boys. *Journal of Consulting Psychology*, 1953, **17**, 373–376.

Myer, A. S. Factors relating to the acceptance of Negro children in a bussing integration program. Paper read at the American Educational Research Association Meetings, 1968.

Naedoo, Josephine C. & Fiedler, F. E. Percepts of self and significant others by Indian and American students. *Indian Journal of Psychiatry*, 1962, **37**, 115–126.

Nagler, S. Clinical observations on Kibbutz children. *The Israel Annals of Psychiatry and Related Disciplines*, 1963, **3**, 127–154.

Narain, D. Growing up in India, *Family Process*, 1964, **3**, 127–154.

Neal, A. G. & Rettig, S. On the multidimensionality of alienation. *American Sociological Review*, 1967, **32**, 54–64.

Neisser, R. *Cognitive Psychology*, New York: Appleton-Century-Crofts, 1967.

Nettler, G. A measure of alienation. *American Sociological Review*, 1957, **22**, 670–677.

Newcomb, T. M. *Social Psychology*. New York: Dryden Press, 1950.

Newcomb, T. M., Turner, R. H., & Converse, P. E. *Social Psychology*. New York: Holt, Rinehart and Winston, 1965.

Osgood, C. E., Suci, G. J., & Tannebaum, P. H. *The Measurement of Meaning*. Urbana: University of Illinois, 1957.

Overall, Betty & Aronson, Harriet. Expectations of psychotherapy in patients of lower socioeconomic class. *American Journal of Orthopsychiatry*, 1963, **33**, 421–430.

Parke, R. D. *Readings in Social Development*. New York: Holt, Rinehart and Winston, 1969.

Patterson, G. R. & Reid, J. B. Reciprocity and coercion: two facets of social systems. In C. Neuringer & J. Michael (Eds.), *Behavior Modification in Clinical Psychology*. New York: Appleton-Century-Crofts, 1971.

Pettigrew, T. Negro American personality: Why isn't more known? *Journal of Social Forces*, 1964, **20**, 4–23.

Piaget, J. *The Psychology of Intelligence*. Translated by M. Piercy and D. E. Berlyne. London: Routledge and Kegan Paul, 1947.

Pierce, C. S. Questions concerning certain faculties claimed for man. *Journal of Speculative Philosophy*, 1868, **2**, 103–114.

Polanyi, M. *The Tacit Dimension*. New York: Doubleday, 1966.

Rabin, A. I. *Growing up in the Kibbutz*. New York: Springer Publishing Company, 1965.

Rachman, S. J. & Teasdale, J. Aversion therapy: An appraisal. In C. M. Franks (Ed.), *Behavior Therapy*. New York: McGraw-Hill, 1969, pp. 279–320.

Rank, O. *Truth and Reality*. New York: Knopf, 1936.

Rapaport, D. The structure of psychoanalytic theory. *Psychological Issues*, 1960, **6**.

Reckless, W. C., Dinitz, S., & Murray, Ellen. Self concept as an insulator against delinquency. *American Sociological Review*, 1956, **21**, 744–746.

Reeves, J. W. *Body and Mind in Western Thought*. Baltimore: Penguin Books, 1958.

Ridgeway, Sarah. The relationship among three measures of self concept. Unpublished master's thesis, University of Maryland, 1965.

Riesman, D. *Individualism Reconsidered*. Glencoe, Illinois: The Free Press, 1954.

Robins, L. & O'Neal, P. Mortality, mobility, and crime: problem children 30 years later. *American Sociological Review*, 1958, **23**, 162.

Roby, T. B. Commitment. *Behavioral Science*, 1960, **5**, 253–264.

Roethlisberger, F. J. The foreman: master and victim of double talk. *Harvard Business Review*, 1945, **23**, 285–294.

Rogers, C. R. *Client-centered Therapy*. Boston: Houghton Mifflin, 1951.

Rokeach, M. *The Open and Closed Mind*. New York: Basic Books, 1960.

Rosenberg, M. *Society and the Adolescent Self-image*. Princeton: Princeton University Press, 1965.

Rosenberg, M. J. Cognitive reorganization in response to the hypnotic reversal of attitudinal affect. *Journal of Personality*, 1960, **28**, 39–63.

Rotter, J. B. A new scale for the measurement of interpersonal trust. *Journal of Personality*, 1967, **35**, 651–665.

Sarason, I. G. *Personality: An Objective Approach*. New York: Wiley, 1966.

Sarbin, T. R. A preface to a psychological analysis of the self. *Psychological Review*, 1962, **59**, 11–22.

Sarbin, T. R. Role theoretical interpretation of psychological change. In P. Worchel & D. Byrne (Eds.), *Personality Change*. New York: Wiley, 1964, pp. 176–219.

Sarbin, T. R. Role theory. In G. Lindzey & E. Aronson (Eds.), *Handbook of Social Psychology*, I (Second Edition). Reading, Massachusetts: Addison-Wesley, 1968.

Schachter, S. *The Psychology of Affiliation*. Stanford, California: Stanford University Press, 1959.

Schein, E. H. *Coercive Persuasion*. New York: Norton, 1951.

Schmitt, R. C. Area mobility and mental health on Cahu. *Social Science Research*, 1958, **42**, 115–118.

Schroder, H. M., Driver, M. J. & Streufert, H. *Human Information Processing*. Holt, Rinehart and Winston, 1967.

Schutz, W. C. *Firo: A Three Dimensional Theory of Interpersonal Behavior*. Rinehart, 1958.

Scott, M. B. The social sources of alienation. *Sociological Inquiry*, 1963, **6**, 1–20.

Scott, W. A. Attitude change through reward of verbal behavior. *Journal of Abnormal and Social Psychology*, 1957, **55**, 72–75.

Secord, P. F. & Backman, C. W. *Social Psychology*. New York: McGraw-Hill, 1964.

Seeman, M. On the meaning of alienation. *American Sociological Review*, 1959, **24**, 783–791.

Sherif, Carolny W. & Sherif, M. (Eds.), *Attitude, Ego-involvement and Change*. New York: Wiley, 1967.

Shipley, T. E. & Veroff, J. A. A projective measure of need for affiliation. *Journal of Experimental Psychology*, 1952, **43**, 349–356.

Skinner, B. F. *Science and Human Behavior*. New York: Macmillan, 1953.

Smith, E. E. The power of dissonance techniques to change attitudes. *Public Opinion Quarterly*, 1961, **25**, 626–639.

Smith, M. B. Untitled memorandum. In S. S. Stauffer, *et al. The American Soldier, Vol. I: Adjustment During Army Life.* Princeton University Press, 1949.

Smith, M. B. Attitude change. In D. L. Sells (Ed.), *Encyclopedia of the Social Sciences.* New York: Crowell-Collier & Macmillan, 1968.

Smith, Mary Dell. Complexity of the self concept and decision-making in homogeneous groups. Unpublished master's thesis, University of Oregon, 1967.

Snyder, E. C. The supreme court as a small group. *Social Forces*, 1958, **36**, 232–238.

Spence, K. W. Cognitive factors in the extinction of the conditioned eyelid response in humans. *Science*, 1965, **140**, 1224–1225.

Srole, L. Social integration and certain corrolaries: an exploratory study. *American Sociological Review*, 1956, **22**, 709–716.

Stark, B. J. A study of marginal men in business organizations. Unpublished doctoral dissertation, University of Oregon, 1969.

Stephenson, W. *The Study of Behavior.* Chicago: University of Chicago Press, 1953.

Stern, G. C. & Scanlon, J. C. Pediatric lions and gynecological lambs. *Journal of Medical Education*, 1958, **33**, 12–18.

Stevenson, H. W. & Stewart, E. C. A developmental study of racial awareness in young children. *Child Development*, 1958, **29**, 399–409.

Stonequist, E. V. *The Marginal Man.* New York: Charles Scribner's Sons, 1937.

Sullivan, H. S. *The Interpersonal Theory of Psychiatry.* New York: Norton, 1953.

Taylor, Charlotte P. Some changes in self concept in the first year of desegregated schooling. Unpublished doctoral dissertation, University of Delaware, 1967.

Terbovic, Natalie J. Interpersonal perception as a function of ratio of reinforcement and self–other orientation. Master's thesis: University of Oregon, 1970.

Thompson, E. H. Complexity of the self concept: contrast and assimilation effects in the perception and acceptance of strangers. Unpublished doctoral dissertation, University of Delaware, 1966.

Thorndike, E. L. & Lorge, I. *Teacher's Word Book of 30,000 Words.* New York: Bureau of Publications, Teachers College, Columbia University, 1944.

Tietze, C., Lemkou, P. & Cooper, M. Personality disorder and spacial mobility. *American Journal of Sociology*, 1942, **48**, 29–39.

Troldahl, V. C., & Powell, F. A. A short-form dogmatism scale for use in field studies. *Social Forces*, 1964, **44**, 211–214.

Vaughan, G. M. The development of ethnic attitudes in New Zealand school children. *Genetic Psychology Monographs*, 1964, **70**, 135–175.

Vincent, C. E. Socialization data in research on young marrieds. *Acta Sociologica*, 1964, **8**.

Wahler, R. G. & Pollio, H. R. Behavior and insight: A case study in behavior therapy. *Journal of Experimental Research in Personality*, 1968, **3**, 45–56.

Watson, J. B. Psychology as the behaviorist views it. *Psychological Review*, 1913, **20**, 158–177.

Watson, J. B. *Behaviorism.* New York: Norton, 1930.

Watson, R. I. The experimental tradition and clinical psychology. In A. J. Bachrach (Ed.), *Experimental Foundations of Clinical Psychology.* New York: Basic Books, 1962.

Wilson, W. C. Development of ethnic attitudes in adolescence. *Child Development*, 1963, **34**, 247–256.

Witkins, H. A., Dyk, R. B., Foterson, H. F., Goodenough, D. R., & Karp, S. A. *Psychological Differentiation*. New York: Wiley, 1962.

Wriston, H. M. *Academic Procession: Reflections of a College President*. New York: Columbia University Press, 1959.

Wylie, R. C. *The Self Concept*. Lincoln: University of Nebraska Press, 1961.

Zajonc, R. B. The process of cognitive tuning in communication. *Journal of Abnormal and Social Psychology*, 1960, **61**, 159–167.

Zajonc, R. B. Cognitive theories of social psychology. In G. Lindzey & E. Aronson (Eds.), *Handbook of Social Psychology*, I (Second Edition). Reading, Massachusetts: Addison-Wesley, 1968, pp. 320–411.

Ziller, R. C. Individuation and socialization. *Human Relations*, 1964, **17**, 341–360.

Ziller, R. C. Toward a theory of open and closed groups. *Psychological Bulletin*, 1965, **64**, 164–182.

Ziller, R. C. The alienation syndrome: A triadic pattern of self–other orientation. *Sociometry*, 1969, Vol. 32, No. 3, 287–300.

Ziller, R. C. A helical theory of personal change. *Journal for the Theory of Social Behavior*, 1971, **1**, 33–74.

Ziller, R. C., Alexander, M., & Long, Barbara H. Self-social constructs and social desirability. Unpublished manuscript, University of Delaware, 1964.

Ziller, R. C. & Golding, L. H. The political personality. *Proceedings of the American Psychological Association*, 1969.

Ziller, R. C. & Grossman, S. A. A developmental study of the self-social constructs of normals and the neurotic personality. *Journal of Clinical Psychology*, 1967, **23**, 15–21.

Ziller, R. C., Hagey, Joan, Smith, Mary Dell, & Long, Barbara H. Self-esteem: A self-social construct. *Journal of Consulting and Clinical Psychology*, 1969, **33**, 84–95.

Ziller, R. C. & Long, Barbara H. Self-social constructs and geographic mobility. Unpublished manuscript, University of Delaware, 1964.

Ziller, R. C., Long, Barbara H., Ramana, K. V., & Reddy, V. E. Self–other orientation of Indian and American adolescents. *Journal of Personality*, 1968, **36**, 315–330.

Ziller, R. C., Megas, J., & DeCencio, D. Self-social constructs of normals and acute neuropsychiatric patients. *Journal of Consulting Psychology*, 1964, **20**, 50–63.

Zimbardo, P. G. Involvement and communication discrepancy as determinants of opinion conformity. *Journal of Abnormal and Social Psychology*, 1960, **60**, 86–93.

Zimbardo, P. G. The effect of effort and improvisation on self-persuasion produced by role-playing. *Journal of Experimental Social Psychology*. 1965, **1**, 103–120.

Zimmerman, Claire & Bauer, R. A. The effect of an audience upon what is remembered. *Public Opinion Quarterly*, 1956, **20**, 238–248.

Author Index

Adler, A., xvi, 5, 63, 64, 67, 134
Adorno, T. W., 42
Alexander, M., 18, 66, 80, 84, 123
Allport, G. W., 79
Ansbacher, H., 5, 6, 28, 135
Ansbacher, Rowena, 5, 6, 28, 135
Aronfreed, J., 7
Aronson, Harriet, 166
Asch, S. E., 22
Ausubel, D. P., 22, 30, 64
Ayllon, T., 165

Backman, C. W., 148, 157, 162, 170, 171, 172
Baldwin, J. M., xiv, 130, 131
Bales, R. F., 56
Bandura, A., 8, 36, 148, 164–167, 169, 172, 177
Bankes, J., 34, 109
Barber, J. D., 78, 80, 89
Barker, R. G., 102
Barnett, L. D., 113
Baver, R. A., 172
Bell, W., 62, 72
Bem, D. J., 149, 160
Bendix, R., 61
Berger, S. M., 177
Berkowitz, L., 67
Bettelheim, B., 114
Biddle, B. J., 166

Bieri, J., 82
Bills, R. E., 14
Blacker, E., 82
Blau, P., 47, 48
Blevans, S. A., 163
Borgatta, E. F., 17
Brehm, J. W., 161
Brim, O. G., 94, 96, 148
Brunswik, E., 4, 143
Burtt, H., 165

Cameron, N., 63, 64, 166
Campbell, J. P., 168
Caplow, T., 52
Carrigan, Patricia M., 64
Cassirer, E., 148
Cattell, R. B., 112
Cayton, H. R., 72
Christie, R. J., 42
Clark, W. H., 84
Cohen, A. R., 161, 163
Converse, P. E., 169
Cook, S. W., 167
Cooley, C. H., xiv, 130
Coombs, C. H., 10
Coopersmith, S., ix, 8, 14, 19, 20, 102
Cormack, M. L., 106
Crowne, D. P., 16
Cumming, Elaine, 69, 71

Davis, K., 54
Davison, G. C., 160
Dean, D. G., 64
Dean, Lois R., 71
DeCencio, D., 12, 22, 23, 109
DeSoto, C. B., 10, 12, 25
Deutsch, M., 41, 42
Diggory, J. S., ix, xiv, 5
Diggory-Farnham, S., 14
Dinitz, S., 170
Ditz, G. W., 54
Doll, E., 113
Drake, St. Clair, 72
Dunnette, M. D., 168
Dyk, R. B., 7, 78, 81

Edwards, A. L., 110
English, W. H., 72
Erikson, E. H., 31, 62, 110, 162
Etzioni, A., 52
Eysenck, H. J., 38, 49, 63, 167

Fairweather, G. W., 17
Faunce, A., 63
Federn, P., 64
Ferster, C. B., 168
Festinger, L., 78, 159, 163
Feuer, S., 62, 65
Fiedler, F. E., 106
Field, P. B., 163
Fishbein, M., 157, 158
Fleishmann, E., 165
Foterson, H. F., 7, 78, 81
Frank, C. M., 164, 177
Freud, Anna, 133
Fromm, E., 8

Gabower, Genevieve, 119, 124
Gallo, P., 42
Gantcheff, Helene, 75
Gardner, B. B., 52
Gerard, H. B., 149, 162, 163, 173
Gergen, K. J., ix
Ghei, S. N., 110, 111
Glanzer, M., 84
Goldiamond, I., 168
Golding, Lynn H., 54, 84, 85, 170
Goodenough, D. R., 7, 78, 81

Gordon, C., ix
Gouldner, 74
Greenstein, F. I., 76
Grigg, I. L., 161
Grings, W., 167
Grossman, S. A., 23, 68, 70, 71, 97, 100, 109

Hagey, Joan, 3, 103
Hallowell, A., 20, 105
Hammer, E., 72
Handel, S., 10, 12, 25
Harris, E., 165
Harrison, A. A., 42
Hartmann, H., 133
Harvey, O. J., 30, 31, 79
Haughton, E., 165
Hebb, D. O., xvii, 143
Heider, F., 98, 159
Helson, H., 124
Henderson, E. H., 11, 13, 20, 75, 97, 98,
    108, 111, 115, 123
Henry, W. E., 69, 71
Hilgard, E. R., 143
Hirsch, Elissa, 88
Hoe, Betty H., 171
Hollander, E. P., 150
Hollingshead, A. B., 20, 119
Homme, L. E., 168
Honegmann, Irma, 88
Horney, Karen, xvi, 115, 135
Horowitz, E. L., 163
Horton, J., 61
Hunt, D. E., 30, 31, 79

Inhelder, B., 25

Jackson, J., 170, 172
Jahoda, Marie, 42
James, W., 5, 130
Janis, I. L., 161, 163
Jones, E. E., 149, 162, 173
Josephson, Eric, 61, 67
Josephson, Mary, 61, 67
Jourard, S. M., xvii, 115
Jung, C. G., 29

Kaffman, M., 113
Kanfer, F. H., 8

Karp, S. A., 7, 78, 81
Katz, D. I., 149
Kelly, G. A., 9, 10, 11, 149
Kelly, R., 16
Kelman, H. C., 164
Killian, M., 72
King, B. T., 161
Klein, G. S., 5, 143
Kris, F., 133
Kuethe, J. L., 12
Kuhn, M. H., 96

Lambert, W. W., 177
Lasswell, H. D., 78
Leary, T. F., 145
Lecky, P., 93, 147
Leventhal, H., 163
Levitt, T., 165
Levy, D. M., 30, 31
Lewin, K., 46, 48, 49, 79, 88, 155
Lewis, J. H., 172
Lieberman, S., 161
Lifton, R. J., 162
Lipset, S. M., 61
Litzker, D. R., 42
London, M., 10, 12, 25
Long, Barbara H., 3, 11, 13, 18, 20, 34, 35,
    66, 75, 80, 84, 97, 98, 103, 106, 108,
    109, 111, 115, 119, 123
Lorge, I., 84

Maccoby, N., 165
Macleod, R. B., xvii
Malcolm, T., 163
Malewski, 163
Mancuso, J. C., xvii
Mandelbaum, D. G., 106
Manis, J. G., ix
Mann, R. D., 18
Marlowe, D., 16
Marston, A. R., 8
Maslow, A. H., 88, 155, 174
McCaffrey, Isabell, 71
McClintock, C. C., 42, 149
McDill, E. L., 62
McGuire, W., 148, 157
McLean, O. S., 14
Mead, G. H., xv, 34, 130, 131, 132

Megas, J., 12, 22, 23, 109
Meier, Dorothy, 62, 72
Meltzer, B. N., ix
Merton, K., 63, 172, 179
Michael, J., 165
Mischel, W., 177
Mizruchi, Ephraim, H., 72
Moreno, J. L., 166, 172
Morgan, J. J. B., 10
Mossman, B. M., 11, 13, 16, 78, 154, 174,
    175
Murphy, G., xiv, 30, 35, 106, 107
Murray, Ellen, 170
Mussen, P. H., 72
Myer, A. S., 116

Naedoo, Josephine C., 106
Nagler, S., 113
Narain, D., 106
Neal, A. G., 62, 66
Neisser, R., 4, 143
Nettler, G., 62
Newcomb, T. M., 149, 157, 169, 171
Newell, D. & S., 71

O'Neal, P., 119
Osgood, C. E., 6
Overall, Betty, 166

Parke, R. D., 172
Patterson, G. R., 75
Perloe, S. I., 163
Pettigrew, T., 72
Piaget, J., 9, 25, 82
Pierce, C. S., 129, 130
Polanyi, M., 10, 149
Pollio, H. R., 167
Powell, F. A., 50

Rabin, A. I., 113
Rachman, S. J., 167
Raiffa, H., 10
Ramana, K. V., 20, 35, 66, 106
Rank, O., 30
Rapaport, D., 133
Reckless, W. C., 170
Redlich, F. C., 20, 119
Reedy, V. E., 20, 35, 66, 166

Reeves, J. W., xiv
Reid, J. B., 75
Rettig, S., 62, 66
Ridgeway, Sarah, 15, 84
Riesman, D., 89
Robins, L., 119
Roby, T. B., 151
Roethlisberger, F. J., 52
Rogers, C. R., xiv, 18, 148, 173
Rokeach, M., 49, 50, 81
Rosenberg, M. J., 19, 103, 158
Rotter, J. B., 42

Sarason, I. G., 33
Sarbin, T. K., 172
Sarbin, T. R., 94, 95, 169, 172
Sarnoff, I., 149
Scanlon, J. C., 171
Schachter, S., 39
Schein, E. H., 162
Schmitt, R. C., 119
Schroder, H. M., 30, 31, 79, 82, 88
Schutz, 38, 49
Scott, M. B., 61
Scott, W. A., 161
Scott, W. R., 47, 48
Secord, P. F., 148, 157, 162, 170, 171, 172
Seeman, M., 61, 63, 64, 65
Sherif, Carolny W., 162
Sherif, M., 162
Shipley, T. E., 38
Skinner, B. F., 165
Smith, E. F., 159
Smith, M. B., 162
Smith, Mary Dell, 3, 84, 103
Snyder, E. C., 51
Spence, K. W., 167
Srole, I., 72
Stark, B. J., 54
Stephens, M. W., 16
Stephenson, W., 175
Stern, G. C., 171
Stern, Marcella, 88
Stevenson, H. W., 163

Steward, E. C., 163
Stonequist, E. V., 46
Strand, Susan, 42
Suci, G. J., 6
Sullivan, H. S., 94, 137

Tannenbaum, P. H., 6
Taylor, Charlotte, P., 72
Teasdale, J., 167
Terbovic, Natalie J., 36, 88
Thomas, E. J., 166
Thompson, F. H., 80, 84
Thorndike, E. L., 84
Thrall, R. M., 10
Tietze, C., 119
Troldahl, V. C., 50
Turner, R. H., 169

Valins, S., 160
Vance, E. L., 14
Vaughan, G. M., 163
Veroff, J. A., 38
Vincent, C. E., 170

Wahler, R. G., 167
Walters, R. H., 36, 165, 166, 172
Watson, J. B., xvii, 4, 150
Watson, R. I., 164
Whalen, C. K., 8
Wheeler, S., 148
Whyte, W. F., 52
Wilson, W. C., 163
Witkins, H. A., 7, 78, 81
Wriston, H. M., 83
Wylie, R. C., ix, xiv, 5, 14, 18, 22, 176

Zajonc, R. B., 82, 84, 177
Ziller, R. C., 3, 11, 12, 13, 16, 18, 20, 22, 23, 31, 34, 35, 54, 61, 66, 68, 70, 71, 78, 80, 84, 85, 97, 98, 100, 103, 106, 107, 108, 109, 110, 111, 115, 119, 123, 147, 170, 174, 175
Zimbardo, P. G., 160, 161
Zimmerman, Claire, 172

Subject Index

Adaptation, 5, 7, 88, 124, 143, 174
Adolescents, 35, 48
Affection, 140
Alienation, 61–75
  definition of, 61, 63
  and inclusion, 139
  measures of, 66–67
American Negro, 72–75, 116–118
  (*See also* alienation)
Apathy, 137
Approach-avoidance, 135–137
Asian Indians, 35, 106–112
Assimilation, 82
Attitudes, 149, 157–165

Behavior modification, 147, 164–165, 167, 172
Behavior problem children, 34, 67–68, 170
  (*See also* alienation)

Closed group, 107, 110–111
Cognitive complexity, 82
Cognitive dissonance, 147, 155, 159, 163
Cognitive mapping, 49, 56, 79, 143
Commitment, 151–152
Complexity of the self, 78–80, 154–155
  and category width, 84
  and decision making, 84
  definition of, 78
  measure of, 84, 184

Confident adequacy, 17
Conflict, 27, 28, 29, 32–33, 47, 48, 62, 64–65, 74, 77, 95, 131–132, 135, 136, 137, 137–138, 174
Consensual validation, 137–138
Consistency, 6, 8, 16–18, 93–101, 104, 119, 137, 142, 147
Control, 139
Control mechanisms, 4, 6, 30, 31–32, 50, 67, 82, 132–134, 137–138, 142, 168, 176

Delinquency (*See* behavior problem children)
Dependence, 30, 31
Depression, 22
Desensitization, 169
Differentiation-Integration, 5, 9, 31, 76, 78, 81–82, 89, 95, 142, 143
  (*See also* complexity of the self)
Disengagement, 65
Dogmatism, 49–50, 81, 93
Dynamic equilibrium, 94
Dynamisms, 137–138

Edward's Abasement Test, 17
Ego, 132–133
Egocentrism, 5
  (*See also* self-centrality)
Ego diffusion, 31

Ego identity, 31
Ego-psychology, 133–134

Field dependent, 7
Foreman, 53–54, 161–162

Group identity, 31
Guilt proneness, 17

Handicapped children, 67

Id, 28, 132–133
Identification, 33–34, 97–98, 107, 110, 164
    measure of, 98, 108, 185
    with father, 108
Ideologue, 81
Imitation, 165–166, 167
Inclusion, 38, 49, 139
Individuation, 97–98
Inferiority complex, 5, 28, 78
Inner directed, 89
Interiorization, 171, 174
Internalization, 164
Introversion-extroversion, 29, 38–39, 49–50, 63

Joint family, 106

Kibbutz children, 112–116

Leveling-sharpening, 5, 143

Majority identification, 104–105, 119, 185
Marginality, 46–57
    definition of, 47
    measures of, 48, 183
Marginal man (see marginality)
Marriage schemata, 174
Meaninglessness (See alienation)
Mobility, 110, 116–123
    and adjustment, 119
    and self esteem, 116
Modeling, 34, 36, 166
Monitoring, 173, 179

Narcissism, 64
    (See also self-centrality)
Need-affiliation, 38, 39–41

Neuropsychiatric patients, 13, 17, 22–23, 64, 68–71, 109, 165
Neurotic personality, 136
Neutrality, 51–52
Non-verbal communication, 149
Normlessness (See alienation)

Openness, 114
    definition of, 114
    measure of, 115, 186

Phenomenology, 47, 57, 173
Popularity, 18, 80, 84, 110
Politician, 19, 76–90
Powerlessness (See alienation)

Q-technique, 175

Rate of change, 154, 174–175
Reciprocity, 74
Responsiveness, 77–78, 81–82, 88, 93
Roles, 52–54, 150, 161, 165, 166, 170–173
    role change, 169–170
    role conflict, 47, 170
    role playing, 161, 166, 172, 177
    role strain, 170

Salesman, 54
Schema, 4
Self, 134
    inferred self, 144
    material self, 130
    social self, 130
    somatic self, 95
    spiritual self, 130
Self-acceptance,
    after marriage, 170
Self-actualization, 155
Self-approval, 5
Self-centrality, 63–66, 135
    definition of, 64
    and geographic mobility, 122
    measure of, 66, 183
Self-esteem, 3–45, 63, 154–155
    and behavior modification, 167
    and caste, 21
    and conformity, 21–22
    and culture, 20–21, 107

Self-esteem (*continued*)
  definition of, 6
  and development, 98–100
  and family, 102–105, 111
  measures of, 9–11, 14, 182
  and persuasion, 163
  and the political personality, 80
  and responsiveness, 77–78
  (*See also* alienation)
Self-fulfilling prophecy, 74
Self-identity, 109
Self-other primacy, 121
  measure of, 121
Self-reinforcement, 8, 17, 48, 62
Self-report, 9, 149
Sharpening, 5
Shy children, 108
Significant others, 6, 10–11
Similarity, 80
Social acceptance, 17, 18–19
Social comparison, 78
Social desirability, 16
Social interest, 5, 27–45, 63, 64, 134, 154–155
  and culture, 107, 114
  definition of, 30

and development, 98–100
  measurement of, 33, 182
  (*See also* alienation)
Socialization, 8, 28, 31, 74, 96–97, 105, 162, 172
  occupational, 171
Social reinforcement, 17, 25, 30, 32, 34, 35, 36, 37, 56, 62, 104, 105–106, 118, 165, 166
Social schemata, 143
Social trust, 27, 30, 40–44
Socioeconomic status, 19–20, 103
Spatial paralogic, 10
Succorance, 110
Superego, 28–29, 132–133
Superintendent of Schools (*See* politician)
Superstition, 79–80

Teachers, 54

Values, 149–150

Who Am I? Test, 96–97
Withdrawal, 71, 73, 136, 137
  (*See also* centrality)

TITLES IN THE PERGAMON GENERAL PSYCHOLOGY SERIES

Vol. 1.   J. WOLPE — *The Practice of Behavior Therapy*

Vol. 2.   T. MAGOON et al. — *Mental Health Counselors at Work*

Vol. 3.   J. McDANIEL — *Physical Disability and Human Behavior*

Vol. 4.   M. L. KAPLAN et al. — *The Structural Approach in Psychological Testing*

Vol. 5.   H. M. LaFAUCI & P. E. RICHTER — *Team Teaching at the College Level*

Vol. 6.   H. B. PEPINSKY et al. — *People and Information*

Vol. 7.   A. W. SIEGMAN & B. POPE — *Studies in Dyadic Communication*

Vol. 8.   R. E. JOHNSON — *Existential Man: The Challenge of Psychotherapy*

Vol. 9.   C. W. TAYLOR — *Climate for Creativity*

Vol. 10. H. C. RICKARD et al. — *Behavioral Intervention in Human Problems*

Vol. 11. P. EKMAN, W. V. FRIESEN & P. ELLSWORTH — *Emotion in the Human Face: Guidelines for Research and an Integration of Findings*

Vol. 12. B. MAUSNER & E. S. PLATT — *Smoking: A Behavioral Analysis*

Vol. 14. A. GOLDSTEIN — *Psychotherapeutic Attraction*

Vol. 15. F. HALPERN — *Survival: Black/White*

Vol. 16. K. SALZINGER & R. S. FELDMAN — *Studies in Verbal Behavior: An Empirical Approach*

Vol. 17. H. E. ADAMS & W. K. BOARDMAN — *Advances in Experimental Clinical Psychology*

Vol. 18. R. C. ZILLER — *The Social Self*

Vol. 19. R. P. LIBERMAN — *A Guide to Behavioral Analysis & Therapy*

Vol. 22. H. B. PEPINSKY & M. J. PATTON — *The Psychological Experiment: A Practical Accomplishment*

Vol. 23. T. R. YOUNG — *New Sources of Self*

Vol. 24. L. S. WATSON, JR. — *Child Behavior Modification: A Manual for Teachers, Nurses, and Parents*

Vol. 25. H. L. NEWBOLD — *The Psychiatric Programming of People: Neo-Behavioral Orthomolecular Psychiatry*

Vol. 26. E. L. ROSSI — *Dreams and the Growth of Personality: Expanding Awareness in Psychotherapy*

Vol. 27. K. D. O'LEARY & S. G. O'LEARY — *Classroom Management: The Successful Use of Behavior Modification*

Vol. 28. K. A. FELDMAN — *College and Student: Selected Readings in the Social Psychology of Higher Education*

Vol. 29. B. A. ASHEM & E. G. POSER — *Adaptive Learning: Behavior Modification with Children*

Vol. 30. H. D. BURCK et al. — *Counseling and Accountability: Methods and Critique*

Vol. 31. N. FREDERIKSEN et al. — *Prediction of Organizational Behavior*

Vol. 32. R. B. CATTELL — *A New Morality from Science: Beyondism*

Vol. 33. M. L. WEINER — *Personality: The Human Potential*

Vol. 34. R. M. LIEBERT et al. — *The Early Window: Effects of TV on Children and Youth*